Henry Harwood

Henry Harwood
Hero of the River Plate

Peter Hore

Foreword by Admiral Sir Jock Slater

Seaforth
PUBLISHING

First published in Great Britain in 2018 by
Seaforth Publishing,
A division of Pen & Sword Books Ltd,
47 Church Street,
Barnsley S70 2AS

www.seaforthpublishing.com

British Library Cataloguing in Publication Data
A catalogue record for this book is available from the British Library

ISBN 978 1 5267 2529 5 (HARDBACK)
ISBN 978 1 5267 2530 1 (EPUB)
ISBN 978 1 5267 2531 8 (KINDLE)

Pen & Sword Books Limited incorporates the imprints of Atlas, Archaeology, Aviation, Discovery, Family History, Fiction, History, Maritime, Military, Military Classics, Politics, Select, Transport, True Crime, Air World, Frontline Publishing, Leo Cooper, Remember When, Seaforth Publishing, The Praetorian Press, Wharncliffe Local History, Wharncliffe Transport, Wharncliffe True Crime and White Owl.

Typeset by MATS Typesetting, Leigh-on-Sea, Essex SS9 5EB
Printed and bound in Great Britain by TJ International Ltd, Padstow, Cornwall

Contents

Foreword by
Admiral Sir Jock Slater GCB LVO DL

There are many officers in the Royal Navy whose name will go down in the annals of naval history, none more so than Henry Harwood whose courageous victory, against the odds, at the Battle of the River Plate in December 1939 was a real tonic for Great Britain in the bleak early years of the Second World War. Churchill, then First Lord of the Admiralty, commented that the victory had 'warmed the cockles of the Nation's heart'.

Much has been written about the battle but a complete biography of Harwood has thus far not been written. Peter Hore is to be congratulated on his detailed analysis for this book, helped not least by some earlier comprehensive research by Harwood's sons, Henry and Stephen.

In many ways, this is ultimately a sad story. Harwood's remarkable victory in the South Atlantic gave him instant promotion to flag rank. On return home, he became an Assistant Chief of the Naval Staff. However, sixteen months later, he was the surprise choice of the First Sea Lord to relieve Admiral Sir Andrew Cunningham, Commander-in-Chief, Mediterranean, as an Acting Admiral, an appointment strongly supported by Churchill, by then the Prime Minister, who much admired Harwood's proven fighting spirit.

Cunningham, who was urgently needed in Washington, did not approve of this appointment, believing that Harwood, still junior on the Flag List, was not the right man for this particular job with British fortunes in the Mediterranean at their lowest ebb. Furthermore, inter-Service relationships at the most senior level were challenging. Nevertheless, Harwood became the Commander-in-Chief and set about tackling the many problems with his customary determination, cheerful optimism and skilful diplomacy.

Amongst the problems and plans that Harwood inherited were the much reduced size of the fleet (with two battleships under repair),

Malta desperate for relief from siege, the lack of satisfactory air support and the intractable issue of the French fleet holed up in Alexandria under Admiral Godfroy. In the months that followed there were a series of reverses which this book covers in detail and despite Harwood's best endeavours, unjustified rumours at the highest level spread that the Royal Navy was not putting its best foot forward to support the Army, inevitably reflecting unfavourably on the Commander-in-Chief.

Sir Dudley Pound, the First Sea Lord, therefore decided to relieve Harwood, offering him the post of Second-in-Command of the Eastern Fleet. Harwood was initially most surprised but delighted at the prospect; however, he soon discovered the basis on which this move had been decided and this must have come as a major blow. His subsequent heart attack effectively ended his front-running career.

Many years later, as a young naval officer, I was privileged to enjoy wide-ranging discussions with my great-uncle, Andrew Cunningham. He spoke with admiration of the victory off the River Plate but, in talking about the Mediterranean, where he had returned as the Allied Commander-in-Chief in 1943, I remember that he clearly felt that Henry Harwood had been hard done by and criticisms of him at the top level, not least by the self-centred, opinionated General Montgomery were not only unjustified, but extremely damaging.

Harwood left a substantial archive of papers and photographs, after his early death aged sixty-two, but this is the first full account of his life. Unfortunately, over the years, his reputation has suffered unfairly as historians, often notorious plagiarists, have chosen to perpetuate erroneous judgements. Peter Hore, after comprehensive study of the Harwood papers and public archives, has set Harwood's character and achievements into perspective and I am pleased that balance has now been restored to the reputation of a famous fighting admiral.

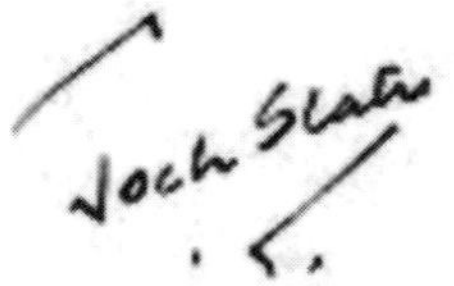

Admiral Sir Jock Slater GCB LVO DL
First Sea Lord 1995–1998

Introduction & Acknowledgements

The first comprehensive account of the Battle of the River Plate was Harwood's report of proceedings in 1939, an edited version of which was published the following year as an Admiralty despatch. The editors noted that the various despatches from the captains of ships did not agree and where they differed, they took Harwood's original despatch as correct.

In the 1950s two official histories of the naval war were published, *The War at Sea* by Captain Stephen Roskill, and *The Royal New Zealand Navy in the Second World War* by S D Waters. Both drew on papers which were then still classified: Waters naturally dwelled on the role of the New Zealand-manned HMS *Achilles*, while Roskill grudgingly wrote that: 'A detailed description of the battle which now took place will be of less interest to posterity than the ocean-wide strategy which led to it, and it is therefore right, without in any way belittling the gallantry and tenacity with which Commodore Harwood's lightly armed cruisers tackled their formidable adversary, that it should occupy a smaller space in these pages'. Provoked by this parsimonious praise, the novelist and historian Dudley Pope wrote in 1956, 'it is not enough to give details of how ... the cruisers found her [*Graf Spee*]; that is not a tenth of the full story'. Maybe also he had an eye on cashing in on the forthcoming film, for Pope sought to see 'to all the British and German documents which I needed', and correspondence in the Naval Historical Branch shows that Pope was indeed granted exceptional access, which he acknowledges in the foreword to his *The Battle of the River Plate*, published in 1956. Pope's book, written using sources in the Naval Historical Branch, is therefore very much the official history of the battle.

However, this is not another retelling of a single battle, but the story of Henry Harwood, one of a handful of senior British naval officers who in the years since the Second World War has lacked a comprehensive biography. Here an account of the Battle of the River Plate is just one episode, one important episode, in Harwood's life. His early life and career is a metaphor for the naval officers of his generation, although the preparation which gave Harwood his special insight into South America and helped to make him the 'Hero of the Plate' is unique. His subsequent career in the Second World War, after he was made Commander-in-Chief, Mediterranean, also deserves closer study.

In 1965 I was awarded the Harwood Prize for modern languages at the Britannia Royal Naval College, Dartmouth. The handsome certificate I was given has not survived, but the books have, and among them is Sir Eugen Millington-Drake's then newly-published ***Drama of the Graf Spee and the Battle of the Plate***. Millington-Drake was the British minister (there was no ambassador) to Uruguay during the battle, who produced a documentary anthology, particularly useful because he translated and included German and Spanish language sources. Little could I know that fifty years later I would use this as a daily reference when Admiral Sir Henry Harwood's sons offered me access to their father's archives.

I am particularly grateful to Henry and to Stephen Harwood and to all the members of their families for access to Admiral Sir Henry Harwood's archive of papers and photographs.

I am also grateful to: Diana Beare, granddaughter of Lloyd Hirst; Robin Brodhurst, for refereeing Part I; Patrick Cogswell, for permission to quote from his father's biography; Mike Coombes, for his research in the Navy Lists; Professor Eric Grove, for refereeing the chapter on Operation Vigorous; Cdr Mike Hill, for his advice on Second World War communications; Cdr David Hobbs, historian of the Fleet Air Arm; Dr Mark Houghton, for information about Vian's illness; Professor Derek Law, for refereeing Part II; Captain Guillermo Montenegro, ARA and professor of naval history; Rear-Admiral Chris Parry, for important clues at Cambridge; Nick Poland, for access to his father's papers about Operation MG2; Jill Quaife, former secretary to Sir Eugen Millington-Drake; Gordon Smith and his successors at Naval-History.net; William Stevens in New Zealand; Peter Turner, proofreader; Dr Jan Witt, historian at the Naval Memorial, Laboe; Michael Wynd, Torpedo Bay Naval Museum, New Zealand; Captain

Hector Gustavo Yori, director of the Uruguayan naval museum; staff and experts at the Churchill Archives, Cambridge, the Imperial War Museum, the National Archives at Kew and the Naval Historical Branch in Portsmouth.

A special note of thanks goes to Julian Mannering and Stephanie Rudgard-Redsell of Seaforth Publishing for faith in my proposal and help in bringing it to fruition.

While the Harwoods have given me full access to their family archives, this is not an authorised biography, and, while I have in places drawn on a draft prepared and privately printed by the Harwood brothers, any and all opinions or judgements expressed in this book are mine and mine alone, as are any commissions or omissions of error.

Peter Hore
February 2018

A note on communications and times

It is important to understand how communications worked in 1939–1945, unlike the modern world of near-instantaneous communications by satellites and the internet. Ships at very close range at sea could communicate by loud hailer. While in sight of each other, ships could also communicate by coloured flag hoists or semaphore in a simple tactical code, or using Morse code by flashing light (V/S) or by wireless (W/T) – as radio was then known. Voice communication by radio-telephony (R/T) was not introduced until later in the Second World War. W/T between ships was sent at high frequency (H/F), ie short wave, which for reliable inter-ship communications was not much more than visual range. H/F could be used to 'bounce' waves on the ionosphere over longer ranges, the bounce varying according to the wavelength used and the height of the ionosphere, which varied by day and night, but there was often a 'silent' gap at medium ranges. Occasionally, freak transmissions which could be received over exceptionally long ranges arose – as happened when HMS *Cumberland*, over a thousand miles away, overheard short-range inter-ship W/T transmissions during the Battle of the River Plate. For long-range transmissions, ships used H/F to 'work' fixed land stations, which were either governmentally or commercially run. Onward transmission by the land stations would be by a worldwide network of cables or specialised, continuously available H/F lines. From this network, messages for ships would be broadcast on H/F at greater signal strength and on multiple wavelengths to give wide area coverage. Thus while short-range communication by flags, light and short-range wireless could be near instantaneous, several hours could elapse between the transmission of a long-range wireless message and its reception, and correspondingly longer for a reply to be received by the reverse process.

To add to the difficulty in identifying when a signal was sent and received, the discipline of keeping a uniform zone time at one place or within a group of ships was not always enforced, and the zone being used was not always marked on signals. Egypt was two hours ahead of London (GMT +2 or B time), and the Plate and the Falklands were four hours behind London (GMT – 4 or P time), London was in GMT (or Z time) but kept British Summer Time (BST, GMT +1 or A time) or from 1940 onwards, Double Summer Time (DST, GMT + 2 or B time).

1
Stubbington Boys

When Mary Harwood sought the advice of a friend, a retired Royal Marines general, on how she should best bring up her only son, Bobby, to be a man, 'Send him into the Navy, May,' was the reply.[1] There had been no ancestors in the Royal Navy since Captain Thomas Harwood had commanded the 56-gun *St Andrew*, flagship of Admiral Sir John Kempthorne, at the Battle of Solebay in 1672,[2] so young Henry Harwood Harwood – to give him his full name – was sent to Stubbington House.[3]

Four generations of the Foster family were owners and headmasters of Stubbington House, a school founded as a crammer in 1841, three years after the Navy had introduced an entrance examination for its cadets. In Harwood's day, Montagu Henry Foster, a son of the founder, had been headmaster since 1866 and the school had outgrown its original, limited ambition. The fees were £60 a term or about £6,500 a term in present-day prices, and the school was never large: the 1901 census lists 124 pupils aged between ten and fifteen from Britain and the Empire. Besides the headmaster and his family there were three live-in tutors (called 'officers' in the census), twenty-nine domestic staff and a dozen outside staff. The school was in a large private house where 'the spacious accommodation, arrangements, playground etc. seem to be quite first rate', and the school had its own water supply and 'artificial light', ie electricity. The masters 'were assigned to subjects rather than to forms ... and the success and reputation of the school are maintained in spite of the presence of a considerable element of probably cheap teachings'. In fact, there was one master to every ten boys, and half of the staff had a university education. German, fencing and rifle-shooting were among the available extras: French was taught to everyone by Mr Brown, who was second master and would teach at Stubbington for some thirty years. Almost the only criticism by school inspectors was that mathematics was taught excessively, while the teaching of English was neglected, and that the 'large and pleasing boys' library' was disorganised. Whether by the quality of the teaching or the natural selection of the boys, Stubbington produced an impressive number of politicians, diplomats, generals and admirals who served Britain well in the nineteenth and twentieth centuries, including the extraordinary number of seven VC-winners (only seven senior schools, all with much larger rolls, have exceeded this), and at least twenty-four DSO-winners.[4]

So many boys joined the Navy as cadets that Stubbington was nicknamed 'the cradle of the Navy'. One of the early students was Admiral Lord Charles Beresford. Others were the Antarctic explorer Captain Robert Scott, Admiral Sir Hugh 'Quex' Sinclair who helped to reorganise MI6 and Bletchley Park in the 1920s and '30s, and several Second World War naval leaders, including Admiral of the Fleet Viscount Cunningham of Hyndhope, Admiral of the Fleet Sir John Cunningham and Admiral Sir Edward Syfret. In more recent times the school also produced Rear-Admiral 'Crap' Miers VC and Admiral Sir 'Sandy' Woodward.

Stubbington prepared boys for entry as a naval cadet to HMS *Britannia*, the naval college, where the standards were high and strict: boys had to be between fourteen and a half and fifteen and a half years old and were to be proficient in mathematics, in English, in two of three languages (Latin, French and German with extra marks for excellence in oral examination), English [*sic*] history, and geography with special reference to the British Empire, and in drawing, with either another of the languages, or with mechanics with either physics or chemistry. When Harwood passed the entrance examination and he joined his fellow cadets at *Britannia* in 1903, just four days before his fifteenth birthday, he had the right to feel among an elite.

The naval college

The naval college was housed in two wooden hulks moored on the Dart. There were seventy-eight cadets in his term, including Evelyn 'Wickie' Wickham, who would become Harwood's close, lifelong friend,[5] and Walter Fallowfield, who would command the heavy cruiser HMS *Cumberland* in the South Atlantic in 1939. Among others of his term were Admiral Sir Robert Burnett who as Vice-Admiral 10th Cruiser Squadron would take part in the Battle of the North Cape in December 1943, when the German battleship *Scharnhorst* was sunk; Vice-Admiral John Godfrey, the future Director of Naval Intelligence in the Second World War, on whom Ian Fleming would base the fictional James Bond's chief 'M'; and Admiral Sir Tom Phillips, another Stubbington boy, who would lose his life commanding the ill-fated Force Z off Malaya in 1941.[6]

Harwood joined a Navy in transition. The training of naval officers at Dartmouth dated from 1863, when the wooden-walled HMS *Britannia* arrived from Gosport creek via Portland. By 1903 Jacky Fisher's reforms of naval training were in full swing, the foundation stone for a new, permanent building on the hill at Dartmouth had been laid, but the new, brick-built college would not be occupied until 1905. Although the cadets were shown in the Navy List, and under King's Regulations command could devolve to a naval cadet, Dartmouth remained in essence a boarding school where parents paid £75 per annum (£8,225 at present-day prices) in fees for tuition and board, plus there were long clothing, uniform and kit lists, and a sextant and a small library to maintain. In addition, personal expenses and pocket money at the rate of one shilling a week (£5.50 per week) were charged to parents.

Harwood spent three terms at Dartmouth and a fourth term at sea in a training cruiser, at the end of which he was marked in mathematics and navigation, extra subjects, seamanship and conduct. One month's seniority, which would eventually count toward promotion to lieutenant was given for each first-class pass, and Harwood gained a total of three and a half months' seniority.

Midshipman

On 15 May 1904 Harwood was appointed as a midshipman to the battleship HMS *London* in the Mediterranean. Though *London* was a new ship, built at Portsmouth, armed with four 12in guns in twin barbettes and twelve 6in guns in sided casemates, and first commissioned in June 1902, she was soon to be superseded in design. Naval construction, like naval training, was in the grip of Jacky Fisher's reforms, and almost the next ship down the building slip in

Portsmouth was the revolutionary HMS *Dreadnought*, whose speed and the layout of her uniform, main armament would make all previous battleships obsolescent.

For centuries, junior officers had been required to keep journals: in Nelson's Navy these had recorded details of the ship's navigation and the weather, but by Harwood's day a midshipman's journal contained details of the ship's activities, essays on matters of interest, and often beautiful pen and ink drawings of ship's machinery, and of harbours and coasts. Harwood had been a keen photographer since he was eleven and his journal contains some of his images. However, his surviving journal does not open until February 1906 and information about his early months in *London* is only available through letters to his mother.

Harwood took every opportunity to see as much of the Mediterranean as his finances allowed, supplemented by birthday and Christmas money and a cheque for £10, a fortune in today's money, which he was reluctant to cash. Athens and Venice were great wonders, and in June 1904 young Harwood led a party of Catholic sailors who travelled to Rome for an audience with Pope Pius X. Aged sixteen, he described the Rome visit to his mother at length:

> We all knelt down as [the Pope] came round and we kissed his ring separately. We were each given a medal blessed by himself and somehow I was given two, one of which I am sending you and I am keeping the other myself ... the paintings and frescoes are simply marvellous; about 20 times better than the Windsor Castle state apartments.[7]

In August 1904 he spent three days in Jerusalem. Maybe some of the gullible stories which he repeated showed a lingering innocence, but he saw the holiest places, reporting home on the Christian sites, and the 'Mohomedan' [*sic*] customs which he had witnessed, and finishing another long letter: 'after that we went to see the Jews' wailing place and then we rode back to the hotel on donkeys and started for Jaffa next morning'.[8] If his favourite adjectives were 'awful' and 'interesting', young Harwood was well aware of the privileges which he enjoyed while the fleet roamed the Mediterranean, telling his mother that he was having 'an A1 time out here seeing all the principal sights of the world which would cost any ordinary person about £100, I see for £2'.[9] The only mention of world affairs in his letters home was a single reference to the Russian fleet having sailed from the Baltic to its defeat at the Battle of Tsushima in 1905.

His powers of observation would soon be sharpened when he started to keep a journal which would be read and supervised by the ship's officers. When Harwood's midshipman's journal opens, it is full of incident. In February 1906 while *London* was in refit in Malta, Harwood joined the armoured cruiser HMS *Leviathan*, another newish ship, with a mixed armament of 9.2in and 6in guns, but like *London* also rendered obsolescent by Fisher's reforms. *Leviathan* left Malta with the Mediterranean Fleet, under its commander-in-chief, Admiral Lord Charles Beresford, to join the Channel and Atlantic Fleets for the combined fleets' spring exercises at Lagos Bay, Portugal, where an anchorage plan in the journal shows fifty-two battleships and cruisers under seven admirals. On passage, ships exercised various drills including wireless telegraphy, when Harwood thought it remarkable enough to record that two ships had communicated while the astonishing distance of forty miles apart.

In April 1906 the Mediterranean Fleet concentrated at Corfu, where King Edward VII and his Queen, in the Royal Yacht *Victoria and Albert*, supported by the Prince and Princess of Wales in the battleship *Renown*, exchanged calls with King George I of Greece. *Leviathan* was despatched to Naples where Vesuvius had erupted and Harwood witnessed lava flows and took photographs of the devastation.

Soon after Harwood rejoined *London* in Malta in April 1906, the Taba crisis broke out: a border dispute between the Ottoman Empire and Egypt over whether Taba, now the northernmost resort of Egypt's Red Sea Riviera, was Turkish or Egyptian. The dispute broke out again later in the twentieth century (with the Israelis taking the place of Turks), but in Harwood's day it was resolved by the Royal Navy. Destroyers were prepared for minesweeping duties, ships' landing parties were exercised, and troopships were escorted to Alexandria. Then, when the fleet threatened to occupy Turkish islands in the Aegean, the Turks withdrew their forces from Taba.

That summer the Mediterranean Fleet midshipmen sat their exams in seamanship and steam, and Harwood came top of 105 candidates.

In August 1906 *London* visited Venice, and Harwood went out to Murano in a gondola to see the glass works, where he bought two glass scent bottles for his mother. Later, at Fiume, a visit to the Whitehead torpedo works and watching torpedoes fascinated him, and his journal entry ran to a page and a half in which he described how torpedoes work, with a diagram of the steering engine. He noted that most of the torpedoes were being built for the Italian navy with a few, which were finished to a lower standard and were cheaper, for Sweden.

In December the commander-in-chief, Admiral Beresford, inspected *London* and presented her with gifts from the City of London, including a silver model of the Tower of London, a silver ship's bell and a silk ensign. These would be in the County-class cruiser *London* when Harwood commanded her in 1932–34. Beresford returned next day to strike sixteen bells at noon instead of the normal eight. On Christmas Eve work ceased at noon and on Christmas Day after church there were captain's rounds and a performance on the quarterdeck by the ship's theatre party. Boxing Day was a normal working day. On 10 January 1907 there was a parade of the fleet's ships' companies on the Floriana parade ground, which was inspected by the visiting Board of Admiralty as part of the ceremonies to mark Beresford's departure as Commander-in-Chief, Mediterranean Fleet. On 6 February the fleet sailed westward to rendezvous with the Channel and Atlantic Fleets in Lagos Bay, and *London* joined the Channel Fleet for passage to Sheerness where she arrived on 19 February 1907 and was decommissioned. The midshipmen were discharged to well-deserved leave.

In April 1907 Harwood joined the battleship HMS *Bulwark* at Chatham, and in May she took part in a review of the fleet by the premiers of Australia, Canada, the Cape, Natal, Newfoundland and New Zealand, who were in London for the Imperial Conference of 1907. While colonies matured into dominions and governments discussed the possibilities of Irish Home Rule and self-governance for India, and the merits of imperial preference over free trade, the Admiralty advocated a single, imperial Navy.

The premiers were taken to see the fleet, though the weather was so bad that the great men huddled miserably under awnings in a dockyard tug, showing little interest, imperial or otherwise. There were exercises in the Channel, during which *Bulwark* narrowly avoided a collision with the battleship HMS *Victorious,* and next day the fleet flagship, HMS *Dreadnought,* led the fleet into Torbay for the annual pulling regatta. In June the fleet visited Norwegian ports on a roundabout route to further exercises at Invergordon.

HMS Bramble *on the China Station*

Harwood left *Bulwark* and was promoted to acting sub-lieutenant. His report described him as 'a very promising and capable young officer'. He then started junior officers' war courses at the Portsmouth training establishments, which lasted until December 1908. He gained first-class passes in all six subjects, which won him a prize and gained him further seniority towards his eventual promotion to the rank of lieutenant. His immediate reward was an appointment to the cruiser HMS *King Alfred,* a sister ship of *Leviathan,* and in charge of the junior officers, cadets and midshipmen, who messed in the gunroom. 'Sub of the gunroom', responsible for the discipline of a group of boisterous youths, was a typical challenge in leadership to set a promising young officer. Then in July 1909 Harwood was awarded his bridge-watchkeeping certificate which enabled him to command a watch at sea. He was ready to begin his career.

Two months later, on 6 August 1909 Harwood took passage to China, where on 27 October at Shanghai he joined the river gunboat HMS *Bramble* as a lieutenant with his seniority backdated to 30 July 1908.

The 700-ton *Bramble*[10] was one of a squadron of British warships which patrolled the Lower Yangtze, the first thousand miles of the 'long river' which flows through central China. There were nine ships in the flotilla, ranging from two of 1,070 tons down to two launches of 85 tons drawing only 2½ft of water. Bramble's captain was Lieutenant the Hon Richard Bridgeman (1879–1917),[11] Harwood was first lieutenant, and the navigating officer was Lieutenant H R Moore.[12] Moore would be Vice Chief of the Naval Staff when Harwood became an Assistant Chief in 1940. There was also a doctor, Surgeon Lieutenant Dyer, and two warrant officers.

It was the custom in the China Fleet for officers' messes to be catered by a Chinese messman, or caterer, who fed the officers magnificently at minimal cost and made a tidy profit for himself. *Bramble*'s wardroom messman was Ah Say whom Harwood, nearly twenty years later, engaged as the wardroom messman of the cruiser HMS *Cumberland*. They exchanged Christmas cards thereafter and Ah Say's prestige in Hong Kong knew no bounds when Harwood sent him a signed photograph of a burning German pocket battleship *Admiral Graf Spee*.[13]

At Woosung in March 1910 Bridgeman was relieved by B G Washington and in October Moore was relieved by John Godfrey,[14] one of Harwood's term-mates in *Britannia*. This was a difficult time in China: the all-powerful Empress Dowager Cixi, one of the last of the Manchus, had died in 1908; civil war broke out amongst regional warlords and pirates, and the Japanese were beginning to exert claims on the Chinese mainland. The task of the Royal Navy was to ensure the safety of British life and property while respecting the role of the lawful Chinese authorities: Harwood's comment was 'We are up here [Changsa, capital of Hunan province] to protect the foreigners and so of course we cannot take any part in any rows once the foreigners are clear, which is a pity'. In April 1910 there was serious rioting at Changsha when the governor's palace and the customs house were burned down and European-owned property was destroyed. *Bramble* was ordered there but the situation had been brought under control by the time she arrived.

Little has been recorded about these events, so Harwood's letter to his mother is unique:

> We found everything quiet at Changsha but things are, I fear, in a bad state out here, not only at Changsha but all over the Yangtze valley and I dare say in other parts of China. The riots at Changsha were a most carefully concocted scheme and everything was done in a most orderly manner. They first of all looted the premises of the Asiatic Oil Company and coolies carried tins of kerosene all over the town. These were poured over all the places they wanted to burn. All the missions were looted and most of them burned afterwards, but in some cases all the contents of the houses were broken up and then thrown outside and a big bonfire made of the lot. In other cases the whole place was burned wholesale. The Customs House and

Governor's Palace were burned. Practically the only place untouched which belonged to Europeans on the mainland was the Customs Mess which was built by local firms. All the hulks which the steamers go alongside were burned and all their go-downs [storehouses]. There is an island halfway across the river where most of the Customs live. They did not burn anything there but everything was looted and the funny thing about it was that nothing was stolen, simply chucked on to the lawn and a bonfire made. The great mistake was made by the Governor who would not give the order for the troops to fire. If this had been done it would probably have stopped the whole thing and any further troubles there are likely to be. Of course he has been chucked out and there is a new man there now.

I went with the Captain to call on him the other day. He has been in several rows before and I believe is one of their most capable men. I am thankful to say he gave us an English lunch but it was rather overpowering as about 27 courses came on, one after the other.

The Captain and Navigator went the other day to a Chinese lunch. I am thankful to say I got out of it as you will see from the following menu: Sharks maw (lips), sharks fins, tripe, seaslugs and seaweed, lotus seeds, fish isinglass, pork, pigeon's eggs, lilies and mushrooms, stewed sinews, bamboo shoots, sweet rice, meat rolls, etc, etc, etc.

Everything was in a common bowl in the centre of the table and each person took pieces of stuff out with their chop sticks. The greatest honour a Chinaman can do you is to well-suck his chop sticks and then to fish you a piece out of the bowl and put it on your plate. I am glad to say I was spared such a miserable performance. They both came back nearly sick!

Harwood was critical of the Christian missionaries, who, despite warnings, had returned to China, and he was sure that they would be the cause of new riots, but, twenty years later when being dined by the Society of Merchant Venturers of Bristol, he praised the British traders for their refusal to abandon their posts:[15]

In 1909 I was in a Yangtze gunboat, and we were sent up a side river of the Yangtze because of a local rebellion. On arrival we found the situation serious, and my captain endeavoured to persuade the consul and all the British residents to come on board, but nothing could persuade them. They said they would, to use a Chinese expression, lose face, and intended to stick it out. We gave them therefore some Very lights as an emergency signal. Sure enough about 11 p.m. the balloon went up, and they all came on board. The next morning however, the situation became a little easier, back they went to their work, to stick it out, and keep up British prestige.

It was probably on the Yangtze, where there was good snipe and duck shooting – and it was the custom to stop the ship so that the officers could land for sport – that Harwood was imbued with his love of shooting. *Bramble* visited many ports in China, including Port Arthur, where the wrecks of Russian ships sunk at Port Arthur during the then recent Russo-Japanese war were still visible. Harwood left *Bramble* to return to the UK, crossing the Pacific with his term-mate 'Wickie' Wickham in a liner to Vancouver, where on arrival they were placed in quarantine for smallpox and subjected to three days' close confinement and sulphur baths before being allowed to continue eastward across Canada and so back to the UK.

2
The First World War

After his foreign service leave, Harwood joined HMS *Vernon* at Portsmouth for the torpedo specialist or 'Long T' course which began on 1 November 1911 and lasted until the end of June 1912. In addition to torpedo warfare, specialists were responsible for ships' electrical systems, mining equipment and wireless telegraphy, although the latter was rapidly becoming a separate specialisation. *Vernon* then consisted of three hulks, *Warrior* (now preserved at Portsmouth) and two wooden walls, moored in Portsmouth where conditions were little better than they had been in *Britannia*.

There were eighteen lieutenants on the 1912 course, including Wickham. He and Harwood took to studying in the evening with the assistance of hot toddies and chocolate biscuits, and were soon joined by William 'Riddles' Ridley,[1] Arnold Maitland-Dougall[2] and Jack 'Crack' Crace, a Stubbington boy.[3] Calling themselves the Hot Toddy Club, every evening they set themselves five questions and did not go to bed until these had been satisfactorily answered. All five remained close friends for life.

In July 1912 Harwood was appointed temporarily to the second-class cruiser HMS *Roxburgh* for the summer manoeuvres, and then with Wickham, Maitland-Dougall and five others he was selected for the advanced torpedo course. This was a mainly theoretical course at the Royal Naval College, Greenwich, which lasted from 1 October 1912 to 30 June 1913. The New Year 1913 saw him shooting in Scotland with Maitland-Dougall and Crace, and for the summer manoeuvres that year he was appointed to the first-class cruiser *Diadem*. It was usual for newly qualified specialist officers to serve for one year instructing at a specialist school and Harwood was sent to HMS *Actaeon*, a hulk in Chatham used as a torpedo school, from August 1913 until July 1914. While in *Actaeon* Harwood submitted a design for a deflection plotting instrument to facilitate torpedo control: this was not adopted, but the Admiralty expressed appreciation of his zeal and ingenuity. By now, golf had become an obsession second only to shooting.

The cruiser HMS Sutlej

In July 1914, during a test mobilisation, Harwood was appointed torpedo officer of the elderly cruiser *Sutlej*, commanded by Captain Henry Doughty.[4] The fleet was meant to demobilise on 25 July but on the initiative of the First Lord of the Admiralty, Winston Churchill, and the First Sea Lord, Prince Louis Battenberg, ships were retained at full readiness during that summer's world crisis. In consequence, when the First World War broke out Harwood stayed in *Sutlej* until March 1915. Her torpedo armament consisted of two 18in torpedo tubes with a range of only 1,700yds, and his action station was as officer of the forward 9.2in gun. Torpedoes could also be fired from the ship's boats, and Harwood recounted how, one day in Queenstown (Cobh), Ireland, they were firing torpedoes from a picket boat when:

> One torpedo went wild and proceeded direct towards the Ordnance Yard. The sentry patrolling the water front suddenly saw it. His first reaction was to come to the charge but as it came closer and closer he took fright, dropped his rifle and ran. We never saw him again and for all he was worth we could have blown up the entire Yard.

Otherwise, *Sutlej* was employed upon a continuous round of intercepting and examining British, Allied and neutral merchant shipping, often in bad weather, to search for contraband goods destined for Germany. It was March 1915 before Harwood was rescued from this drudgery by an appointment to *Vernon* to run that year's torpedo specialist course. Like many officers in such appointments he found himself dealing with 'mad inventors':

> One of these was a man called Billington who had the German rights for the Beck searchlight.[5] The crux of the matter came when he produced from his pocket an inch of carbon. All our hands went out to grab it and that gave us the secret we wanted. There was another one, a milliner from Ealing, who claimed to have invented

a beamless searchlight. He tried it out on the poop of the Vernon and when it was switched on he proudly said 'You see, no beam.' We all replied 'Yes, but no light!' He ended up by reporting me to the First Lord of the Admiralty as a menace to the country's welfare. In due course his letter reached my basket and I had the greatest pleasure in sending the Admiralty a suitable draft reply to this well-meaning but rather vacuous milliner.

So far, all of Harwood's appointments had been to elderly or obsolescent ships, but on 17 August 1915 he became torpedo officer of the brand-new battleship *Royal Sovereign* which was building in Portsmouth dockyard. As was customary in the Royal Navy, the engineer officer and then the principal departmental heads joined before the captain, who did not appear until the following spring. *Royal Sovereign* had been laid down on 15 January 1914 and launched on 29 April 1915: her lengthy building period owed something to a change of policy in Admiralty, which at the beginning of the war had halted work on new capital ships – indeed *Royal Sovereign* was one of the last battleships to be completed during the First World War. Seven ships of the class had been ordered, but two were completed as battlecruisers and the others were subject to much modification during the war. Armed with eight 15in guns in twin turrets, and fourteen 6in guns, *Royal Sovereign* had a torpedo armament of only four 21in torpedo tubes, but relatively complex requirements for electrical supply, which presumably justified the appointment of a torpedo officer.

Captain A T Hunt[6] commissioned *Royal Sovereign* in early May 1916, but she was still suffering teething problems with main engines and was left behind three weeks later when Admiral Sir John Jellicoe ordered the Grand Fleet to sea. Harwood left no record of his frustration at having missed the Battle of Jutland, nor much record of when she took part in a bungled attempt to ambush the German High Seas Fleet on 18 August 1916. Hunt was relieved in July 1917 on promotion to rear-admiral, when he reported on Harwood as 'a most excellent torpedo officer, worthy of early promotion', a great tribute to Harwood who, with only one year's seniority as a lieutenant-commander, was well short of the promotion zone.

Captain H M Doughty, who had been Harwood's captain in *Sutlej*, succeeded Hunt and was in command in April 1918 when the High Seas Fleet sortied to attack shipping off Norway. This was the last time *Royal Sovereign* and the Grand Fleet deployed together, until on 21 November 1918 they met the surrendered German fleet and escorted it into internment. Harwood described the internment to his uncle, Harry Harwood:[7]

> We left Rosyth at 2am last Thursday and the fleet formed up in two lines. The Germans were led in between us and we turned and steered for the Firth of Forth. On arrival at Rosyth the Germans were anchored in their billets and we anchored all round them. The next item on the programme was an inspection to see that they had no ammunition or torpedoes on board. The Commander, Gunnery Commander, Engineer Commander and myself went over and did this.
>
> The next day we all went over again with a large number of assistants to carry out a more detailed inspection. We found no signs of explosives which was satisfactory. It really was a most extraordinary proceeding. We went alongside in our picket boat and were piped over the side in the usual manner. We were received by several of their officers and their men were all aft smoking and lounging on the Quarter Deck. They have on board what they call 'Members of the Soldiers' and Workmen's Council'. They wear white and red bands on their arms. The officers have to get all their orders signed by the Council but once they are signed the officers have full power to carry them out. On the whole there is still quite a lot of discipline left although the men seem to spend all their time in smoking on the quarter deck.
>
> Needless to say we were very formal. Grave salutes and no shaking hands etc. and only strictly business remarks were passed. We were treated quite courteously and especially so by the men. It is very hard to understand, but I can't help thinking that the German sailors think they are on our side against their officers. For instance, the men were much more inclined to show us details of the ship than the officers were. Their ships were filthy and can't have been painted for years. I hear that in one case the Captain and First Lieutenant both burst into tears.

> On the whole we saw practically everything we were told. All the inspections being satisfactory they left in batches for Scapa Flow, each batch being led and escorted by a division of the Fleet. We left Rosyth at noon yesterday with 4 Germans (***Bayern, Markgraf, Kaiser Wilhelm*** and ***König Albert***) astern of us and the remainder of our division astern of them. We arrived here (Scapa Flow) at 9am this morning after an uneventful trip. Our Navigator at once went on board and took them to their internment billets. I don't think they will get away easily now. Even if any escape they will only get on to Orkney Island so they cannot do much harm. Meanwhile I fear we have to stay in this beastly place watching them.

On Doughty's recommendation, Harwood was awarded an OBE in the post-war honours list for his valuable services in ***Royal Sovereign***.

3
First Acquaintance with South America

Harwood joined the light cruiser HMS *Southampton* on 5 April 1919 as her first lieutenant and torpedo officer. Built before the war, armed with eight 6in guns, four 3pdrs and just two 21in torpedo tubes, she was one of the coal-burning Town class: her four funnels gave her a distinctive appearance. Her captain was Theodore J Hallett,[1] and she was the flagship of the Commander-in-Chief, South America, who was Rear-Admiral A T Hunt, who had been Harwood's captain in *Royal Sovereign*. As was the custom, whereby senior specialist officers also held staff appointments reporting to the admiral, Harwood held the dual appointment of staff torpedo officer to the commander-in-chief. Post-war the squadron comprised *Southampton*, two or three other cruisers, and the minesweeping sloop *Petersfield*. *Petersfield* served on the China Station and now on the South America Station as the commander-in-chief's yacht or headquarters, and was especially useful in the shallow waters of the River Plate, the wide estuary between Argentina and Uruguay where the rivers Uruguay and the Paraná meet, and known in Spanish as the Río de la Plata or River of Silver.[2]

The world then was separated by the Admiralty into stations into which the Royal Navy's worldwide responsibilities were distributed. The South American Station had, under different names and with differing boundaries, been in existence since the early nineteenth century, and it was under the protection of the Royal Navy that the Monroe doctrine had flourished. Following the break-up of the Spanish Empire in South America in the early nineteenth century, British Foreign Secretary George Canning claimed to 'have called the New World into existence to redress the balance of the Old': he wanted to keep other European powers out of the New World, fearing that British trade would be harmed if the New World were colonised by other Europeans. Canning's proposal to the USA for a joint declaration of policy, which separated the New World from the Old, was rejected by the USA in favour of a unilateral statement which became known as the Monroe Doctrine: 'that the American continents, by the free and independent condition which they have assumed and maintain, are henceforth not to be considered as subjects for future colonization by any European powers'.

However, during the Pax Britannica of most of the nineteenth century, when the USA was militarily weak, the Monroe Doctrine was maintained by the Royal Navy. Several countries owed their independence from Spain to British efforts and there was much goodwill towards Britain, as well as significant British communities in South America. British government supported political development, while British firms profited, building an immense, informal, commercial empire in South America. Britons owned extensive mining concessions and enormous sheep and cattle ranches, and meat-canning factories; most of the railways were British-owned and British-run. British investment had enabled Argentina to become one of the wealthiest nations of the world. In 1914 Harrods of London had even opened a branch in Buenos Aires, and during the First World War the British-owned canning factory at Fray Bentos, on the river Uruguay, had supplied over 250 million tins of bully beef to the Allied troops in France. Post-war, matters began to change, with South American countries starting to tax British profits more heavily and the USA, enriched by the war, seeking to gain economic control of an area which was considered to be in its sphere of influence.

Harwood dismissed his time in *Southampton* lightly:[3]

> I spent the rest of the war in the *Royal Sovereign* and after it was over I began to remember one of my theories about naval life which was to alternate between Harwood working for the good of the Service and the Service working for the good of Harwood. The chance to get back to my theory came when I was offered the appointment of 1st Lt and T of the *Southampton* and Fleet Torpedo Officer of the South American Squadron. It was a great life. Our bag for the commission exceeded 23,000 head of game. I might add that you won't get that sort of thing if you go out there now. The CinC, Admiral Hunt, had the excellent idea of having one of his two ships

on each side of South America and so the drill was to send the other ship a letter across the Andes and go on leave for a fortnight until the reply came back.

His visits to both coasts of South America, the ports where there were British interests and large 'Anglo' communities, and wild regions such as Tierra del Fuego and the Magellan Straits are told through Harwood's photograph albums. *Southampton* spent much of her time in the Plate estuary and landed guards to parade through the streets on the national days of the Argentine and of Uruguay. Port visits started with an exchange of official calls by his admiral, followed by dinners with long-winded speeches; Harwood noted that the admiral had to rely on an interpreter to translate and read his speeches for him. There were three interpreters in *Southampton*, Lieutenants John S Horn and Arthur H L Terry, and Paymaster Lieutenant-Commander Lloyd Hirst. Hirst had joined the Navy in 1904, had been secretary to the senior naval officer on the South American Station, and by the time of the Battle of Coronel (when a British squadron had been annihilated by a German squadron commanded by Admiral Graf von Spee) and the first Battle of the Falklands in 1914 (when von Spee's squadron had been annihilated) he had already been the station intelligence officer for four years.[4] Only a heavy sea had prevented him on the eve of Coronel from joining HMS *Good Hope* a few hours before she was sunk. Hirst spent the next four years either on the South America Station or on the South American desk of the Naval Intelligence Division in the Admiralty and post-war he would retire from the Navy to live in the Argentine. There, in the interwar years, he held the dormant appointment of Assistant British Naval Attaché to Buenos Aires and to Montevideo. Hirst and his family would become firm friends of Harwood, and between these two men few had greater knowledge of the region. Hirst would later play a part in the Battle of the River Plate at the start of the Second World War.[5]

The squadron was entirely dependent on local support facilities, and *Southampton* was docked twice in South America, once on 27 April 1920 for a routine docking at Bahía Blanca, Argentina, to repair underwater damage, and again in January 1921, at Talcahuano, Chile. Groundings seem to have been commonplace: Harwood's diary tells us that the Spanish battleship *España* needed to be docked after hitting a rock and that *Petersfield* went aground on a sandbank in the Plate for three days. No one seems to have been overly worried and Harwood's only concern was that in consequence of *Petersfield*'s mishap, he and his admiral arrived in Buenos Aires after the shooting season in Argentina had closed.

Opportunities for weapon training were taken on the rare occasions when two or more ships of the squadron were together and there was a squadron exercise off Maldonado on the River Plate in the summer of 1920. There were few operations, but in 1920, when there was a border dispute and risk of a war involving Peru, Bolivia and Chile, HMS *Weymouth* was sent to exercise off the border for a few days until the tension dropped. The presence of local navies is implied, a Japanese training squadron visited the Falklands, the Italian battleship *Roma* visited Santos in Brazil, and the US Pacific squadron visited Valparaíso at the same time as *Southampton*. Hunt's report of proceedings noted that 'the conduct of our liberty men was exemplary compared to others, particularly the Americans'. Discipline in *Southampton* does indeed seem to have been good: generous leave was given and even when the ship visited Rosario, 350 miles from the sea, for nearly three weeks in August and September 1919, the sick list was short, no punishment warrants were read, and much football was played.

Shooting and fishing

Sport, shooting and fishing filled Harwood's diaries. Admiral Hunt was an obsessive sportsman and a very good shot, and Harwood's first duty on arrival at a new port was to make the necessary contacts and arrange transport. Lieutenant John H Edelsten, the flag lieutenant, was also a sportsman and under the pseudonym 'Banderas' would write a book about their exploits.[6] The ship's bag of birds for the commission included 16,000 tinamou (related to a partridge), 4,000 duck and teal, 2,600 snipe and lesser numbers of other species down to eighteen swans and eleven rhea. There were 835 animals of various sorts including twenty deer, 714 hare, two wild goats, and two alligators. All this entailed much walking over mountainous ground and standing in cold, wet marshes. Sometimes the local railway company would provide a headquarters train, sometimes special coaches were attached to scheduled trains, while at other times a separate locomotive was provided, which would stop and wait while the officers did their shooting. In January 1920 Hunt, accompanied by Harwood and Edelsten, was allocated a carriage from Callao on the Ferrocarril Central del Perú (Central Railway of Peru) to shoot in the Andes, when they crossed a 15,583ft pass at Chiclo, before descending to the shooting grounds at between 10,000 and 12,000ft. Mountain sickness took its toll: walking was painful and every gunshot was head-splitting.

An opportunity for a similar trip came the following December when the admiral was invited to attend the opening of the Bolivian National Assembly in La Paz. There was shooting around Lake Titicaca, again affected by altitude sickness, and a call on the Bolivian army which included a day's shooting. Harwood played golf at 13,000ft and the ship's team beat the La Paz local British at tennis, but it was difficult to get around the dance floor at that altitude. Harwood later recounted:

> Another example of British push and enterprise which I always recollect with pride, I experienced in the Andes in Bolivia. We were crossing Lake Titicaca, a lake 12,000 feet up in the Andes, and after dinner I was talking to a Peruvian who said to me 'You English ought to be very proud of this steamer. In about 1850, long before any railway was established in these parts, this old ship was brought up in sections on pack mules, 12,000 feet up into the Andes. She was assembled up here by your men, and here she is still the most reliable of our Lake steamers'.

On 10 March 1921 a signal arrived out of the blue saying that the squadron was to be paid off. There was gloom all round. Everyone had been looking forward to another shooting season and the planned 1921 squadron exercise period at Maldonado had to be abandoned. *Southampton* went to Montevideo and then to Buenos Aires where last shooting and fishing expeditions were arranged, and much champagne flowed at a succession of sad farewell parties. Harwood spent his last dollars unsuccessfully at the races. However, he was given excellent reports, and promoted to commander at the young age of thirty-three.

This was a formative period in Harwood's life, when he developed a great affection for South America and its peoples and realised the importance of learning Spanish, in which he would become reasonably proficient. When in the late 1930s he commanded the South American Division himself, he would never suffer the indignity of needing a lieutenant to translate for him, as Hunt had. He got to know many of the British community, as well as local officials and naval officers. His love of shooting and fishing never left him. He had made firm friends with Lloyd Hirst, who helped him greatly in Montevideo in 1939, and with John Edelsten, who would become his chief of staff in the Mediterranean in 1942. Perhaps most important of all, he gained a knowledge of the shoal waters of the River Plate.

4
Working with Dudley Pound

After a brief appointment to the cruiser HMS *Dartmouth* for passage home and foreign service leave, Harwood joined the Royal Naval College, Greenwich, for the staff course at the end of September 1921. He was one of nine commanders and thirteen lieutenant-commanders on the course: also on the course were Wickham, whose name had been on the same promotion list, and John Edelsten from recent *Southampton* days.

After the First World War there had been an effort to improve in-career education of naval officers. The lieutenants' course, which had been suspended in 1911 was reintroduced,[1] and the study of naval history was encouraged by the appointment of Geoffrey Callender to the first chair in history at the Royal Naval College, Greenwich.[2] Attendance at the staff college was then much rarer than it has become in the twenty-first century. Selection then was a mark of high merit: the students spent a year on their course, though details of the syllabus do not seem to have survived. Harwood's course director was Captain Reginald Plunkett-Ernle-Erle-Drax,[3] whose judgement of Harwood was that he was 'mentally and physically active. Sound, good judgement. Better at concrete than at abstract problems but will make a staff officer of more than average ability'.

The naval staff

Harwood was appointed in August 1922 to a desk on the naval staff of the Admiralty. The naval staff was relatively new, having been created by Prime Minister Asquith and First Lord of the Admiralty Winston Churchill in the pre-war years. Post-war, a parliamentary paper detailed the distribution of duties amongst the naval staff,[4] which quickly developed into a core of officers responsible for the use of the fleet, and was organised along lines which largely stood the test of the twentieth century. Its tasks included the collection and dissemination of naval intelligence, the framing of long-term plans, naval tactics, strategy and policy. Under the First Sea Lord, who was also the Chief of Naval Staff, was a Deputy Chief of the Naval Staff who headed six divisions: operations, plans, naval intelligence, trade, gunnery and torpedo.

Harwood joined the plans division, which handled all large questions of naval policy and maritime warfare, in particular naval aspects of imperial policies; international law; general plans prepared to meet the possibility of fresh conflicts or a need for particular operations; types and numbers of ships and submarines; new scientific developments and, in consultation with the Imperial General Staff and the air staff, combined operations. Wartime events had shown a need to keep work concerning possible future operations separate from the conduct of current operations, and the plans division had been set up to plan future operations and oversee the provision of material.

Post-war, work on operations passed to the operations division and the plans division developed an expertise in naval policy and, later, budgetary matters. In the 1920s plans division became very heavily loaded by League of Nations business, together with other international treaty and disarmament matters: it played a considerable part in the international negotiations which sought greater stability and security, while at the same time safeguarding the interests of Britain and the Empire. Given Britain's standing as a naval power, the naval staff had far greater responsibilities for current international business than did its opposite numbers in the Army and RAF. Plans division also kept in very close touch with the naval intelligence division.[5]

In 1921 the First Sea Lord and Chief of Naval Staff was Admiral of the Fleet Lord Beatty,[6] Vice-Admiral Roger Keyes was Deputy Chief of Naval Staff, Captain Dudley Pound was Director of Naval Plans, and Captain George d'Oyly Lyon was the Deputy Director,[7] and among his fellow 'desk officers' were two Stubbington boys, Commander Tom Phillips and John Godfrey.[8] Many of these officers would impact upon Harwood's subsequent career, especially when in 1939 Pound had become First Sea Lord, and Lyon, Commander-in-Chief, South Atlantic. Pound was a shooting man, and Lyon was a sportsman who played first-class cricket and rugby for England; not surprisingly Harwood's game book for the winter of 1922/23 shows that he took every opportunity to pursue his love of shooting. Harwood's precise duties, when he was at his desk, are not known, but the most pressing problems of his days on the naval staff were trying to reconcile the requirements of the naval defence of the British Empire with the 1922 Washington Treaty, whose limitations on tonnage and size bore little relation to the Royal Navy's perceived requirements for imperial trade protection.

Marriage

Harwood became engaged to Joan Chard, the daughter of the late Selway Chard, a former surgeon, and his wife Ethel, who were then living at Broadwater, outside Worthing in Sussex. He was in his thirties and she in her early twenties: the two grandmothers had plotted a meeting over lunch, when apparently Harwood, who had an appointment on the golf course, was furious to realise that he had been set up. The grandmothers had done their matchmaking well and the marriage took place on 24 April 1924 at the Roman Catholic church of St Mary and All Angels in Worthing. For their honeymoon in April and May, the couple went to Paris and then down to the Pyrenees, where they stayed at San Sebastian and Pau and visited Lourdes. Harwood took his golf clubs and his fishing rod, but his fishing book records that he caught only one small fish. On return they took a lease on a house in Seymour Place in London.

Harwood left the Admiralty on 1 December 1924, when Dudley Pound wrote of him: 'Is keen and possesses initiative and imagination. Above average as a staff officer at the present time and should develop into a first class one if he can get to the bottom of a subject and not roam around it as he is inclined to do at present. Has done excellent work in the Plans Division'. Keyes, who in the spring of 1925 was going as Commander-in-Chief, Mediterranean Fleet, took Pound with him as his chief of staff and Pound wanted his plans team to go with him, including, despite the lukewarm report which he had written, Harwood.

Harwood and his new bride made their way overland, via a skiing holiday in Switzerland and then by Venice, Rome and Naples, to Malta where they rented 24 Strada-i-Torre [Tower Road] overlooking Sliema. In Malta, Joan was quickly incorporated into the life of Malta naval wives and welcomed into the Malta Amateur Dramatic

Company, where they began a lifelong friendship with Ella and Kay Warren who were considered the social queens of Malta. Joan returned to England for the hottest part of the Malta summer of 1925 and was presented at Court in July.

The Mediterranean 1925/26

Meanwhile, Harwood spent several months as Squadron Torpedo Officer, 3rd Battle Squadron, whose chief, Rear-Admiral Hugh Watson, was also Flag Officer, Second in Command, Mediterranean.[9] The flagship was the battleship HMS *Iron Duke,* and within a week of joining her, the fleet was in Greek waters and Harwood was organising shooting parties for Watson and his chief of staff, Commodore Barry Domvile.[10] After Easter in Malta, the fleet visited the Western Mediterranean and in May Keyes took over as commander-in-chief. When Watson was relieved, he reported on Harwood as being 'of exceptional ability' and that he was 'an excellent staff officer with a thorough knowledge of the tactical aspect of torpedo armament'. When Harwood heard this, he remarked, 'Good, because it stamps me as staff not material', in other words, his career would be in operations and not technology.[11]

On 4 August 1925 Harwood took up his long anticipated appointment as Fleet Torpedo Officer in the battleship HMS *Queen Elizabeth*. G K Chetwode (later to be Harwood's admiral in the cruiser *London*) was captain of the flagship,[12] and Hallett (who had been Harwood's captain in *Southampton*) was Captain of the Fleet. Harwood's fellow staff officers were a distinguished group: besides Pound they were Phillips as Fleet Operations Officer; Lieutenant-Commander George Creasy (a future Admiral of the Fleet who married Harwood's second cousin, Monica Ullathorne) was Phillips's assistant;[13] Commander Bruce Fraser (the future wartime Commander-in-Chief, Home Fleet 1942–44, Eastern Fleet 1947–48, and then First Sea Lord) was Fleet Gunnery Officer;[14] and Lieutenant-Commander Stephen King-Hall, an enterprising officer with a talent for organising amateur theatricals to a near-professional standard and later a Member of Parliament, was Fleet Intelligence Officer.[15]

The Mediterranean Fleet was Britain's premier fleet, with an average strength of two battleship squadrons of four ships each, two cruiser squadrons, one or two aircraft carriers, four destroyer flotillas and a submarine flotilla. The main business of the fleet was preparation for war, with sport and diplomacy as secondary purposes, though peacetime restrictions on fuel consumption and ammunition expenditure bore heavily on fleet exercises. When not embarked in the fleet flagship, HMS *Queen Elizabeth*, the commander-in-chief administered the fleet from shore offices in the eighteenth-century Auberge de Castille in Valletta (now the prime minister's offices). Keyes, as commander-in-chief, had a laissez-faire attitude and preferred 'parties and polo', while his chief of staff, the soon-to-be promoted Rear-Admiral Pound, who was then in his full vigour, ran the fleet from day to day.[16] While Pound's energy was admirable, as one keen observer, Royer Dick,[17] put it, 'dancing till early in the morning, shooting and working', Pound found it difficult to delegate and the staff found his interference upsetting.

The fleet sailed for the Eastern Mediterranean shortly after Harwood joined, and once in Greek waters shooting started again in earnest, particularly during a fortnight in Kalamuti Bay where good bags of quail were had. Harwood soon became known as one of the best shots in the ship, while Pound found time to produce a guide book, *Shooting in the Mediterranean*, to which Harwood undoubtedly contributed. Nevertheless, Harwood was frustrated, as surviving letters to his new wife show:[18]

> Fed up with the whole damn thing and wish to goodness I had never shifted over [from *Iron Duke*]. Everything seems to be confusion and makes the impression of being frightfully smart. Result, I am fed up. Staff officers appear to be looked on as midshipmen. One always to be on watch. What we should do nobody knows. Pound does everything himself. Duty Staff Officer fetches him a pad, hands him a pencil and runs message from him to CinC. Yesterday, three times, I was sent off to tell CinC something. I did absolutely nothing except stand up on the bridge and run messages. After 21 years at sea this bores me.
>
> Any exercise Pound runs. I might be a mere cipher and not worth looking at. Keyes (CinC) quite good and would, I think, like to be human. But feels he should not be. Pound deadly serious, sense of

humour vanished. Looking for trouble to find out what's wrong in everything and everywhere. Trying to draw everybody's work on to himself. Grossly overworked. Such is life in the Navy. The dear old *Iron Duke* was peaceful, cheerful and human. So different, and it means such a lot.

Dear old Hallett [captain of the fleet]. God bless him. The only spark of humour. Strolls about, gets into odd corners and spins a yarn. Then feels perhaps he shouldn't and goes off with a serious countenance and then comes back and has another yarn.

Fraser. You know him. Always cheerful. Phillips (Tom) – Fleet Operations Officer (FOO) – rather bored and bolshie but quite hard working and has no intention of being anything but just right, at the back however he and I will sigh a bit.

Perfect confusion, beautifully worded orders as to how the happiness of the Fleet depends on us etc. No information as to how we are to do it. No short cuts or aids such as we had in *Iron Duke.* i.e. condensed programmes so we could see at a glance what to do. Each staff officer working on his own and generally Pound doing his work as well without telling him.

And such, my love, is what your poor B has struck. Fame, Glory, you may call it. But give me a light hearted job. They are always more efficient.

One problem which faced Harwood and his fellow staff officers was the possibility that Kemal Atatürk, the leader of Turkey, might seize the Mosul oilfields in northern Iraq, in defiance of the British Mandate for Mesopotamia (ie Iraq) and Palestine, which had been awarded in 1920. There was not much new thinking about the response: it was thought that the fleet might, as it had attempted in 1810 and in 1915, force the Dardanelles to threaten Constantinople from the Sea of Marmara, the only new twist being that the Army would land in European Turkey and at the Gulf of Alexandretta (modern Gulf of İskenderun) in the easternmost Mediterranean on the border between Turkey and Syria. When it was realised that the fleet lacked a landing force and that the Mobile Naval Base Organisation (a forerunner of today's Commandos) was little more than a paper one, a Royal Marines Striking Force was organised from within the fleet and exercised in June 1926.

By then the Turkish crisis was over and a new problem was the growing power of Japan, seen as a threat to Singapore and Malaya.[19] A plan was prepared to force a passage through the Malacca Straits while escorting a fast, military convoy, and an exercise, codenamed MU, to simulate this was held in the Aegean in August 1926. The exercise found that the Straits could not be forced against determined opposition and that the better option was the permanent stationing of ships in Singapore.[20]

There were also persistent threats of trouble between Jews and Arabs in Palestine, of a Muslim rising in French North Africa, and of a coup against Mussolini in Italy. As always, the fleet had to be ready to protect and possibly evacuate British nationals in the event of political trouble or a natural disaster anywhere in the Mediterranean. Given these practical problems, exercises in the protection of slow merchant convoys against attack by submarines or aircraft were not prevalent.[21] Instead, the fleet prepared to refight aspects of the Battle of Jutland – even though Pound himself frequently told young officers about 'the awful lack of initiative at Jutland and insist[ed] that the fleet must be trained on new lines'.[22]

Pound drove the fleet hard, so hard that the lower deck gave him the nickname 'Twenty-four ounces', because he always wanted more than his sixteen ounces for his pound.[23] Harwood's view was: 'This fleet and Pound have gone exercise mad. The amount we have to do is awful and everybody is fed up with it'.[24] For several weeks, Harwood's comments in letters to his wife continued in the same vein: 'Pound still deadly serious. I don't think he can dislike me suddenly, but he is very off-hand. The same all round with us all.'[25]

In another letter Harwood wrote:[26]

> Pound arranged all sorts of drills on the way [to Argostoli, Kefalonia]. Everybody is fed up with so much exercising. He is too clever and headstrong and does not take heed of the personality side. If men or officers don't want to work, I don't mean lazy but just want to rest, they must be led and not driven. That, to my mind is the crux of the situation now. It could be done but driving exercise after exercise won't do it. Where we differ from the Atlantic Fleet is they have a month's rest every four, i.e. during each leave period. This

> fleet leads a hectic life all summer and while at Malta there is very little peace for the sailors although the officers have a great time ... This is a most disturbing ship. Everybody looks fierce, busy and bored stiff. Nobody seems to like to relax except Hallett and Fraser – a good fellow and he and I are great friends. Phillips struggles manfully, hating every moment of it. Poor old Phillips. He thinks of his sloop out in Africa when he was a little god.

Harwood was learning by example how things should not be done: 'Things are settling down, but not pleasantly ... Everything seems to be in a muddle and sticks at Pound. He tries to do too much. Thinks he is omnipotent and that nobody else can be trusted. It's quite all right in theory but bad in practice.'[27] And he was becoming increasingly frustrated: 'Fed up with Pound. However quite affable, but disagreed hotly. Phillips (Tom) trying to do my job with Pound. Fed up with Phillips. Fed up with the whole damn lot.'[28] He was also learning how to deal with Pound:

> A trying morning. Pound, as he did at Admiralty, generally manages to deal with the wrong person. This led to Phillips and he crossing my track over something I was keen on. Result, I had to go and see him. He was rather hostile at first, then argued and finally we narrowed the trouble down to a definite point of disagreement. Naturally he had the decision to make so I had to accept it. Ended peacefully, though as a result I got through another point I badly wanted.[29]

Pound and Harwood seemed to reach an understanding and a little later Harwood was able to tell his wife, 'Left at 10pm for Lemnos. A lovely moon light night and I sat on deck and talked to Pound. He suddenly became most affable. I suppose as the subject was shooting he relaxed.'[30]

There were still difficulties, not least some caused by ***Queen Elizabeth*** being restricted to a top speed of 11 knots on the grounds of economy, and Harwood, in the privacy of his letters to Joan, continued to be critical, especially of Pound:[31]

> Spent the afternoon in exercises. Now, with this economy, every moment at sea has to be employed; not a minute wasted. At 9pm we started one of my torpedo exercises. The weather was bad and we had to reduce the number of torpedoes (fired) from 3 to 1. A perfect pandemonium ensued. Everyone talking and giving orders and making signals. The CinC was awful; grumbling, – do this, do this, – make this signal, – what's she doing? I retired into the background and every time I was sighted something unpleasant happened. All over nothing. The exercise went perfectly. There were no delays or hitches other than those made by the panickers. I got a copy of all the signals made. One third were unnecessary, one third would not have been necessary if Pound had not altered my orders, and the other third were normal. Really it turned an interesting little exercise into a perfect misery. To start with, I don't believe he had even read the orders for the exercise, so no wonder he did not know much about it. The next minute, peace perfect peace reigns; it's an extraordinary state of affairs.

However, the intimate and revealing letters between Harwood and his wife dried up, presumably because in October 1925 she returned to Malta while *Queen Elizabeth* was refitting in Malta dockyard and the staff worked from the commander-in-chief's offices ashore. When in mid-January 1926 the refit was over, Joan remained in Malta and developed a great interest in the archaeology and architecture of the islands. In May 1926 Joan was in Syracuse, Taormina and Rome during the visit of the newly modernised battleship *Warspite*, which had replaced *Queen Elizabeth* as flagship, and she was in Venice in early July, from where she went home for the birth of their first son, Henry, born in London on 25 August 1926.

Meanwhile, the Hot Toddy Club kept in touch. 'Wickie' Wickham was the captain of the minesweeping-sloop *Cornflower* which had recommissioned at Malta in the spring of 1925; 'Riddles' Ridley was Squadron Torpedo Officer in the light cruiser HMS *Coventry* and took part in many visits and exercises of the Mediterranean Fleet in 1925/26; and Maitland-Dougall passed through Malta in the cruiser HMS *Emerald*. Only the Australia-born 'Crack' Crace was left in Britain, commanding HMS *Osprey*, the anti-submarine school at Portland.

The fleet was in the Aegean again in September and made the most of the available shooting. On 6 September Keyes, Pound, Harwood and five other guns shot 195 partridge on Imbros. In October Harwood was sent home to visit the Admiralty, which enabled him to see his newly born son. In December Pound was relieved and went home to become Assistant Chief of the Naval Staff and a junior member of the Board of Admiralty: in his nearly two years in the Mediterranean Fleet he had recorded 100 days' shooting,[32] most of them with Harwood.

Harwood, who had learned much from working and living closely with the other rising stars of his generation, was relieved as Fleet Torpedo Officer a few weeks later at the end of January 1927. His relief was none other than 'Crack' Crace – who was succeeded at the anti-submarine school by another of the Hot Toddy Club, Wickham. Harwood might have been surprised to read Keyes's report on him that he was 'a very able and hardworking staff officer. Possesses initiative and imagination. Has done excellent work on my staff.'

5
The War College

From early February to mid-April 1927 Harwood was on leave before his next job appointment as commander (ie second in command) of the new heavy cruiser HMS *Cumberland*, which was building at Vickers-Armstrong's yard at Barrow-in-Furness. She was one of the first of the eagerly awaited County-class or 'Treaty' cruisers designed and built under the terms of the 1922 Washington Treaty. The treaty had specified 10,000 tons as the maximum size of a cruiser, and an unintended consequence was a new arms race to build the best 'Treaty' cruisers. Subsequent naval treaties sought to address this by limiting overall cruiser, destroyer and submarine tonnage. Three-funnelled ships of nominally 10,000 tons displacement, fast and with long-range, and armed with eight 8in guns, the County class were the very latest in British cruiser design.

The Harwoods rented a house in Barrow while *Cumberland* was being made ready for sea. Harwood's job was to prepare her for commissioning, drafting orders, preparing the internal organisation, welcoming aboard her complement, and setting the tone in the new wardroom of officers. She successfully commissioned on 15 December 1927, under the command of Captain Arthur Snagge,[1] and in the New Year of 1928 she sailed to join the 5th Cruiser Squadron on the China Station.

The China Station

The Commander-in-Chief, China was a famous fighting admiral, Vice-Admiral Sir Reginald Tyrwhitt, who had distinguished himself as commander of the Harwich Force, a flotilla of light ships based on the east coast during the First World War.[2] Tyrwhitt flew his flag in the heavy cruiser HMS ***Hawkins*** and his fleet enjoyed bases in Singapore, Hong Kong and Weihaiwei, in the northeast of China. Ships on the

China Station usually consisted of several older cruisers and destroyers, and the Chinese rivers, as Harwood knew from his pre-war days, were patrolled by a flotilla of suitable, shallow-draught gunboats, all in their distinctive livery of white hull and dark funnels.

The situation in China had deteriorated since Harwood had been there twenty years before. After the death of Sun Yat-sen in 1925, the Kuomintang (Chinese Nationalist Party), or KMT, had broken into left-wing and right-wing factions, the latter led by Chiang Kai-shek. In north China there was a bewildering kaleidoscope of constantly changing alliances between various warlords, leaving a vacuum which the Communist Party of China filled. Offshore, there was widespread piracy, while inland there were anti-foreigner demonstrations and riots along both the West River and the Yangtze, the main artery of Chinese trade. In 1927 there were forced evacuations of women and children at Hankow (Hankou) and Kiuchiang (Jiujiang), where there were British concessions, and even the concession at Shanghai, one of several extraterritorial treaty ports, was threatened. The China Fleet consisted of an aircraft carrier, four cruisers (reinforced to eight), nine destroyers, twelve submarines, and several gunboats of improved class to the *Bramble* which Harwood had known. Other navies, the Dutch, French, Italian, Japanese, Spanish and US also had ships on the station. While urging Tyrwhitt to exercise restraint, the British government sent several thousand imperial reinforcements which Tyrwhitt virtually commanded through Major Lord Gort, the Army chief of staff. Tyrwhitt the warrior proved a considerable diplomat in protecting British lives and property against all-comers, including the increasingly bellicose Japanese.[3]

By the time *Cumberland* arrived on station, the troubles had temporarily died down, and it was even safe for Tyrwhitt to make a summer visit to Weihaiwei in his yacht, *Petersfield*. Harwood's time in *Cumberland* was short, no letters have survived, and he was selected for promotion to captain in December 1928 and relieved on 15 March 1929. Arthur Snagge gave him an excellent confidential report: 'A most brilliant and efficient officer ... Intellectual and technical ability are combined with a fine personal character and forceful power of command'. Tyrwhitt obviously agreed and would write to Harwood after the Battle of the River Plate: 'My dear Harwood. I can't tell you how pleased and delighted I was to hear of your glorious action ... It was an additional pleasure for me to see your success as I was instrumental in your promotion to Captain which, incidentally, you earned handsomely.'[4]

Joan travelled to Egypt in April 1929 to meet her husband on his way home, and they visited Cairo and travelled up river to Luxor and Karnak, then crossed by ship to Athens where they toured the classic sites, including Marathon and the temple of Poseidon at Sounion; then through Serbia to Venice, which they enjoyed visiting again, before moving on to Lake Como, returning via Lausanne to England.

HMS Warwick *in command, home waters*

On 1 August 1929 Harwood was appointed in command of the destroyer HMS *Warwick*, a small wartime destroyer in the Home Fleet. He was second in command of the 5th Destroyer Flotilla and thereby senior officer of the 10th Destroyer Division. This would normally have been a commander's appointment, but a new policy had recently been introduced to give junior captains experience of destroyer command. The Home Fleet spent much of the autumn of 1929 in Scottish waters and Harwood was able to get some shooting. In London and in New York the stock markets crashed, setting off the Great Depression.

The spring cruise of 1930 was centred on Gibraltar, and in the summer Harwood took two ships, *Warwick* and *Velox*, on a goodwill visit to Bristol. Two of his first public speeches date from this visit. He told the Society of Merchant Venturers:[5]

> A year ago I was again in the Yangtze in a Cruiser, the conditions there were appalling. At Chin Kiang [Chenkiang or Zhenjiang] the British concession was overrun and in the hands of the Chinese, but our merchants were still undeterred, they worked ashore, when they could, by day, and lived by night in a small motor boat in the lee, I am glad to say, of a British gunboat.

At home, Prime Minister Ramsay MacDonald's second Labour administration was focused upon domestic policy and wanted to reduce the naval budget yet further. At the Lord Mayor's banquet in

Bristol, Harwood showed that he knew how to deliver a nicely turned plea for the Royal Navy, using phraseology which might be timeless:[6]

> In these times of financial reductions it is a great encouragement to us to realise that interest in the Navy is being maintained by the British public in general and by one of the leading shipping ports in particular. I would like to assure you that the efficiency of the Navy is being maintained, our exercises, naturally cut down by financial stringency, are being carried out on progressive and up to date lines. Equally however, with you all, we watch with sympathy and understanding the various efforts that are now being made to increase the chances of peace. On the other hand I feel that I should not be honest to my own convictions if I did not remind you of the fact that there is a limit beyond which the Navy could be reduced with safety. Should war unfortunately occur it must be remembered that the food supply of these islands will not last three weeks unless the fighting services acting in co-operation are able to insure its safe passage. The cost of these services is the insurance premium which the three fighting services ask from the Empire.

On leaving *Warwick* in August 1930 the flotilla leader, Captain R N C Hallifax,[7] reported on Harwood as 'a man of tact and intense loyalty who had brought his ship to a high state of efficiency and done much to increase the efficiency of the division'.

Imperial Defence College

Earlier in 1930, the London Naval Conference hosted by Great Britain, France, Italy, Japan and the United States had reviewed the effect of the 1922 Washington Naval Treaty and explored the possibility of further naval disarmament. After three months' meetings, general agreement had been secured on the regulation of submarine warfare, a five-year moratorium on the construction of capital ships, and the extension of the limitation on aircraft carriers provided for by the earlier treaty. The USA, Great Britain and Japan agreed a limit on battleship tonnage in the ratios of 10:10:7, as well as limits on numbers of cruisers, destroyers and submarines.

Uninvolved in these talks and seemingly unaffected, on 22 September 1930 Harwood started a two-month tactical course at Portsmouth, and he also took a gun in a shoot at Stubbington. Then in January 1931 he was appointed to the recently established Imperial Defence College, at that time located at Buckingham Gate.[8] This was a year's course for officers of captain's rank from all three services who were considered likely to be promoted further. Harwood made full use of the IDC shoot near Sudbury. At the end of the course, the director, Air Marshal Robert Brooke-Popham,[9] reported on Harwood as having good mental powers and making good use of them: 'Harwood has a strong personality and would always make his presence felt'.

Meanwhile, the Harwoods rented Tubbenden Lodge at Orpington, a substantial six-bedroom Victorian house overlooking Mr Cook's chicken farm, home of the Buff Orpington. The Harwoods' second son, Stephen, was born in London on 16 December 1931. To fill in time before his next job, Harwood attended the senior officers' technical course in the early months of 1932.

HMS London, *Mediterranean and Malta*

On 28 March 1932 Harwood was appointed to command of the County-class cruiser HMS *London*, a sister ship of *Cumberland*, wearing the flag of the admiral commanding the 1st Cruiser Squadron in the Mediterranean, Rear-Admiral George Chetwode, who had been captain of *Queen Elizabeth* when Harwood was Fleet Torpedo Officer. His second in command was an old friend from South America days, and fellow student on the naval staff course, John Edelsten, who had already been executive officer for two years; their time together in *London* was short, but undoubtedly she was 'a splendid ship and a very happy one'.[10]

At the beginning of the 1930s there was little to distinguish the activities of the Mediterranean Fleet from those in the 1920s, though the strategic situation of the Mediterranean Fleet was changing: Mussolini was becoming more vocal and a pro-Italian movement was growing in Malta. As arbiter of peace and imperial police force from the Pillars of Hercules to the Hellespont and the Pyramids, the Mediterranean Fleet was larger than the next two major Mediterranean naval powers, France and Italy, with whom relations were good. It was noted that the Italian men and ships were improving and they were described in official reports as 'impressive', 'striking' and 'very creditable'. The fleet's routine, however, was largely unchanged since Harwood's previous service. There were two or three cruises each year; annual combined fleet exercises with the Home Fleet based each spring on Gibraltar; tactical exercises on passage; goodwill visits to Mediterranean ports; and weapon training in the Maltese exercise areas, followed by maintenance at Malta at the end of the year. The Invergordon Mutiny, in 1931, seems hardly to have affected the Mediterranean Fleet.[11]

When Harwood arrived, the commander-in-chief was Admiral Chatfield,[12] who was worried about the increasing obsolescence of his capital ships; faced with a difficult choice whether he should have battleships or aircraft carriers, he opted for the former. In confined waters he thought carriers would be more valuable than battleships, but did not want to give strength to the 'false theories' that battleships were of 'questionable utility'.

In October 1932 Admiral Sir William Fisher, known as 'WW', relieved Chatfield.[13] Fisher, who had long experience of the Mediterranean, used his influence to support Lord Strickland, the leader of the Malta Constitutional party.[14] Harwood, a Catholic, would also have appreciated Fisher's support of Bishop Mikiel Gonzi in opposing the pro-Italian faction.[15] Fisher built up a strong rapport with the Maltese people and supported many local charities, particularly the church at Mgarr (built and paid for by the local population through the sale of eggs), and he also persuaded the Malta Union Club, hitherto a preserve of the British, to admit Maltese members.

The far-sighted Fisher was also intent upon making his fleet ready for war, and exercises at sea and in harbour became more realistic. Fuelling at sea and air defence of the fleet were being investigated and increasing importance was placed on damage control. However, Fisher rang alarms in the Admiralty and wider in Whitehall when he voiced the idea that in the event of a war with Italy, Malta might become untenable, and he demanded increased high-angle, ie anti-aircraft, guns for his ships, and more practice. Nevertheless, 30 May 1932, when Harwood's *London* was launch ship for a Fairey Queen, a radio-controlled target plane, was a frustrating day; after six hours' manoeuvring to find the right conditions the target was launched at 14:30 and promptly shot down on only its second run, thus depriving the majority of the fleet of their much-needed shooting practice.[16]

Fisher organised debates between his officers, the motion for one being whether the Mediterranean Fleet could operate in the Mediterranean in the face of an air threat. Whether Harwood spoke for or against the motion is not known, but Bertram Ramsay (who would then have been the captain of the battleship HMS ***Royal Sovereign***) remembered Harwood as a cruiser captain who was beginning to make his own name. Nearly twenty years later Ramsay wrote:[17]

> Just a few lines to say how glad I was to hear of your appointment as ACNS(F) ... Knowing your independent views and tendency to say and do just what you think right, without ulterior motives, I feel that it is a matter for general congratulation that you will now be in a position to exercise those characteristics to some purpose. You may, and almost certainly will, find yourself in a minority on occasions, even as at that notable meeting in the Canteen at Malta when debating WW's motion that the Mediterranean Fleet 'could proceed to and remain in, any part of the Mediterranean, disregarding the threat of air attack.'

Meanwhile, in August 1932 the Prince of Wales and his brother George visited the fleet at Corfu, and ***London*** was inspected by the heir to the throne; each flying in the back seat of a Fairey F, the princes witnessed a torpedo air attack on the fleet – though Prince George's aircraft became temporarily lost when the carrier HMS ***Glorious*** ran into a fog bank. Sporting prowess was still regarded as an important indicator of a ship's efficiency and morale, and the annual fleet regatta, a series of pulling (rowing) and sailing races, was usually held each summer at a remote anchorage in Greek waters. Harwood managed to keep ***London*** ahead of the rest of the squadron in both weapon training and sporting achievements. She was 'cock of the fleet' in the 1933 pulling regatta and won more sporting trophies that year than any cruiser before her.[18] Harwood the photographer now possessed a cine camera, a novelty in those days, and filmed ***London***'s regatta crews, showing the film to his crews in slow motion so that they could learn from mistakes. He also used the crib on boat racing which had been written and printed by George Chetwode, when he commanded the battleship HMS *Warspite* in 1926/27, and which Harwood kept annotated until 1938.[19]

Joan and Henry lived in a rented house in Sliema. Their Austin 16 car was shipped out from England, which enabled picnics in the country and swimming at the numerous sandy beaches round the island. Stephen, less than one year old, remained at home under the care of the two grandmothers. On 14 July 1933 Harwood enjoyed a second audience with the Pope, travelling to Rome with a group of sailors, mostly from HMS *London*, to meet Pope Pius XI. He described this in a letter to Joan:[20]

> Arrived at bronze doors on right of Vatican at noon. Capt Potter, PMO, Enright, a Pay Cadet, Bruce Cooke and Self.[21] Im Thurn did not come at the last moment ... We all knelt down as he came round and gave his hand and we kissed his ring ... He then came to the corner and made a long speech, quite enjoying himself doing it. The Vice Rector then translated it. How pleased he was to see us and how it pleased him to think of the distance we had come. He always liked sailors because they represented to him courage and discipline and he said he always felt that sailors, with the bad weather they had to put up with, were nearer to God than anybody else. He said when he gave the Blessing it would apply to everybody we thought of; our wives, mothers, children, friends etc., those who wished to have joined our party and couldn't come, our ships and those in them, our houses etc. etc. Very charming. The whole way through the translation he was nodding to emphasise the points he wished to make. He can understand but not speak English. He then gave us his blessing and I was told he could be given three cheers which I did. He then came over to Potter who was the senior officer and shook hands with him and went off. As only crowned heads are supposed to shake hands with him we all chaffed Potter.

When Chetwode was superseded in June 1933, he wrote of Harwood as having an outstanding personality with an excellent power of command, that he had produced a most efficient ship with happy and contented personnel, and he recommended that Harwood be given as much sea time as possible as he was an exceptionally able officer who was certain to rise to the highest ranks of the service. Fisher endorsed this report: 'Concur. Undoubtedly an able officer'; however, he followed this with the withering comment 'Too corpulent and placid to be inspiring'.[22]

Harwood's admiral for his last six months in command of *London* was Rear-Admiral J K im Thurn,[23] whose report was of 'a good Captain with a quick brain and plenty of common sense. A very capable staff officer, quick, accurate and methodical. Strong personality with a tendency to be dogmatic but accepts loyally an over-ruling decision. Good social qualities. Plays golf, is a good shot and keen on fishing'. Fisher's endorsement was: 'Concur. A very competent Captain', but again he found fault: 'His bodily activity is not the equal of his mental and he will have to watch the former'.[24]

War College, 1934–36

Harwood was relieved in *London* on 13 February 1934 and, after foreign service leave, was appointed 30 April 1934 as a student on the senior officers' war course (SOWC) at the Royal Naval College, Greenwich. Established in 1900, the SOWC taught captains and senior commanders tactical and strategic naval war games, they studied and wrote reports on various problems, and heard lectures from distinguished visitors on a range of politico-military issues.[25] After three months' study, Harwood was appointed to the directing staff under Vice-Admiral Ragnar Colvin, a Stubbington boy; the two other captains on the staff were A G Talbot and J M Mansfield.[26]

Although the Conference for the Reduction and Limitation of Armaments (or General Disarmament Conference) had broken down in 1934, arms limitation does not seem to have featured as a topical object of study on the SOWC. Of more concern was the Anglo-German Naval Agreement, signed in 1935, which limited the German navy to a ratio of 35:100 to the Royal Navy, and also that the Germans were already commissioning a new class of three heavy cruisers or Panzerschiffe. Under an earlier treaty, the 1919 Treaty of Versailles, supposedly these were limited to being 10,000-ton ships, but they were armed with six 28cm (11in) guns in two triple turrets; as a secondary armament they carried eight 5.9in guns. Though they were not fast ships, their diesel engines gave them long range: the British called them pocket battleships. The comparable British 'Treaty' cruisers were the County class, also 10,000 tons, capable of higher speeds but of shorter range and armed with eight guns of smaller size, 8in. While the Admiralty insisted that seventy cruisers were needed for the defence of the Empire and trade, there was continuing financial stringency in Britain, and the last two heavy cruisers of the interwar years, *York* and *Exeter*, were smaller still at 8,500 tons and with one less turret of 8in guns. The new class were light cruisers: the *Leander*-class cruisers of the 1930s, two of which were *Achilles* and *Ajax*, were armed with eight, even smaller, 6in guns; their main armament was only fractionally larger than the German pocket battleships' secondary armament.

Another debate which raged in Whitehall in the 1930s was over the control of the Fleet Air Arm, but naval aviation does not seem to have been on the syllabus of the SOWC either. Harwood's principal contribution to the SOWC was a series of six lectures in the summer of 1936 on the attack and defence of trade.[27] He opened with a definition of terms, a discussion of international maritime law, and a historical review of war on trade and then looked in depth at raider warfare by the Germans in the First World War, identifying three phases when they had used regular warships, armed merchant ships and submarines. In his discussion of British countermeasures he concluded that 'Often our strategy was at fault, and we followed the raiders round, about four days astern of them, instead of protecting the focal area and making the raider come to us'. Patrols, he told his students, were essential but uneconomical; no attempts were to be made to patrol trade routes 'but instead patrol focal and terminal points'. Covering forces for patrols were essential. He summed up the tactics which should be used by the raiders: originality, initiative and surprise; go for fruitful areas and vital supplies; avoid action, even with an inferior enemy, unless satisfied that you can destroy him without him damaging you at all; strike suddenly, strike hard, advertise your presence and then shift your area; and conserve seaworthiness and ammunition because you are sure to have to fight one day.

The defender, Harwood told his audience, must protect vital areas, concentrate at some suitable point, not start looking for a needle in a haystack, and never give up the chase. It was during a war game on raiders that Harwood explained what tactics he would use. A Canadian student, Commander J A Heenan recalled:[28]

> The main object of Captain Harwood's lectures concerned the navies of the world vis-à-vis the Royal Navy. Germany's pocket battleships had then emerged which Captain Harwood called the greatest challenge the Royal Navy ever faced. He was referring to our bases overseas and trade routes, where, for their protection we had only cruisers, which singly were no match against the pocket battleship. However, Captain Harwood, in his lectures and drawing board, explained the tactics he would employ in fighting a pocket battleship with three cruisers (which were just those employed by him in the Battle of the Plate).

In one game a single heavy cruiser met a pocket battleship and hastily withdrew to shadow. Harwood recalled: 'We made great play with the damage done by one hit to the ***Dresden*** by the ***Kent*** [at the Battle of the Falklands in 1914] and how it kept her off the trade-routes for 3 weeks. We drew the conclusion that whenever possible one must attack to try to get even that one hit ... In the post mortem the captain of this cruiser got an imperial bottle'.[29] Harwood had certainly owned the tactic as his own idea, writing to Joan after the Battle of the River Plate:[30]

> Dudley Pound says [on 11 January 1940] 'Even if all your ships had been sunk you would have been right' ... You see, a raider is thousands of miles from his base. Attack him. Make him use his ammunition. Hit him, and he can't repair his damage without going in and risking internment. Reduce his efficiency and upset the morale of his crew. He is then weaker and some other unit can come later and dispose of him. It is not easy to sink a raider, lovely of course to do so, to lame him is most valuable. It is a combination of all these reasons that makes it essential to attack and, as it turned out, forced him into Montevideo either to internment, scuttling or even an escape but in a much weaker condition than he originally was. He is therefore easier to find again and be finished off. At his

> best he may only be able to limp home to Germany. He is cleared off the trade routes. Our ships, cargoes, merchant marine are saved. Read the above carefully. The principles are as old as sea warfare. I merely applied them with dash and the offensive sprit ... The other side of the story is luck and fate. I was not touched.

Harwood, of course, would apply these tactics with a nuance: he would divide his force and attack from two or more sectors. 'I discussed how best to do it with Captain Woodhouse of the *Ajax* and we decided that we must split and attack from either flank and in effect we did a shoot on these lines at Bermuda before the war'.[31] This would split the enemy's fire control and also provide opportunities for torpedo attack. 'It is just the old principle,' he told Pound, 'of damaging a raider thousands of miles from his base, making him use up all his ammunition, upsetting his maintenance services and giving him severe damage to repair which can only be done in harbour'.[32]

Other subjects on which Harwood gave lectures was one called 'Co-operation, Concentration and Economy of Force', a talk which opened with words which may have come back to him when he met General Bernard Montgomery: 'Co-operation fails when it is due to (a) inefficiency (b) tactlessness, jealousy or psychological inability to co-operate or (c) a clash of strong and forceful personalities who look at the problem quite honestly from different view-points.'

Harwood also lectured on the problems of fighting a naval war with, separately, France, Germany, Japan and Russia. There were lectures by others on India and Afghanistan, the Balkans, and on West Africa; the economies of Germany and Italy; how to write a staff appreciation; the use of armed forces in civil disturbances; the personalities of great leaders; the economies of Italy and Germany; and international law. Quite when Harwood learned that his next appointment would be in South America is not known, but there were sheaves of handwritten notes about South America.

Harwood made the most of two years' family life in the comfortable house at Orpington, playing golf at Royal St George's, Sandwich, and in April 1935 he reached the finals of the club's pro-am Sidgwick Cup. His handicap was 7. He left Greenwich on 24 July 1936, when Admiral Colvin reported on him as 'a most able officer of strong and forceful personality who had done much to relate the academic side of the course to the practical requirements of Senior officers ... a strong character and tenacious of his opinions but always loyal in furthering the policies imposed on him from above. His social and physical qualities were excellent'.

When Harwood knew that in his next appointment he would be dual-hatted as captain of the heavy cruiser HMS *Exeter* and commodore of the South American Division, part of the Royal Navy's small America and West Indies Fleet, he applied for leave to study Spanish for two months at his own expense, and he and his family spent the summer holidays of 1936 at Ramsgate, where a Spanish priest from the local Catholic church taught him.

Meanwhile, the third and last of the German pocket battleships, *Graf Spee*, had been commissioned on 6 January 1936.

6
The Commodore

Harwood was forty-seven years old when he took command of the 8in cruiser HMS *Exeter* on 17 September 1936; he also took the rank of commodore 2nd class and command of the South American Division of the America and West Indies Station. In those days, when Britannia ruled the waves, the world was divided by the Admiralty into naval commands or stations. The Royal Navy's North American Station had, under one name or another been in continuous being since the early eighteenth century, but Harwood's distinct command was a revival of an earlier formation: the Commander-in-Chief South America (later Pacific) had been stationed in Valparaíso, Chile, in 1826–65, and then in Esquimalt, Canada, in 1865–1905, while the Commander-in-Chief, South East Coast of America had had his headquarters in the Falkland Islands 1838–1905.

Harwood's division consisted of the cruisers *Exeter* and *Ajax*. His commander-in-chief was Vice-Admiral the Hon Sir Matthew Best, who flew his flag in *Exeter*'s sister ship, HMS *York*;[1] there were two more cruisers in Best's North American Division, the light cruisers *Orion* and *Apollo*, and the sloops *Dundee* and *Scarborough* (the former commanded by Harwood's friend John Edelsten). Together these ships made the 8th Cruiser Squadron.

Though there was much goodwill towards Britain, there were other European settlers in South America and by the late 1930s Nazi Germany and Mussolini's Italy were beginning to exert influence in South America through their communities. Harwood summarised the purposes of the South America Division, which had been reinstituted in 1936 in response to the Abyssinian crisis, under six headings. He was to assist diplomatic representatives to enhance British prestige in the area; to produce a pro-British atmosphere so that 'in the event of war they will grant us at least benevolent neutrality and deny this to our enemies'; to influence the various local officials and nationals; to assist British trade generally; to deal with the strategic and intelligence aspects of a future war; to ensure the safety of British lives and property in the event of an emergency; and to foster friendly relations with local navies.

As for the Royal Navy, as the author Warren Tute wrote in his historically based but fictional account of a visit by a cruiser to South America, 'the Royal Navy enjoyed a matchless reputation all over the world. It could almost be said to have no enemies. It was held in quite extraordinary esteem even by those who had fought us, and who would soon be fighting us again'.[2]

In 1935 there had been one naval attaché to cover the whole of South America, Captain P J Mack.[3] The appointment of a second attaché had been warmly debated between the Admiralty, supported by the Foreign Office, and the Treasury, who opposed the idea, in the late 1920s,[4] but in 1937 Captain S H T Arliss was appointed naval attaché on the west coast of South America and accredited to Chile, Peru and Ecuador,[5] leaving Mack to concentrate on the east coast. Beside their overt day jobs of liaison with other navies and a responsibility to the British ambassadors, naval attachés were intelligence-gatherers and reported to the Director of Naval Intelligence in the Admiralty. In 1938 Mack would be relieved by Captain Henry McCall,[6] and beginning in 1938 as tension increased in Europe, several additional consular posts, mostly cover for naval intelligence-gathering, were established after the usual arguments about which department, the Admiralty or the Foreign Office, would pay in peace and war.[7]

All the while, Lloyd Hirst, Harwood's friend from time in HMS *Southampton* in the 1920s, had settled into the Anglo-Argentine community as the representative of Marconi, and in 1935 he had help to start up Radio el Mundo, an influential news broadcaster in Buenos Aires. In late 1939 Hirst would be recalled to uniform as McCall's assistant naval attaché.[8]

HMS Exeter *sails*

On New Year's Eve 1936 *Exeter* sailed from Plymouth. Harwood's second in command was Commander C Philip Clarke, a fellow torpedoman, who was both efficient and popular.[9] His secretary was

Paymaster Lieutenant Victor Weekes who would follow Harwood in all subsequent appointments.[10] His operations officer, also known as Staff Officer (South America) was Lieutenant-Commander Tom Wisden, followed by Lieutenant-Commander F M Beasley, a qualified Spanish interpreter. The Sub-Lieutenant of the Gunroom was David Wickham, Harwood's godson and son of Harwood's friend 'Wickie'.[11] Earlier, the Mayor of Exeter in full regalia had visited the ship and suggested that the city should give a party for the ship. Harwood replied: 'Not yet. We have not yet justified your trust'.

On 13 January 1937 King Neptune and his court boarded *Exeter* for the traditional ceremony of crossing the line. His Majesty awarded Harwood 'with the Order of the Barnacle in recognition of his years of loyal service and his dutiful return to the Court of Equator bringing with him many loyal subjects of long standing and a greater number of aspirants to that honour.' The insignia of the order was a clinker 'about the size and shape of a banana worn round the neck on a broad ribbon of bunting, which the Old Man wore all day and afterwards hung it up in his cabin.' The ceremony can be quite rough and one young officer lost his temper and hit out at the Bears who were administering 'medicine' and mock shaves before dunking the novitiates in a bath of seawater. 'It was,' remembered Warrant Electrician Reginald Cogswell 'the only time I heard him [Harwood] shout in anger. He called the young officer by name; sternly ordered him out of the water, and at the top of his voice gave him a piece of his mind; then told him to go round again and behave himself.'[12] This is indeed the only time anyone would remember Harwood being angry.

On 18 January *Exeter* arrived at Montevideo, and a few days later she rendezvoused off Punta del Este, Uruguay with the commander-in-chief, Best, in *York* and with *Ajax*. Best explained his intention that he would visit the major ports of South America on the east and west coast in alternate years, while Harwood and his division of ships would circumnavigate the continent each year, leaving time for a fleet exercise in the West Indies and maintenance in Bermuda. Best sought to downgrade the importance of Harwood's visits, but Harwood objected, using arguments provided by Hirst. Hirst, who had recently published a memoir of his service in the First World War, *Coronel and*

After, endorsed with a preface by Admiral Sir Herbert Richmond, produced a robust response. Hirst wrote:[13]

> The policy of stationing a ship permanently in these waters has much more to recommend it than sending a cruiser occasionally from the West Indies to cruise around the continent. Her officers have a much more intimate knowledge of the waters they are to fight in, a better knowledge of the language and of local resources, and which is more important, a better perception of the psychology of local officials. The South American is proud and susceptible and only by constant contact can the right way be learned in which to deal with him. It takes two or three meetings to break down his reserve, but in the course of such meetings many personal friendships can be formed, which in time of war are translated into many invaluable services to a belligerent warship.

Then, while Best put the new arrival through her paces, Eugen Millington-Drake, the British minister in Montevideo spent a night onboard *Exeter*, before the three ships visited Montevideo. The first test of Harwood's newly acquired Spanish was when Best and Harwood began to pay their official calls and to entertain Uruguayan dignitaries.

On the way north via Brazil to Barbados and Bermuda, the fleet conducted tactical exercises, in one of which *York* played the role of commerce raider while *Exeter* and *Ajax* shadowed. At Bermuda in March the 8th Cruiser Squadron held its annual exercises, and when Harwood's force attempted to intercept a merchantman, 'enemy' cruisers appeared, opened fire and Harwood was told he was 'dead', leaving his commander, Clarke, to assume command. After further visits, *Exeter* returned to Bermuda where Joan had arrived in the Elders & Fyffes' banana boat *Bayano* and the Harwoods rented the Old Post Office on Somerset Island for a few weeks.

Best was relieved as commander-in-chief by Vice-Admiral Sydney Meyrick,[14] and the American and West Indies Squadron sailed for a summer cruise up the western seaboard of North America while *Exeter* remained at Bermuda to host the visit of the sail training ship *Presidente Sarmiento*, making one of her last cruises under sail. On 21

June *Exeter* sailed for Panama but was diverted to Trinidad where serious riots had broken out, the Butler Riots. Averaging nearly 29 knots, she arrived at Port of Spain two days later, and seamen and marines were landed in support of the local militia. *Exeter* passed through the Panama Canal between 9 and 11 July and visited several ports: Balboa, the port of Panama City; the US naval base at San Diego; Esquimalt, base of the west coast Royal Canadian Navy; Victoria, which was celebrating the seventy-fifth anniversary of its foundation, and where Harwood recalled that he had been placed in quarantine for yellow fever in 1911; and San Francisco, passing under the Golden Gate Bridge, which had only recently been completed. *Exeter* moved southwards, to the Mexican port of Manzanilla, and the oil port of Talara in the desert country of northern Peru, where the British oil workers were as happy to have strange faces to drink with as the ship's company were to drink their beer. *Exeter* worked her way along the ports of Peru and Chile, through the Magellan Straits to the Falkands, to Buenos Aires, and spent Christmas 1937 alongside in Montevideo. The relatively small British community were focused on their family Christmases and the sailors were left to make their own amusements, but it was during this visit that the Uruguayans came to look on *Exeter* and Harwood as theirs.

There were Spanish- and English-speaking lunches and dinners at which Harwood spoke and he found his feet as a diplomat. His ability to speak Spanish, his previous knowledge and love of the area, and his friendly manner made him welcome and respected in all South American diplomatic and service circles and, importantly, with the local press. In Chile he was quick to remind his guests of shared values and history: '[It is a] great pleasure to see you on board a British cruiser. In past times the English and the Chileans have co-operated gloriously in the early struggles for the independence of this country. These visits and celebrations show the same spirit of friendship and co-operation and are those the heroes of old would wish to see.'[15] The local newspapers began to pick up his words: 'For more than a century Chilean and English officers have shown the same spirit of co-operation. I am sure Admiral Cochrane, General O'Higgins and the other heroes of old would give a smile of satisfaction to see the English sailors and Chilean soldiers celebrating together the victories they have won'.[16]

For the Argentines he had a slightly different formula of words:

> Last week we took part in the parades and celebrations for the unveiling of the Canning Memorial and I well remember the friendly discussions about that great English diplomat. Later on you welcomed many Englishmen who have contributed to the development of your country. It gives me great pleasure to see the cordial relations which exist between our two nations and I hope they will grow even closer in the future.[17]

To English-speaking audiences in Canada, the USA and among the business communities of South America, he had a stronger message: that collective security had failed, Britain and America had been the only countries to disarm; their example had not been followed by other leading powers, and had merely encouraged the aggressor nations in their grabs for other people's land. Notes of his speeches survive; only strength could deter aggression; Britain was now re-arming, new ships and equipment were being produced and the Navy could be relied on to protect British and Empire commerce with their trading partners; Britain had no material or territorial ambitions, her purpose was to ensure world peace and prosperity and to develop trade.

Exeter's visit to Buenos Aires in early December 1937 was typical of many. The ship was open to visitors three times; once to the British community, once to the Argentine commercial community and once to the general public. There was a children's party and the officers hosted a dance for 100 onboard; there was a dance for the ship's company ashore. The Pacific Railway Athletic Club gave an *asado* (barbecue) for 100 men, the Centre of British Engineering arranged two outings, each for forty chief and petty officers, and Anglo Frigorífico hosted a party for 150 men. The Apostleship of the Sea hosted a reception and took a party to the shrine of Our Lady of Luján, the Lourdes of South America. TOC H hosted a reception at the Anglican Cathedral and there was a formal church parade led by 100 men and the band of *Exeter*'s Royal Marines. There were cricket matches against the Hurlingham Club, against the Buenos Aires Cricket Club and against other local sides, as well as a football match (despite the midsummer heat) against a team from the Bank of London and South America

(BOLSA). Ship's teams participated in the Tigre Boat Club regatta. Smaller scale parties and sporting events for both officers and ratings were included in the official programme and much private hospitality developed.

The President of Argentina, Agustín Pedro Justo, invited Harwood and his officers to lunch and afterwards visited the ship, and Harwood first met and befriended the head of the Argentine navy, Admiral José Guisasola. Harwood had little time to himself, but played some golf and shot some game: he joked, reading from a letter out from John Edelsten, 'It is reliably reported that the partridges, duck and snipe of South America have formed a League of Birds and may be expected to apply the principles of Collective Security' – a reference to the League of Nations.[18]

The policy and purpose of 'showing the flag'

To the twenty-first century mind these visits might seem frivolous and self-indulgent, but they served Harwood's purpose, they reinforced British prestige, reassured British merchants, and assured the security of British trade. Harwood put the matter simply to his ship's company: 'Our task in South America is to so impress and please its people that they will incline favourably to the interests of our nationals.'[19]

When, concerned at the costs of such visits, the Admiralty suggested that only the commander-in-chief himself should attract full ceremony, Harwood gave Meyrick his considered view: on the contrary, the present policy was too passive and did not exploit the full prestige value necessary to counter the vigorous anti-British campaign being conducted against British interests by the totalitarian powers (meaning Germany and Italy). South Americans set great store by formality and exchange of hospitality, they understood the rank of commodore, which they treated as a junior flag officer, and they would be offended if he visited their ports without offering and receiving the customary ceremonial. Ship visits should strengthen local British communities and draw together the weaker ones, while providing an opportunity for British commercial interests to meet local officials and dignitaries on board visiting ships. It should not be necessary to give expensive banquets for the officers or to raise large sums for the entertainment of ratings. Once introductions had been made, relationships would develop and ships would reciprocate to the best of their ability. Children's parties were always popular and visits by schools and societies with a British connection should always be arranged if possible. There was no doubt that these events played a valuable part in consolidating goodwill and engendering friendship, but the expense of all this entertaining could be a heavy drain on the pockets of officers and of the commodore himself. Harwood was able to turn the table on the money-pinchers at home: sporting fixtures were important and transport for these could be expensive – a grant from command funds for this purpose should be considered. Harwood struck another blow: it was important that the commodore and his senior officers, especially his Staff Officer (South America), should speak Spanish, and all officers should be encouraged to reach a conversational capability in the language.

The year 1938 saw further visits to Mar del Plata and the Argentine naval base of Puerto Belgrano, before *Exeter* turned northwards along the Brazilian coast to São Paulo, Rio de Janeiro and Bahia. Next was Trinidad, where Exeter rendezvoused with the commander-in-chief in *York* with *Apollo* and *Orion* in company, and Bermuda, where, while *Exeter* was docked and refitted, Harwood's family joined him. Harwood was prosecutor at the court martial of a 'blighter of a Paymaster Lieutenant who did no work for two years when we were there' and this took up a great deal of his time, but he was still able to play golf at Mid Ocean and enjoy being with his family. At Bermuda those of *Exeter*'s ship's company who had stayed on from the previous commission were relieved by a new draft of 157 men, and *Exeter* sailed for her 1938/39 cruise on 2 July.

The first call was at Pernambuco, the most northerly port in Brazil, where three children of the British colony were christened onboard, and then Rio de Janeiro, for the third time, where Harwood chaired a meeting of the British Chamber of Commerce. There he stressed the growing power of the Royal Navy and its ability to protect British interests, and explained the role of the Navy in the current Spanish Civil War. Then it was Rio Grande do Sul, Punta del Este, Montevideo and Puerto Belgrano, where *Exeter* was joined by *Ajax* under her new captain, Charles Woodhouse.[20] Puerto Belgrano was an unprepossessing place, but the British community from Bahía Blanca,

Argentina's third largest city situated only ten miles away, laid on a masterly programme of social and sporting activities. Harwood spoke in Spanish to the officers of the Argentine armed forces, to the local Rotary Club, and gave a presentation at the university. A performance ashore by the ship's concert party was much appreciated.

The Munich Crisis

Between visits the two ships exercised and worked up as the Munich Crisis, Hitler's demands to annex German-speaking Czechoslovakia, developed. A Practice Order Book was issued, and simulated attacks on passing British merchant ships were conducted. Then on the evening of Sunday, 25 September 1938 *Exeter* sailed, darkened and at a high state of readiness, making her way northwards at speed, showing herself off the principal Brazilian ports and calling at Rio and Pernambuco to refuel. On 30 September the British Prime Minister, Neville Chamberlain, returned from Munich with an agreement signed by him and by Hitler – the piece of paper which gave 'peace for our time'. Chamberlain's appeasement won time for Britain to prepare for war, and gave impetus to Harwood's preparations. An organisation for naval control of shipping was stood up, and Harwood, who already routinely used to send an officer and a doctor from *Exeter* to board ships flying the Red Ensign, met as many merchant captains as possible, and studied the pattern of merchant ship movements. Intelligence-gathering efforts were increased, anti-sabotage measures were investigated as tactfully as possible, and British committees were formed and briefed.

The remainder of the autumn programme saw *Exeter*, usually with *Ajax* in company, visit Buenos Aires, Montevideo, the Falklands, South Georgia and ports in Chile. During visits, Harwood spoke in English or Spanish to businessmen, including Rotary clubs, university students, at mayoral receptions and, of course, to guests onboard. The full text of one of Harwood's speeches has survived, a talk to the British Chamber of Commerce at Montevideo. When Harwood asked the Admiralty for guidance on a speech he was to deliver, he was advised to stress that new and modernised ships and equipment were now entering service, and also the country's policy of maintaining a strong and efficient navy to safeguard British interests in both hemispheres.

They could be assured that in the event of war there would be early introduction of a convoy system and that the build-up of the Singapore naval base was proceeding to plan. He should, however, avoid mention of the Spanish Civil War in view of the government's policy of non-intervention.

While at Montevideo, the Marquess of Willingdon,[21] a former Viceroy of India, was on a goodwill mission to South America, and there was a march-past at which Willingdon, flanked by Harwood and Woodhouse, took the salute.

For light relief, *Exeter* visited the Falklands in November 1938, where there were reunions with old friends, informal dances ashore, visits to the ship by the 'kelpers', a children's party when each mess provided tea for a dozen children, and a concert party ashore which raised money for a local charity. At the end of the month *Exeter* took the Governor of the Falklands, Sir Herbert Henniker-Heaton, on a visit to the colony's dependencies. The governor and the commodore struck up a particular friendship based on their having the same initials, HHH.

Ajax and *Exeter* sailed for Punta Arenas on 6 December. That day *Exeter* conducted a speed trial and in the afternoon off Tierra del Fuego she overtook a four-masted barque under full sail, a wonderful sight on a southern summer evening. Harwood reduced *Exeter*'s speed and the two ships came within hailing distance: she was one of the famous German P-liners, *Padua*.[22]

Earthquake at Concepción

They spent Christmas alongside in Puerto Montt: 'we were not looking forward to it in the least, for ... it offered little or no opportunity for extensive gaiety,' said *Exeter*'s commission book. In the New Year a series of visits began to Chilean ports and on 24 January 1939 the two ships arrived at Valparaíso, known to the sailors as 'Valps', who were 'looking forward to a repetition of the good times that we had experienced during our first visits'.[23] Reginald Cogswell was one of those who did not go ashore that night, but at about 23:30, as he swung himself into his bunk, he missed and fell to the deck. He blamed his own unhandiness and an unusually strong surge by *Exeter* on her anchor cables.[24] Those ashore, where the theatres and cabarets were in full swing, felt extensive vibrations which threw civilians into a panic, but left British sailors for the most part unperturbed.[25] Harwood was at the casino at nearby Viña del Mar, where he described the noise as like an express train, while the ground shook for about a minute and a half. There was little panic as people made for the door, and Harwood took shelter under an arch from the falling roof.

Next morning, in a rare lapse for the commodore, Harwood appeared on the quarterdeck in his shirtsleeves. Cogswell recalled that his commodore 'was something of a knob-fiddler and very fond of picking up signals from distance stations on his own very sensitive Eddystone receiver', and had heard via a wireless station in the Argentine that an earthquake had wrecked Concepción. Harwood hurried ashore to consult the British ambassador in Santiago by phone, while *Exeter* continued to complete her much-depleted stores and both ships were ordered to raise steam for full power. Plans to grant thirty-six hours' leave were not cancelled until 15:00 when the signal for general recall was hoisted. At 19:00 on 25 January *Exeter* sailed for Talachuano, 200 miles to the south, leaving *Ajax* to embark further equipment. Overnight landing parties were got ready, field utensils were checked, barricoes filled with water, and first-aid equipment was readied. *Exeter* anchored at daybreak, thirty-six hours hours after the earthquake had struck.

Harwood went ashore to investigate in person and shortly afterwards three platoons of sailors and marines, a medical party and a demolition party were landed. The road from the jetty at Talcahuano showed ominous cracks and Concepción, five miles away, was in ruins: 'terror had come in the night where only a fortnight before the bands of *Exeter* and *Ajax* had played for the youths and maidens to dance.'[26] There had been a major earthquake further inland at Chillán which killed thousands, followed by another a few minutes later at Concepción. Estimates vary, but there were hundreds of dead and wounded. There was no water nor electricity, and the town centre had been razed. Only the main plaza was recognisable, where the one remaining tower of the cathedral had been twisted on its base and leaned at a crazy angle. The roads were filled with debris – even modern shockproof buildings had suffered when their foundations dropped several feet, but the wooden huts of the poorer quarters had, mercifully, not caught fire. Field kitchens and first aid posts were set up in the plaza, while the platoons spread out to dig in the ruins and to pull down dangerous edifices. Such small parties could make little impression on the wreckage, but they set to with a will and their example helped to move the inhabitants from their lethargy. Paymaster Midshipman H R 'Bobby' Vine described the situation in a letter to his parents:

> I have never seen such a tragic or terrible sight as met our eyes when we got near the place. Literally every building, except one or two, had crumpled up and smashed itself across the roads. Lines and lines of bodies lay covered in sacks. These were placed in the main plaza. One thing I noticed was a dead horse which presumably had been pulling a farmer's cart along the main street before the disaster. The horse had fallen into a big crack where the road had opened up and only its head was visible above the road level. We dug and hacked among the broken buildings, heaving out furniture, bodies and other rubbish; a frightful job. The heat was terrible; flies everywhere for the drains had been smashed and the smell was awful. We worked bare to the waist, giving our water to the Chileans who were homeless and had no water or food, and, some of them, no clothing.

In the early evening of the second day *Exeter* sailed to Valparaíso, carrying about three hundred European and North American refugees, and perhaps as many Chileans. Vine continued:

> We got back to the ship just before dark. They were embarking refugees by the hundred including the British residents who were given priority over everyone else. I had to get each refugee to sign his or her name, sex, age, residence etc. This was an awful job but it gave me the opportunity to study the poor wretches. Most of them had lost friends and relations, were starved and very thirsty. We served out water from a tub at the head of the port gangway. 700 Chileans were embarked and quartered amidships, everything was done to make them comfortable. The aged and ill were taken to the sickbay and given a cot. Any men who looked dirty were given a steam bath behind a screen right aft under the ensign staff. This was

> done to kill off any bugs or disease. The officers all gave up their cabins for the British women, the Mids[hipmen] their hammocks for the girls, and the Commodore's cabin was used to accommodate the children. The men slept in the wardroom, gunroom and warrant officers messes. We did not sleep at all. However the trip was very pleasant as most of us knew many of the Britishers from our former trips to Talcahuano.

Exeter and *Ajax* made two trips carrying refugees northwards and, on the second, carrying the Chilean army southwards to take over from the British sailors the task of disaster relief. There was fog off the coast; despite this, Cogswell observed his commodore do 'what I never knew a captain do before or since ... he left his bridge to the commander and walked about among the people ... smoking a cigarette and joking in his comic Spanish.'[27]

By 28 January the Chilean battleship *Almirante Latorre* and her destroyers had arrived and taken over the relief effort. The press overflowed with praise for the British effort: one reporting that 'the British Navy terrible in war yet kind and gentle beyond undemanding to those in need ... the heart of Chile floods out in gratitude.' The Chilean government too was grateful for the prompt and effective assistance given by Harwood's ships, thus cementing already existing strong support for Britain and the Royal Navy. Harwood was awarded the Grand Cross of the Order of Merit in gold and *Ajax*'s Woodhouse was made a commander of the same order, and forty-one officers and senior ratings were awarded lesser orders. Eventually every member of the two ships' companies received a miniature medal.

'All because,' Cogswell wrote, 'two ships all ready to go had been in the right place at the right time. Two fast ships, well manned and well provided for, and commanded by a resolute officer who could make up his mind and set matters in train.'[28]

Harwood's ships left Valparaíso on 3 February 1939 and, making several visits, worked their way northward to the Panama Canal. At Colon on 27 February they met their commander-in-chief in HMS *York* with *Orion* and six Canadian destroyers in company, and exercised in the Caribbean en route to Kingston, Jamaica and Bermuda. On 11 March *Exeter* arrived at Bermuda, for inspection by Meyrick's staff and two months' docking. There were also inter-ship sporting competitions. Vine commented: 'The Commodore is in a very good temper as we have pinched all the cups from the other ships which, together with all those we won in South America, makes the deck outside his cabin look like a silver ware shop.'

Joan arrived in SS *Bayano*: one of her fellow passengers was the fiancée of Sub-Lieutenant Noel Kemble, who had been one of Harwood's midshipmen in *London*. The daily orders for the day they arrived read '0930. Barge to Hamilton for Commodore's wife and Sub's sweetie'. Noel and Elizabeth were married on 6 May 1939, Harwood gave her away, and the couple left for their honeymoon in the commodore's barge.

The North American cruise

Joan and other *Exeter* wives followed in the four-funnelled Cunard liner RMS *Aquitania* when the squadron steamed north for visits to the eastern seaboard of the USA during the visit of King George VI and Queen Elizabeth to the World's Fair in New York. In the Great War (1914–18) the protection of the valuable trade in the River Plate had been a paramount aim of the Royal Navy, something which Hirst would have reminded Harwood,[29] but it was at that World's Fair in 1939 that Joan remembered her husband being enthralled by a map of world shipping routes showing the concentration of seaborne trade in the Plate estuary.

Hospitality for all the visiting ships was generous and ceaseless, including a dance given by the British War Veterans' Association for 500 sailors from the British ships, when four bands including *Exeter*'s Royal Marines and the Dagenham Girl Pipers played. At Philadelphia the Harwoods met some of the richer Americans, who, Joan recorded in her diary, were 'very Walley' (a reference to the divorcee Wallis Simpson who had married Edward VIII after his abdication), and asked them out to their country estates. Joan stayed with a Miss Silvis, who very kindly took her for long drives around the surrounding country. The entertainment offered to the ship's company continued unabated.

At Baltimore on 7 June *Exeter* held a memorial service for those drowned in the submarine *Thetis*, recently lost in the Thames estuary. Harwood, with four officers and the Royal Marines band, travelled overland to Washington to attend the British Embassy garden party for the King and Queen, when young Vine noted that Harwood was engaged in a long talk with the King. On the way back to the ship, the Harwoods were also shown round the Harwood-Hammond house in Annapolis, once owned by a co-descendant of Captain Thomas Harwood. Miami from 27 June to 11 July proved the most hectic and enjoyable climax of the North American cruise, where, more to Harwood's liking, he caught a 32lb sailfish.

The preceding account of Harwood's time on the American Station may seem like all play, but there was hard work too. In the latter half of the commission, with war looming, Harwood in *Exeter* kept *Ajax* close enough for the two ships to exercise together whenever possible and to provide mutual support in an emergency, and his commander-in-chief, Meyrick, seized the opportunity to exercise the whole squadron. *Exeter* became particularly proficient at her gunnery.

On 18 July *Exeter* reached Bermuda, via Nassau and Haiti, to act as host ship to a French cruiser squadron consisting of the cruisers *Georges Leygues*, *Gloire* and *Montcalm* under Rear-Admiral René-Émile Godfroy, who was to prove such a problem to Harwood later in the Mediterranean. On this occasion Harwood and Godfroy got on well and discussed how best to fight a pocket battleship. Hospitality was exchanged between the ships and on Sunday, 23 July the Exeters 'were well and truly regaled with the best of food, washed down by litres of good French wine'.[30] But all was not well, Cogswell observing: 'The visit of the French cruisers was nothing to feel satisfied about. The officers were polite enough, but that is the business of officers to be polite. The [French] matelots were surly; a tension was present.' Harwood was obliged to clear lower deck and to speak to his people. Pointing to the French ships in Grassy Bay, he reminded them that most of the French knew what it was to live in an occupied country 'something no Englishman had known for a thousand years'. He spoke of the heavy threat lying over Europe and the danger to France. Such a threat was reason enough for anxiety and being out of temper. The Exeters, Harwood told them, must be patient and understanding – the French might soon be allies in war.[31]

On 8 August *Exeter* sailed from Bermuda dockyard for the last time with her long paying-off pennant streaming behind her, its length indicating the two years and eight months she had been in commission.

Nevertheless, war was in the air. While *Exeter* had been away from home, the Munich Crisis had passed, but Britain had been re-arming against the threat of Nazi Germany, and the Germans had tightened their grip on Europe. In March 1938 Austria had been annexed, then German-speaking Sudetenland. In March 1939 the rest of the Czech lands were occupied, and a puppet state set up in Slovakia. Also in March 1939 Hitler made his claim on Danzig and the Polish Corridor, a strip of land which separated East Prussia from Germany. Germany strengthened its alliance with Mussolini's Fascist Italy and signed non-aggression or trade treaties with Denmark, Estonia, Latvia, Romania, Norway and Sweden. Unbeknownst to Britain and France, a pact was being prepared which would carve up Eastern Europe between Germany and the Soviet Union.

While *Exeter* was in mid-Atlantic, signal traffic increased so markedly that Harwood was obliged to put his cipher officers on a twenty-four-hour watch to handle the increased volume.

Ring off main engines

When *Exeter* berthed in Devonport on 17 August 1939 she had steamed some 100,000 miles in less than three years. Some of her people were owed up to two and a half months' leave, and next day the majority of the Exeters went on leave, some never expecting to see or serve with each other again.

7
Eve of Battle

For the summer weeks of 1939, Joan had leased a house at Chub Tor on Dartmoor, near Yelverton Golf Club. However, the boys saw little of their father, young Henry Harwood remembering overhearing his father explaining to a tearful Joan that war was inevitable and that he expected to be at sea again soon. Within four days of *Exeter*'s arrival after so many months away, she was ordered to prepare for sea. She took on stores and ammunition, about fifty of her crew changed (since commissioning over two years before she had gained too many 'chiefs' (senior ratings) and had not enough 'indians' (junior ratings)), fuel tanks were filled to the brim, and on 24 August she slipped down the Hamoaze to an anchorage in Plymouth Sound. Young Henry Harwood's thirteenth birthday treat was lunch onboard. The last letters were written before the mail was closed onboard, and while *Exeter* lay at anchor, the polished muzzles of her guns were painted over and anything that would catch the glint of the sun disappeared, boats took visitors ashore and were then hoisted inboard. Speculation onboard was that she was going to a fleet rendezvous at Portland or Scapa Flow, but that evening Harwood mustered the ship's company on the quarterdeck: 'he came aft, his face normally a countenance of good-natured authority, turned hard and stern,' to tell them they were going back to South America.[1]

However, Harwood would no longer be their commanding officer. Instead they would have as their captain, Frederick Secker 'Hooky' Bell, 'a tall gaunt man with dark face and the look of a bird of prey'. While Harwood remained as a commodore, Captain Bell would relieve him of his responsibility for command of the ship and become chief of staff, while Harwood concentrated on his duties as Commodore, South Atlantic. Lieutenant-Commander Ralph Medley had recently joined as Staff Officer Operations, and Victor Weekes continued as commodore's secretary. Harwood had been told that he would be appointed commodore 1st class in recognition of the fact that he would be commanding a cruiser squadron, but the promised elevation never came, and his promotion was a nagging worry.

After dark on 25 August 1939, *Exeter* sailed from Plymouth, and by 31 August she was off Freetown, Sierra Leone.

August 1939 – 'Let slip the dogs of war'

Under war plans, Harwood's South America division, reinforced to squadron strength, came under the Commander-in-Chief, South Atlantic, Vice-Admiral George Lyon, who had been Harwood's immediate superior in the plans division in the early 1920s. From his base at Freetown, Lyon commanded the oceans south of a line running due west from Dakar in Africa to the South American coast, round the Cape of Good Hope and into the Indian Ocean as far as Durban. Harwood was responsible to Lyon for the 4,000 miles of American coastline from Cape Horn and the Falklands to the most eastern point of Brazil. His principal tasks were to protect Allied shipping and to intercept enemy merchant ships. In practice, this meant patrolling the approaches to the River Plate and Rio de Janeiro, the shipping routes in between these places, and Recife in Pernambuco province where ships to and from Europe took their departure or made their landfall.

The potential threat was from raiders, whether these were surface warships, U-boats or armed, disguised enemy merchant ships. The Admiralty knew of the emphasis which the Germans would place on cruiser warfare through its reading of the two-volume history of German raiders in the First World War. This had been written by no less than Erich Raeder in 1922 and 1923, and had been translated into English by the naval intelligence staff.[2] In 1928 Raeder would become an admiral and commander-in-chief of the Weimar Republic's navy, the Reichsmarine, and in 1939 he became Grossadmiral of Hitler's Kriegsmarine (renamed in 1935). Under Raeder's plan for the expansion of the German navy, Plan Z, war with Britain was not expected so early as 1939, and in 1939 just two ships, the sisters *Deutschland* and *Graf Spee*, were ready for operations in the Atlantic at the outbreak of war. Raeder noted that these: 'if skilfully used, should be able to carry out cruiser warfare on the high seas for some time ... however, [they] cannot be decisive for the outcome of the war'.[3]

There were a score of U-boats available for operations in the North Atlantic, but none were yet ready for distant deployment. There were plans for up to twenty-six merchant ships to be converted into armed raiders but 'to avoid suspicion the conversion of selected [ships] ... was to be left until the actual outbreak of war.'[4] The British also perceived a threat by German volunteers from the well-organised German communities in South America to the Falklands.

The German supply ship *Altmark*, commanded by Captain Heinrich Dau, was ordered on 27 July to take on three months' supplies and sailed on 2 August from Germany; she took on 9,400 tons of diesel fuel at Port Arthur, New Mexico, and sailed again on 19 August to disappear into the vastness of the Atlantic.[5] On 21 August 1939, that is four days before Harwood in *Exeter* left Plymouth, *Graf Spee*, under Captain Hans Langsdorff, departed Wilhelmshaven, bound for the South Atlantic. Since taking command in October of the previous year, Langsdorff, an officer of the old Imperial Navy who had fought at Jutland, had taken part in several minor operations and two deployments into the Atlantic and the Western Mediterranean.[6] Now *Graf Spee*, besides her war complement, carried additional men as potential prize crews, and also a team from the Beobachtungsdienst (B-Dienst) from German naval intelligence, responsible for intercepting, decoding and analysing British wireless communications.[7]

Langsdorff took a northwesterly course along the west coast of Denmark and Norway before turning west into waters between 60° North and the Arctic Circle, and then south to make the open Atlantic. Langsdorff's orders were explicit: he was allocated a primary operational area covering the South America to Cape Verde and Biscay trade routes, and a second area covering Capetown and the southern Indian Ocean. This was almost the same area that had been granted to the British commander-in-chief based in Freetown. In his area, Langsdorff was to intercept and damage British supply routes, conducting trade warfare according to prize regulations. This meant safety of the crews of merchant ships had to be assured before they were sunk and that passenger ships were not to be sunk. Engagements with enemy naval forces, even if inferior, were to be avoided, unless this furthered the main purpose of the operation. One aim was to oblige the British to disperse their fleet away from a concentration in home waters against the German navy, and 'frequent changes ... in the operational areas [would] create uncertainty and restrict enemy merchant ships [including] temporary departure into distant waters'.[8] The orders were laced with Nazi prose, his commander-in-chief, Raeder, telling Langsdorff 'he expected aggressiveness from his officers ... rather death with honour than strike the flag'.

Graf Spee arrived at her planned waiting area without being reported. However, the voyage was ill-starred, for on 26 August Bosun's Mate Matzke was swept overboard and, though Langsdorff looked for him for three hours in the heavy seas, Matzke was given up as lost.

September: 'The game's afoot'

When *Exeter* called at Freetown briefly on 1 September to fuel, Harwood met his new commander-in-chief, Lyon, flying his flag in the light cruiser HMS *Neptune*, and sailed again that evening.

War was declared on 3 September and in less than three hours, one of Harwood's ships, *Ajax*, intercepted and sank the German merchantman *Olinda*, whose crew were transferred to a British tanker for landing in Montevideo. The following day *Ajax* had another success in stopping and sinking the merchantman *Karl Fritzen*. On 5 September the destroyers *Hotspur* and *Havock* sailed from Freetown to join Harwood and they would be followed three days later by the heavy cruiser *Cumberland*, one of Harwood's previous ships and now under the command of one of his term-mates in *Britannia*, Walter Fallowfield.

Meanwhile, after a brief stop in the Cape Verde islands, *Exeter* arrived at Rio on 7 September for a short visit during which Harwood called on the Brazilian minister for foreign affairs, and met the British ambassadors to Brazil and to the Argentine (who was passing through). During this call, Harwood drew attention to the sinking without warning of the passenger liner *Athenia* by a German U-boat on the first day of the war, and reasoned that since British warships would protect all ships against similar attacks, they deserved preferential treatment for repairs and refuelling. Otherwise, under The Hague Conventions the warships of belligerent nations were only allowed to visit a neutral port to take in sufficient fuel to allow them to reach the nearest port of their own country, which was the Falklands, over a thousand miles away to the south, and they were only allowed to visit a port of the same neutral nation once every three months. The Brazilian minister was sympathetic and gave permission to refuel at more frequent intervals, provided that such visits were made discreetly and at different ports.

Another transient in Rio was Vice-Admiral José Guisasola, commander-in-chief of the Argentine navy. He and Harwood discussed the problem of refuelling for the British warships. Harwood did have a tanker, the Royal Fleet Auxiliary *Olwen*, but needed calm waters to refuel from her, and thanks to Harwood's existing relationship with him, Guisasola was sympathetic and strongly advised Harwood to use the lee of Rouen Bank in the River Plate, as it offered calmer conditions than English Bank, and was clear of all normal shipping routes. There was little time for other niceties, and learning that three German merchant ships were assembling off the coast of Patagonia, Harwood sailed at 01:00 on 8 September for the Falklands, ordering *Ajax* to meet him there.

There were further ill omens for *Graf Spee* when on 8 September, in the late morning in the mid-Atlantic, she crossed the Equator without performing the usual rites to mark the crossing of the line and the centuries-old custom of paying respect to King Neptune. Shortly afterwards there was an alarm and, anxious not to be spotted and recognised by a merchant ship, *Graf Spee* reversed course across the Equator before resuming her southward voyage, thus insulting his aquatic majesty, King Neptune, not once but three times.[9]

Next day *Exeter* and *Ajax* rendezvoused. Harwood ordered *Ajax* to the Falklands to guard against any possible invasion, to land her prisoners, and for a self-maintenance period, while for the next week and a half *Exeter* would patrol off the Plate.

Meanwhile, *Cumberland* was following a great circle route from Freetown towards Rio de Janeiro,[10] but though Fallowfield had ordered his aircraft to fly off while at Freetown for a reconnaissance along the coast, and though the Atlantic weather continued balmy with winds Force 2 or 3, a long swell and with good visibility, and thus good for further aerial reconnaissance, no aircraft was flown off while on passage. Fallowfield did, however, order a large zigzag (a track along a base course with large and irregular variations of course intended to prevent a U-boat from obtaining a firing solution for its torpedoes); *Cumberland*'s log records no sightings of other ships, friendly or otherwise, during the next week.[11]

However, *Cumberland* herself was sighted. Four days later, at dawn on 11 September there was 'one of these strange and dangerous coincidences that happen in war': Langsdorff in *Graf Spee* had arranged a rendezvous with his tanker, *Altmark*, in an area which lay across *Cumberland*'s route. Langsdorff had ordered a dawn reconnaissance by his Arado 196 seaplane, while both German ships were lying stopped and the transfer of fuel and stores was about to begin. *Cumberland*, despite weather suitable for flying, had not launched any of her aircraft. Consequently, while making a triangular search, the Arado crew spotted *Cumberland*, on a base course of 250°, but at the moment when she was making a large alteration to port as part of the pre-planned zigzag. *Cumberland* was only some twenty miles away, not far over the horizon to the north, and any further alteration of course would bring her south and directly towards *Graf Spee* and *Altmark*. The Arado crew, anxious that they themselves might be spotted, dived and returned to *Graf Spee* at low altitude to make an immediate report, not by wireless which might have been detected, but by flashing light. *Graf Spee*'s wireless operators listened tensely on British frequencies for any increased traffic, while Langsdorff scanned the horizon for smoke, but it was soon clear to him that *Cumberland*'s lookouts had not seen the Arado. Langsdorff felt safe to resume refuelling from *Altmark*.

Had Fallowfield been using his aircraft to reconnoitre around his course, or had his track been a few miles further south so that he approached from the east, he might have stumbled upon *Graf Spee*. Langsdorff would have been confronted with the problem of risking damage in a fight with a faster but inferior ship armed with 8in guns, or of fleeing despite his superior 11in guns. This was a scenario which Harwood had foreseen when at the War College: Fallowfield's duty, according to Harwood's tactical thought, would have been to shadow or to close and engage his enemy in hope, if not of sinking him, of at least inflicting sufficient damage as to curtail his raider operations. Whichever response Langsdorff chose, *Cumberland*, using her powerful wireless, would have sent an enemy locating report and thus caused a concentration of force against this lone raider. Fallowfield's moment of glory had not come: *Graf Spee* avoided detection, and *Cumberland* continued blithely on her route westwards across the Atlantic.

When Fallowfield arrived at Rio on 15 September, Harwood ordered him to refuel and then to organise 'run-out' convoys using *Havock*. The convoys were to leave at dawn and would be covered against U-boat or raider attack until sunset, and to disperse during the night, so that by dawn on the next day they were well dispersed. Harwood ordered *Hotspur* to join him in the Plate for similar purposes. Should a German pocket battleship show herself off the coast, *Cumberland* was to abandon the limited convoy scheme and join *Exeter*.

On 17 September *Hotspur* joined *Exeter* off the Plate and on the 19th Harwood visited Montevideo. It was a hectic visit: 'It started at 5am and ended at 2am, and then to sea again at 6am. Official calls, conferences, interviews; all very busy and very important. It was good to get back to sea again with its modicum of boredom and sleep,' wrote Harwood. However, he did call, with the ambassador Eugen Millington-Drake, on the Uruguayan foreign minister, and did discuss refuelling for his ships. They drew attention to the sinking of *Athenia* and Germany's breach of international law against sinking ships on sight. The foreign minister may have been nervous, but Millington-Drake was confident that Harwood's destroyers would be able to visit for repairs, even if they could not refuel more than once every three months. These talks would pay off at the beginning of the following month when Harwood was able to send *Olwen* into Montevideo for stores and repairs; nevertheless, Lyon warned Harwood against departure from strict laws of neutrality in case the enemy were also to gain some advantage from reciprocal concessions.

Domestic affairs

Harwood's farewell letter home had been poignant. He blamed 'the blunderings of politicians ... They are the cause of our agony,' but he remained, 'An optimist and hope[d] for the best,' signing his letter, 'All my love and may we soon be together again. Ever Your B – utterly miserable'.[12] As he settled into the routine of patrols and letters to Joan, he expressed the tedium of being almost constantly at sea:[13]

> A dull life. Occasionally we chase merchant ships to see who or what they are ... My flag captain [Bell] is a great comfort to me and a really nice person. We lunch and dine together in my sea cabin ... Days on end at sea and never more than 24 hours in harbour ... We are rolling about badly now. My wireless is about my only comfort. I live in my sea cabin ... I am quite well, busy occasionally. Nothing to do at other times. I dream and think of the days to come. We have had a hard deal with being apart so much, but the high spots have been high and we must live on the past and the future ... I remember those happy times; Cairo, Luxor, Venice in 1925. Athens. No use getting miserable. I hope for the future. How lucky you came to America otherwise I would only have partly seen you for seven days this year. I have no news to tell you, even if I could. Everybody works hard; long hours closed up on watch. I have had a bunk put in my shelter on the bridge and occasionally sleep there. I never see my after cabin and live in my sea cabin.

Harwood was still addicted to his listening in his sea cabin to news broadcasts:

> I have my wireless up there and listen and listen to news. In fact I hear the same one about 6 times over, always hoping for some new bit ... We are all just existing in a groove. On the whole, cheerful in a sort of way. Sims [*Exeter*'s engineer officer] has just rung me up. He has found another news [broadcast] in English in the middle of the day. This is our real amusement.[14]

He was worried about Joan, who was moving home and having an air raid shelter built, and he was worried about his finances, telling her, 'I am saving money and am sending it home to my bank ... do not worry about it. Please eat properly and well and take enough nourishment. It is essential in times of strain. Your health, my beloved, is essential to us all. You must not worry and fret.' There was also uncertainty about his rank: 'I have no idea yet if I am a Commodore 1st or 2nd class. It makes a lot of difference financially to me ... is most unfair if they leave me a 2nd class one, and, besides, I have had my best uniform all altered to it. They told me at the Admiralty that I would be a 1st'.[15]

Harwood's anxiety grew when mail from home came irregularly and in despair he wrote to Joan: 'Why did I decide that afternoon to take the job of CSA [Commodore South America]. 3 years of hard work ended with this and so.'[16] He must also have been worried about promotion. Several of his 'batch', other captains with similar seniority in the Navy List had already been promoted to rear-admiral, and he reassured Joan, 'I think they will make new Admirals this January and I really do think I must be included at last'.[17] He need not have worried overly, for in January that year, after the Admiralty had called for a special report on Harwood, his commander-in-chief, Meyrick, had rated his chances of promotion at 95 per cent, equal to that of Captain H M Burrough and above those of Captains A L St G Lyster and four others of his batch:

> I can strongly recommend him for retention on the Active List ... and confidently recommend him for Flag Officers' appointments in important sea commands ... young for his age, very active and has outstanding ability to bring a broadminded view to bear on matters of policy and public affairs ... and has shown readiness to act on his own initiative.[18]

These were all qualities which Harwood was about to display again.

Rumours abound

There were rumours of German merchant ships assembling off Patagonia, either to rush the Falklands or arming themselves as raiders, and from Buenos Aires, the naval attaché, McCall, reported intelligence that local German authorities were trying to warn German ships at sea that the Falklands Islands Company's passenger ship ss *Lafonia* was on her way to the Falklands with British reservists. So, after the first local convoy left Montevideo on 22 September accompanied by *Hotspur*, Harwood ordered her to escort *Lafonia* to Port Stanley and to replace *Ajax* who was now steaming north. As the volume of shipping was greater in the Plate than at Rio, Harwood ordered *Havock* south to cover *Hotspur*'s absence.

Two days later McCall had other intelligence that German merchant ships and a U-boat were to meet some 120 miles southwest of

Ascension Island. Harwood, anticipating Lyon's orders, sent *Cumberland* to the German rendezvous and ordered *Ajax* to replace her off Rio; while refuelling on the 25th in the Plate, Harwood's precious tanker *Olwen* grounded, but sustained no apparent damage. Meanwhile, Lyon ordered a concentration of ships from Freetown to join *Cumberland* and search on 28 and 29 September around the German rendezvous, but they found nothing. Lyon's forces returned to Freetown with *Cumberland* low on fuel.

The month ended with *Exeter* accompanied by *Olwen* in the River Plate, and *Ajax* off Rio running convoys to the north. Harwood's destroyers were ordered home on the 28th to meet a serious shortage of destroyers in the Home Fleet, while Harwood had yet to concentrate his cruisers as a single force.

In Germany, Hitler hoped that Britain and France would accept his occupation of Poland and would not go to war, and it was not until the 26th that Langsdorff was ordered to begin commerce raiding. Raeder embellished the order: 'England is in need of successes; any gain of prestige by England is therefore undesirable ... attacks on shipping by the pocket battleships are to be carried out to the fullest extent'. This prompted Langsdorff to note in his war diary that he considered it necessary to avoid any engagement with one of the heavy cruisers, meaning *Exeter* or *Cumberland*, since a single lucky hit might put an end to *Graf Spee*'s career as a raider, even though it was highly probable that the heavy cruiser would herself be heavily damaged by *Graf Spee*: this was the same scenario which Harwood had envisaged when teaching at the War College.

On 30 September *Graf Spee* claimed her first victim, the 5,000-ton Booth Line SS *Clement*. However, *Clement* bravely broadcast a message of distress, warning that she was being attacked by an enemy surface raider, an RRR message, which was picked up by other ships and relayed ashore.

The RRR signal – meaning 'I am under attack by an enemy surface warship' – came from a handbook, *Defence of Merchant Shipping*, or DMS, which stipulated:

> it is the Master's first and most important duty to report the nature and the position of the enemy by wireless telegraphy ... confidential books and papers should be thrown overboard in a weighted bag ...

> [and ships should] make a distress message immediately by wireless telegraphy ... all wireless operators shall be thoroughly familiar with the requirements for transmitting distress messages ... so that they may be instantly ready to carry out the correct procedure in emergency. This applies not only to the form of the message but also to the frequencies ... Masters should personally ensure, by means of frequent exercise, that all operators are efficient in this respect.

In the case of an enemy warship, the different parts of the distress signal were the position of the ship, her name, and the nature of the attack or distress 'expressed by one of the following words: MINED, BOMBED, TORPEDOED, GUNNED'. The distress message was prefixed by the letters RRR, repeated three times. Ships and shore stations hearing such a message were to repeat it.[19]

These distress signals, the RRR messages, were to prove the best source of intelligence about raiders. Otherwise 'the cruise of the *Graf Spee* illustrated the extreme poverty of intelligence', and for many months in 1939 her identity was confused with her sister ship *Scheer*. In the event, several of *Graf Spee*'s nine victims were to risk their lives by sending out such a message, which eventually allowed the Admiralty's Operational Intelligence Centre (OIC) painstakingly to reconstruct the German's track.

After their capture, *Clement*'s master and chief engineer were taken onboard *Graf Spee*, while the rest of the Clements were allowed into their boats. The capture was marred when *Graf Spee* missed in two attempts to hit *Clement* with a torpedo as she lay stopped: a torpedo was fired at half a mile range and passed ahead, a second passed astern.[20] *Graf Spee*'s attempt at sinking *Clement* by gunfire, witnessed by her master as a prisoner on the bridge of the German ship, was also unimpressive: some twenty-five rounds of 5.9in were fired at a range of 2,500yds with little effect, and finally five 11in rounds were needed to send *Clement* to the bottom. Under the German raider doctrine it was also necessary for *Graf Spee* to make her presence known, and Langsdorff's B-Dienst team, using the call sign of another pocket battleship *Scheer*, now wirelessed the position of the boats, and received an acknowledgement from a Brazilian steamer. As *Graf Spee* left the scene, she stopped a neutral Greek freighter and insisted that she take onboard *Clement*'s master and chief engineer, and having thus advertised her presence on one coast of the South Atlantic, Langsdorff now made off eastwards into mid ocean.[21]

October 1939 – bound in shallows

By 1 October *Clement*'s distress signal had been reported to the Admiralty in London, and next day survivors from *Clement* landed in Brazil with reliable accounts of what had happened, though they misidentified the cause of their nemesis as the *Admiral Scheer*.

At the start of the war, British policy for dealing with the pocket battleships had been the dispersal of shipping, evasive routeing, and patrols in focal areas, where cruisers would be deployed in pairs against a superior enemy. It is likely that Harwood had read the translations of Raeder's history of cruiser warfare and therefore knew German strategy. His personal view was that focal areas should be protected 'to make the raider come to us'. He thought that following raiders around often 'four days astern' was wrong, but in the Admiralty in early October there was a shift in policy, and instead of patrols in focal areas, on 5 October 1939 the war diary recorded the formation of nine British and French hunting groups. Three of these groups were to be deployed in Lyon's sea area: Force G, consisting of the heavy cruisers *Cumberland* and *Exeter* under Harwood's command; Force H, consisting of the heavy cruisers *Sussex* and *Shropshire* off the Cape of Good Hope; and Force K, consisting of the aircraft carrier *Ark Royal* and the battlecruiser *Renown*, which would operate in the southern mid-Atlantic under the direct control of the Admiralty. Such was the effect of the appearance of one pocket battleship off South America: all told, in order to form the hunting groups, four British battleships or battlecruisers, three aircraft carriers and five cruisers had been withdrawn from home waters and from the Mediterranean. Raeder's policy was working.[22]

The groups were to keep wireless silence while searching, unless their presence had been disclosed, and given wide discretion in their movements, which meant that commanders-in-chief would not necessarily know where friendly ships in their areas were. As a sop to previous policy, the Admiralty cautioned that groups were not to be enticed from areas where trade was thick. Harwood's views on this change of policy were not recorded, but it would be hunting for the proverbial needle in a haystack, with the only clue available being the occasional RRR signal from a brave merchant ship under attack.

By 5 October Harwood had concentrated his ships, *Exeter*, *Ajax*, *Havock* and *Hotspur*, off Rio. His plan was that if he met a pocket battleship by day, to shadow until dusk when he would close and attack in the dark hours. If he made contact at night, his destroyers would at once close the enemy's beam and attack with torpedoes. He had also learned that the New Zealand-manned cruiser *Achilles*, under Captain W E Parry, would be joining him from the west coast of South America.

That same day a vital clue as to *Graf Spee*'s whereabouts was missed.[23] *Graf Spee* had claimed her second victim, Tyneside Line's 4,600-ton *Newton Beech*, who before she was stopped and boarded sent out a distress message. The wireless signal was weak but was nevertheless picked up by the modern, efficient and well-run Brocklebank's *Martand* several hundred miles to the north. A few hours later *Martand* met *Cumberland*, who was again on passage from Freetown, this time to the River Plate to join *Exeter*. *Martand* reported by flashing light that she had just received a distress message from an unknown ship being attacked by a raider in position 9° 20' South 6° 19' West. However, after a brief visual inspection of *Martand*'s modern lines, Fallowfield resumed his course, deciding neither to explore nor to report the warning that he had received via *Martand*. Fallowfield's opportunity for glory had again passed.[24]

Not even on 9 October when Fallowfield rendezvoused at sea with Harwood in *Exeter*, nor on 14 October when he called on Harwood at anchor in Samborombón Bay, did Fallowfield think to mention this vital intelligence. It was not until the end of the month, when he wrote his report of proceedings for October that he thought to mention the exchange of signals with *Martand*.[25]

Meanwhile, *Graf Spee* had boarded the third victim, the 4,200-ton cargo steamer SS *Ashlea* and, after transferring her crew to *Newton Beech*, sank *Ashlea* on 7 October with scuttling charges. When it became clear that *Newton Beech* was too slow to keep up, her crew and that of *Ashlea* were embarked in *Graf Spee* and *Newton Beech* also was sunk by scuttling charges. Embarrassingly, her maize kept her afloat for several hours. Next, *Graf Spee* captured ss *Huntsman* and before sinking her on 10 October, using her wireless, Langsdorff's B-Dienst team sent a distress message purporting to come from *Newton Beech* saying she had been attacked by a U-boat, and giving a false position.

On 22 October *Graf Spee*, now a hundred miles south of St Helena, sighted her fifth victim, the Hain Line's 5,300-ton *Trevanion*, who also sent an RRR before she was boarded, a message which was picked up and relayed to Freetown. Though garbled, *Trevanion*'s massage was the first intelligence of *Graf Spee* since 30 September.[26]

Exeter was scheduled for self-maintenance in the Falklands, and on 27 October Harwood transferred his broad pennant to *Ajax*, the Exeters giving him three cheers as he left. He was sorry to leave her after nearly three years, but welcomed the opportunity to meet new people. Harwood wrote to Joan:[27]

> Here I am in *Ajax*. Very comfortable and all except a bathroom, forward. Sea cabin not quite so big but adequate. Woodhouse (Captain) and I lunch and dine in it. Woodhouse has been very nice and done everything possible to make me comfortable. Between you and me, I am much happier here. Everybody in *Exeter* was getting on my nerves. I got ruder and ruder. Awful. I tried not to be but inside I itched and itched at them. I liked Bell ... I was very sorry to leave but now I am here I am much happier. Have not lost my temper once and no need to. Woodhouse is a most capable captain and everything organised perfectly. He knows the game and there is no need for me to supervise. I just play the part of an Admiral in his flagship complete with staff.

That day *Graf Spee* was south of Tristan da Cunha, heading east and then passing well south of the Cape, to show herself in the Indian Ocean.

November – on such a full sea

By 1 November Langsdorff had informed Raeder that he intended 'to break through into home waters in January 1940 for engine overhaul'.[28] So lean were *Graf Spee*'s pickings in these weeks that the Admiralty on 3 November informed Lyon that all German capital ships were, apparently, already in German waters. The Admiralty took the opportunity to order that the ships of Forces G and H should swap, which would give *Cumberland* and *Exeter* the opportunity to refit at the dockyard in Simonstown, and which would give Harwood, who would remain on the South American coast, two heavy cruisers, *Shropshire* and *Sussex*, with longer range. On 6 November *Ajax* entered Buenos Aires: Harwood's first time ashore for forty-six days, though much of the time was spent on official calls and at the dentist. There was time for Harwood to discuss with the Argentine minister of marine and with Admiral Guisasola the issue of using English Bank for refuelling, and both men suggested that he could also use the sheltered waters of Samborombón Bay, closer inshore. This was most acceptable as it did not suffer the heavy seas which ran across the shallow banks or the swells, which in a gale on 10 November caused a new tanker, RFA *Olynthus*, to smash into the starboard side of *Exeter*. This incident and bad weather delayed the departure of Force G for its new area.

On 15 November and in another ocean, *Graf Spee* fell on her next victim, George Brown's small, 700-ton *Africa Shell*, close inshore in the Mozambique Channel. As he had with his first sinking, Langsdorff made sure that his presence was known and, having advertised himself, he doubled back into the South Atlantic.

On 16 November the naval officer in charge at Simonstown reported the sinking of *Africa Shell*, but the conflicting reports from eye-witnesses were unclear as to whether the raider was a pocket battleship or a heavy cruiser. Whichever, this was *Graf Spee*'s sixth victim and, although a number of other merchant ships were overdue, only the second confirmed sinking by a raider which was known to the Admiralty.[29] The effect was just what Langsdorff and Raeder wanted: a further change in disposition by the British. Force K, several thousand miles away in Freetown, was sent towards the Indian Ocean, and the exchange of Forces G and H was cancelled. Force G, whose sailing had been delayed by bad weather, was already on its way to South Africa when it turned back towards South America and Rio.

Harwood ordered *Achilles* to refuel from *Olynthus* on 22/23 November in Samborombón Bay and then to relieve ships in the Rio area, so that *Cumberland* and *Exeter* could come south to refuel on the

26th and to patrol the Plate while *Ajax* visited the Falklands. On passage, *Ajax* flew aerial reconnaissance over Bahía Blanca and arrived in Port Stanley on the 27th. *Cumberland* and *Exeter*, after long periods at sea, were in need of refit and Harwood was determined to start a programme of self-maintenance by sending each in turn to the Falklands. So, leaving *Cumberland* in the River Plate, *Exeter* was sent to join *Ajax* and arrived in Port Stanley on the 29th.

December 1939 – the game is up

After a few days in the Falklands, *Ajax* sailed on 2 December making for the River Plate. This was the same day that Langsdorff scored his greatest success, stopping the 10,000-ton *Doric Star*, bound from Auckland to London. However, *Doric Star* sent her RRR message, enabling the Operational Intelligence Centre (OIC) correctly to link this sinking to the same raider that had sunk *Africa Shell*. The OIC deduced that the raider had returned to her previous hunting ground, where she had already sunk *Newton Beech*, *Huntsman*, *Ashlea* and *Trevanion*. This was the turning point in the hunt for the raider, and post-war Harwood gave full credit to the brave wireless operator of the *Doric Star* who, in spite of gun- and machine-gun fire, stood by his office until he knew he had transmitted his raider report.[30]

Next day Langsdorff attacked Furness Withy's *Tairoa*. She too sent out an RRR message: this gave the OIC the direction of the raider's movements. For once, Lyon and Harwood possessed a clear idea of *Graf Spee*'s whereabouts and her movements.[31]

The capture of the enemy's merchant ships was not a one-way business and on the evening of 5 December *Ajax* caught the 9,600-ton German liner *Ussukuma*, which had left Bahía Blanca the previous day, and promptly scuttled herself. The next morning, prisoners from *Ussukuma* were transferred to *Cumberland*, who was on her way to Port Stanley both for her self-maintenance period and to reinforce those islands in case the Germans decided to commemorate their defeat (and the death of Admiral Graf Maximilian von Spee) at the Battle of the Falklands on 8 December 1914 by raiding the Falklands.

Ajax then refuelled in Samborombón Bay from the faithful *Olynthus*, while Lyon, thinking that the still unnamed raider might be working northward, juggled the ships of Force H and Force K under his command, and the Admiralty sent the submarine *Severn* south with orders to protect South Georgia.

On 7 December Langsdorff claimed his last victim, *Streonshalh*. He had destroyed nine British merchant ships totalling 50,089 tons and without loss of life. The cargoes these ships carried were maize, sugar, manganese ore, pig iron, zinc concentrates, meat, wool, lead, wheat and dairy products, illustrating the dependency of the British Isles upon imports. The identity of his ship remained unknown to the British, though most thought that probably she was the *Scheer*. However, on 8 December the name *Graf Spee* appeared for the first time in the Admiralty war diary in the text of a signal from McCall in Buenos Aires. On the same day news of *Ashlea*'s sinking two months before reached London.

The correlation of forces

So far, Harwood's cruisers had operated singly or in pairs, but now in mid-December he was able to concentrate three of his ships. Even so, Force G was the weakest of the hunting groups which were looking for the German raider.

Graf Spee was at least 12,000 tons displacement, far more than the 10,000 tons allowed by the Washington Treaty, powered by diesel engines and with a designed speed of 28 knots, though during the battle she never did more than 24 knots. Her main armament was six 11in guns in two triple turrets firing shells of 700lbs weight with a maximum range of 40,000yds, but a rate of fire of only two to three rounds per gun per minute. Her secondary armament of eight 5.9in guns, in single, open mountings, four aside, firing 100lb shells to a maximum range of 24,000yds, used a separate control system to the 11in guns. She also carried two quadruple 21in torpedo tubes on her quarterdeck. Her armoured belt was 3in thick, sufficient to keep out shells of 8in calibre and below, and her 11in gun turrets were protected by 5½in of armour. She had excellent stereoscopic rangefinders. Unknown to Harwood, *Graf Spee* carried a primitive radar ranging system, but her single Arado seaplane was out of action by the day of the battle.

Against her, the heavy cruiser *Exeter* was 8,400 tons displacement with a maximum speed of 32 knots. Her six 8in guns in twin turrets fired shells of 256lbs to a maximum range of 30,500yds with a rate of fire of about six rounds per gun per minute. She carried two single 4in guns in open mountings and three 21in torpedo tubes each side. Her armoured belt was of similar thickness to *Graf Spee*'s, increasing to 5½in over the engine rooms, but her turrets were only lightly armoured. She carried two Walrus amphibious aircraft.

His two light cruisers, *Ajax* and *Achilles*, were of 7,270 tons displacement and also capable of 32 knots. Each carried eight 6in guns in twin turrets, firing 112lb shells at a rate up to eight to nine rounds per minute. Their gun range, armour protection and maximum speed were broadly similar to *Exeter*. *Achilles* had four single 4in AA guns, two each side in single mountings, while *Ajax* had four each side in shielded twin mountings. Each ship carried four 21in torpedo tubes aside. *Ajax*, but not *Achilles*, carried a single Seafox sea plane.

Graf Spee's overwhelming superiority in weight of fire could cripple one of Harwood's cruisers with a direct hit from long range. While the British ships had an advantage in speed, only *Exeter*'s shells could, possibly, penetrate *Graf Spee*'s armour. None of the British ships had any radar equipment. Harwood's first problem, if he met a German pocket battleship, would be to get within effective gun range before any of his ships were put out of action. Much would depend on the skill and tactics of the two opposing commanders.

The rendezvous

Harwood's choice of a rendezvous for Force G was no matter of chance. *Doric Star* had given her position as over three thousand miles from South America, *Tairoa* had indicated a position some 120 miles further to the southwest: Harwood realised that *Graf Spee*'s next objective might be the valuable British shipping on the South American coast. He sketched a diagram on a signal pad, and estimated that at a cruising speed of 15 knots the German could reach the Rio de Janeiro area by 12 December, the Plate by the 13th or the Falklands by the 14th. More than 1,500 miles separated these areas, but the most important of the three was the focal area of the large and very valuable grain and meat trade off the River Plate. Harwood therefore decided to concentrate all his available forces off the River Plate by 12 December. Cancelling his previous dispositions of 3 December, he ordered *Achilles* to meet *Ajax* in the Plate area at 10:00 on the 10th, and he ordered *Exeter* to leave the Falklands on the 9th. On her way north, *Exeter* was to cover *Lafonia*, which was bringing back to Buenos Aires the British contingent which had volunteered for service in the Falkland Island Defence Force. Having made these dispositions, Harwood ordered wireless silence.

At 06:00 on 12 December *Achilles*, *Ajax* and *Exeter* met 150 miles east of Médanos Point, south of the River Plate. The three cruisers then proceeded towards a position in the centre of the thickest of the British diverted shipping routes off the Plate. That evening there was no Nelsonic meeting of captains, Harwood already knew his people well. Instead, he signalled by flashing light:

> My policy with three cruisers in company versus one pocket battleship. Attack at once by day or night. By day act as two units, 1st Division [*Ajax* and *Achilles*] and *Exeter* diverged to permit flank marking. First Division will concentrate gunfire. By night ships will normally remain in company in open order. Be prepared for the signal ZMM which is to have the same meaning as MM except for Division read Single Ship.

Harwood amplified this signal:

> My object in the signal ZMM is to avoid torpedoes and take the enemy by surprise and cross his stern. Without further orders ships are to clear the line of fire by hauling astern of the new leading ship. The new leading ship is to lead the line without further orders so as to maintain decisive gun range.

On the evening of 12 December Harwood exercised this manoeuvre.

Langsdorff was indeed on his way westward to the Plate, where German intelligence told him that a convoy of merchant ships was being formed. So far, Langsdorff's almost invariable practice had been to fly off his Arado seaplane at dawn each day. It was a reliable aircraft, but on 11 December the seaplane landed badly, ingested seawater and the engine block had cracked. This was the second engine, the first one already having been damaged. Her crew took the opportunity for some much-needed maintenance and the Arado sat on its launcher, wingless and engineless, looking 'like a trussed turkey waiting to be put in the oven'.[32] Consequently, on the morning of Wednesday, 13 December 1939 *Graf Spee* was not flying aerial reconnaissance.

At 05:20 on the morning of 13 December the British cruisers were about 340 miles east of Montevideo. As the day broke, they undertook their normal daily wartime routine of dawn action stations. Some twenty minutes later the ships' companies fell out from action stations and reverted to their usual degree of readiness. Passing his orders by flashing light, Harwood reformed his squadron in single line ahead, in the order *Ajax*, *Achilles*, *Exeter*, zigzagging on a mean course of 060°, speed 14 knots. There was a gentle breeze from the southeast, with a low swell and a slight sea from the same quarter, and visibility was about twenty miles.

In *Graf Spee* Langsdorff was in his sea cabin, close to the bridge, on a course of 155°, speed 15 knots, his intention being to alter on the hour to 335°, in order to sweep a large area in his search for merchant shipping. At 05:52 a lookout spotted against the brightening, eastern sky 'at first two and then four thin masts at approximately a distance of 310 hectometres'.[33] Looking east, the officer of watch saw the black masts against the brightening eastern sky.[34] Langsdorff gave orders to maintain course and speed, and to go to action stations while he climbed high in the ship to the flying bridge.[35] The sun rose at 05:56 in a cloudless sky, giving extreme visibility.

At 06:00 *Graf Spee* was cleared for action, while in the British warships many men had already fallen out from action stations and those who could had gone back to their bunks and hammocks to snatch a few more minutes of sleep. From his vantage point, Langsdorff made out the furthest right of three ships to be a heavy cruiser, presumably *Exeter*, and at first he thought that the two ships on the left, because of their low superstructures, were destroyers. Suddenly, Langsdorff recognised them as light cruisers. He could see that they were signalling and must have assumed that he had been spotted: because of the speed advantage of the British ships, which meant that as shadowers they could never be shaken off, he was committed to fight. He decided to attack at once, in order to close and overwhelm the British ships before they could work up to full speed. *Graf Spee* was in an advantageous lee position for a gunnery duel, and when the engine room reported ready for full speed Langsdorff ordered an alteration of course to 115° at 06:12.

For eighteen minutes, at more than a quarter of a mile a minute, *Graf Spee* had been closing the British ships from out of the dark, western horizon without having been seen. It was probably a puff of dirty, diesel exhaust as *Graf Spee* increased speed that was seen in the British ships. Leading Signalman Bill Swanston in *Ajax* was first to report a telltale plume of smoke, but at 06:10 *Exeter* hoisted the flag signal: 'smoke 320 degrees'. In *Ajax*, Harwood had a pre-prepared signal to send ashore and, still maintaining wireless silence, he ordered *Exeter* at 06:14 to 'Investigate smoke bearing 324 degrees. If this is a British merchantman bound for the Plate due to get into harbour soon, transfer your signal to her'.

Hardly had this signal been made when at 06:15 the hull became clear over the horizon: Bell in *Exeter* shouted at his gunnery officer, 'There's the f***ing *Scheer*, open fire on her!' and a minute later he signalled Harwood, 'Enemy in sight 320 degrees'.[36]

8
The Battle of the River Plate

Almost simultaneously, the enemy was sighted by each of the British cruisers. Action stations was sounded off by buglers and battle ensigns were hoisted as six hundred men in each ship dashed to their action stations. In *Achilles*, a signalman with a flag under his arm ran aft shouting, 'Make way for the Digger flag!', and hoisted a New Zealand ensign to the mainmast head to the accompaniment of loud cheers. For the first time, a New Zealand cruiser was about to engage the enemy.[1] Harwood, who had been in his sea cabin, put on a uniform jacket over his orange pyjamas and stepped onto *Ajax*'s bridge. His orders had been simple 'attack at once, by day or night', and he found that Captain Woodhouse was already acting upon his signal ZMM.

The first blows

Ajax and *Achilles* continued together northeastwards to cross the enemy's bows, while *Exeter* made a large alteration of course to the north and then westward, so that the enemy would be engaged simultaneously from widely different bearings and from opposite sides. The German would be compelled either to split his main armament of 11in guns to engage both divisions or to concentrate his fire on one and leave the other unengaged. At first Langsdorff chose to divide his fire and at 06:17, at 197hms, fired first at *Exeter* and then at the light cruisers, before concentrating his main armament on his more dangerous opponent, *Exeter*.[2]

Even while the signal ZMM was being executed, Harwood signalled to the world 'Immediate one pocket battleship 034 degrees south 049 degrees west course 275.'

The British cruisers were rapidly working up to full power and were steaming at more than 25 knots when *Exeter* returned fire with her four forward guns at 06:20. *Achilles* opened fire at 06:21 and *Ajax* two minutes later: the light cruisers quickly developed a high rate of accurate fire, obliging *Graf Spee* to reply with her 5.9in guns. However, the 8in salvoes from *Exeter* appeared to worry the enemy more, and after shifting targets rapidly once or twice, Langsdorff concentrated his six 11in guns on *Exeter*.

Graf Spee's third salvo at 06:23 straddled *Exeter* amidships, killing the crew of the starboard torpedo tubes, damaging communications, and riddling the searchlights and aircraft. Both aircraft were being prepared for catapulting, but as they were now extensively damaged and a fire hazard, they were manhandled over the side. One minute later, *Exeter* received a direct hit from an 11in shell on the front of 'B'-turret, putting its two guns out of action. Splinters swept the bridge, killing or wounding many except Captain Bell and two others. *Exeter* was no longer under control from the bridge and Bell hurried to the after conning position, where he found that all communications had been cut: steering orders would have to be passed along a human chain, and for the next hour *Exeter* was conned in this difficult manner, the captain fully exposed to the blast from the after pair of 8in guns and to enemy fire.

At 06:25, fearing a threat of a torpedo attack from the light cruisers on his opposite side, Langsdorff turned to port and northwards. Harwood in *Ajax* followed the German's movement. He made no manoeuvring signals to Parry in *Achilles*, who nevertheless had 'no doubt whatever regarding your intentions' and remained in close support, not attempting to keep accurate station but conforming with Harwood's movements. While developing maximum gunfire, the light cruisers dodged punishment from the enemy's fire by frequent alterations of course. As they closed the range and drew ahead of *Graf Spee*, it was clear that the concentrated fire of their sixteen 6in guns was worrying the German, who briefly at 06:30 again split her main armament and fired one 11in turret at them. *Ajax* was straddled three times and the 1st Division turned away slightly to throw out the enemy's fire. *Graf Spee* was also firing alternately at the two ships of the 1st Division with her 5.9in guns.

At 06:32 *Exeter* fired her starboard torpedoes, but these went wide when the German ship made a sudden large alteration of course to port and steered westwards under cover of a smokescreen. The two 6in-gun cruisers immediately hauled round to close the range and regain bearing.

At 06:34 Harwood broadcast the first of several enemy locating reports, intended to keep the OIC in London and his commander-in-chief informed of the battle.

The chase

Graf Spee had been steering towards her adversaries, but after turning away to avoid *Exeter*'s and then *Ajax*'s torpedoes, she began making a smokescreen and continued the turn to port until she was heading westwards.

If there was one weakness in the South American Squadron, it was that very little use had been made of the seaplanes in *Exeter* and *Ajax*, but at 06:37, between blasts from *Ajax*'s 6in guns, Lieutenant E D G Lewin was catapulted off in his Seafox. Fifteen minutes later he was able to establish wireless communications and, by spotting the fall of fire, help concentrate the 1st Division's guns.

At about 06:38 *Exeter* turned to starboard to fire her port torpedoes and was hit by two 11in shells. One struck 'A'-turret, putting its two 8in guns out of action, the other burst inside the ship amidships causing very extensive damage and starting a fierce fire. From aloft in the Seafox it seemed that *Exeter* was completely wreathed in smoke and flame. She had suffered severely: both forward 'A'- and 'B'-turrets were disabled and the after 'Y'-turret was in local control; she was burning fiercely amidships; several compartments were flooded; her compasses had failed and Bell was using a magnetic compass brought from one of the ship's boats to con his ship. Nevertheless, *Exeter* was kept resolutely in action, turning to the east so that port torpedoes could be fired as soon as the tubes came to bear on the enemy, and although listing and down by the head, she came onto a parallel, westward course, and opened fire with her two remaining 8in guns.

On the opposite side of *Graf Spee*, on her starboard quarter, *Ajax* and *Achilles* had now worked up to full power and were closing at 31 knots, firing as fast as they could.

Harwood recalled this phase of the battle:[3]

> The whole thing ... was to try and make him [Langsdorff] divide his fire. We succeeded. He started with one turret on the *Exeter* and the other one on us. Then he shifted to the *Exeter* and then he came back to us. When we saw that he was going in to try and finish off the *Exeter* we opened the A arcs [turned to bring more guns to bear] and gave him all we had with sixteen 6in guns. So he remained undecided, but there is no doubt that he ought to have finished off one or other of the forces on his flanks. After the hits on *Exeter* he ought to have finished her off. Perhaps he thought he had, as we did when she disappeared in a great cloud of spray, smoke and flame. But she came out and remained in the action – her finest achievement – and so the enemy remained undecided.

At 06:40 an 11in shell fell short of *Achilles*, but splinters showered the bridge, wounding Captain Parry, and the control tower, where Washbourn,[4] the gunnery officer, was cut in the scalp and momentarily stunned, but calmly set about clearing away the dead and wounded and soon had the control tower back in action.

'After 06:40 the action became virtually a chase.'[5] *Graf Spee* turned away to the westward under cover of a smokescreen, while the two 6in gun cruisers hauled round to the northwestward in pursuit, Harwood accepting that this meant being unable to bring the after guns to bear on the enemy. *Ajax* and *Achilles* were now on the starboard quarter of *Graf Spee*, while *Exeter* was on the enemy's port beam, still in action with her two remaining guns.

Harwood ordered maximum speed, and at 06:56, when his light cruisers were still eight miles astern of *Graf Spee*, he ordered a turn outwards, to starboard, to bring all guns to bear again. Despite fire control problems and a loss of the gunnery control wireless, the sixteen 6in guns of the 1st Division were maddening *Graf Spee*, who could only bring one main turret and her 5.9in guns to fire intermittently on the British ships, which were obscured by *Graf Spee*'s own smoke.

By 07:00 *Exeter* was on fire, flooding and listing, with one turret remaining in action but still with full power.

At 07:10 Harwood turned his ships westwards to close *Graf Spee* again. At 07:16, under cover of more smoke, *Graf Spee* made a large alteration of course to the south and headed towards *Exeter*, ten miles away, as though to finish off that much-damaged ship. Terrier-like, Harwood responded with a turn towards the enemy, and the rapid shooting of his light cruisers scored a number of hits and started a fire amidships in *Graf Spee*. The German turned back to the northwest until all her 11in guns were bearing on her tormentors. At 07:20 the range was five and a half miles when Harwood felt able to open his gunnery arcs again, and the division's rate of fire worked up to between eight and nine rounds per minute from all sixteen guns. None penetrated *Graf Spee*'s armoured belt.

At 07:24 *Ajax* fired her port torpedoes, Harwood recounting later, 'The result was instantaneous. Over went *Spee*'s wheel and she disappeared once again behind smoke towards Montevideo'.[6] But a minute or so later, with the range down to four miles, Ajax received her first direct hit: an 11in delayed-action shell struck her after superstructure and penetrated 42ft, putting 'X'- and 'Y'-turrets out of action. Almost simultaneously, *Graf Spee* fired torpedoes, but *Ajax* and *Achilles* turned sharply away eastwards.

All this time, *Exeter* was dropping behind as her damage increasingly affected her speed, but her captain kept her angled so that her only functioning, after turret could bear and fire on *Graf Spee*. However, at about 07:30 flooding caused power to the turret to fail, and *Exeter* made off at slow speed to the southeast to repair damage and make herself seaworthy.

When the light cruisers turned back at 07:32 to resume their pursuit, *Graf Spee* was headed westward and had begun to zigzag and to make smoke. In *Ajax* Harwood recalled:

> We did not see a lot of her [*Graf Spee*] during this phase. When we did get a glimpse of her, she appeared to be listing to port but the next time she appeared for a moment out of the smoke she was listing to starboard. We then realised that she was zig-zagging in the smoke and we were seeing her as she heeled over on the turns.[7]

Again at 07:36 *Graf Spee* altered course to the southwest in order to bring all her 11in guns to bear on the British cruisers, but *Ajax* and *Achilles* stood on, until by 07:38 the range was down to 8,000yds.

At this moment, when *Graf Spee*'s shooting was still very accurate and she did not appear to have suffered much damage, Harwood was told that *Ajax* had only 20 per cent of ammunition remaining and only three guns in action. He decided to break off the action and to try and close in again after dark. Accordingly, at 07:40 *Ajax* and *Achilles* turned away to the eastward under cover of their own smoke: while in the turn, a shell from *Graf Spee* cut the main topmast of *Ajax* clean in two, destroying the wireless aerials, and causing a number of casualties. However, *Graf Spee* made no attempt to follow them, but steadied on a westerly course for the Plate. Six minutes later the British cruisers hauled round and began to shadow the enemy, *Ajax* to port and *Achilles* to starboard, at a distance of about fifteen miles. In the prevailing conditions of extreme visibility, the conspicuous control tower and bridge of *Graf Spee*, as well as her continuous funnel smoke, made it an easy matter to shadow her at long range.

The rough circle which *Ajax* and *Achilles* had steamed and fought had brought them by 08:00 to a position barely twenty miles northwest from where they had first sighted the enemy.

The action had lasted barely an hour and half, and there was disappointingly little apparent damage to *Graf Spee*: Harwood remarked to Woodhouse, 'we might as well be bombarding her with snowballs'. However, the German report of the damage, particularly to *Graf Spee*'s upper deck during the phase of close-range fighting, when the British 'fired very fast, their fire being at times very effective, the ship receiving in this part of the action a large number of hits', fills ten pages of the *Gefechtsbericht*, or battle report. There were many dead and wounded too, including Langsdorff, who had fought his ship from the exposed flying bridge. He had been wounded twice, once in the arm, and again when he was blown to the deck and concussed. His second in command had been called to the flying bridge to take over, but Langsdorff soon recovered and insisted on continuing to command from the same exposed position.

Later during the day, Langsdorff was able to tour *Graf Spee* and see the damage caused by the light cruisers' relentless attack. He saw the hole in *Graf Spee*'s bows, he heard varying reports of the amount of usable fuel left, of the destruction of the galleys, and the loss of flour for baking and fresh water. It seems his morale collapsed and on returning to the bridge Langsdorff told his navigating officer, 'We must run into port. The ship is not now seaworthy for the North Atlantic'.

In *Ajax* her wireless aerials were still down, and Harwood ordered *Achilles* to broadcast hourly the position, course and speed of *Graf Spee*, while wondering, 'Why is she running into the Plate? Has she got a submarine there? Or something else? I could not believe that she was going to intern herself.'[8]

HMS Exeter

By 08:14 *Exeter* was out of sight to the southeastward and Harwood ordered his aircraft to tell her to close. At 09:10 the aircraft reported: '*Exeter* is badly damaged, but is joining you as best she can.' Two minutes later *Ajax* recovered her aircraft, which had been in the air for two hours and thirty-five minutes. Captain Bell in *Exeter* did his best to rejoin but, having only an inaccurate boat compass to steer by, he decided instead to steer towards the nearest land, some two hundred miles to the westward, and speed was reduced while bulkheads were being shored and the ship's list corrected. When in the afternoon Harwood heard more of the extent of her damage, he ordered her to proceed to the Falkland Islands at whatever speed was possible without straining her bulkhead: 'Do as you think best but consider proceeding to Falklands at slow speed. I don't want you to get caught by *Scheer* [*Spee*]'.[9] *Exeter* later reported that one gun of her after turret could be fired in local control and that she was making 20 knots, and she would arrive at Port Stanley at noon on 16 December.

HMS Cumberland

Cumberland, it will be recalled, had been refitting at Port Stanley more than a thousand miles away, where Harwood had planned seven days' self-refit at eight hours' notice for steam for each ship of his squadron. A sixth sense told Commander E C H Featherstone, her engineer, that this was 'too good to be true', and Featherstone had arranged for the refit to be staggered. Work on 'B' boiler room and the forward engine room had been completed on the morning of 13 December, and work was about to begin on 'A' boiler room, when at breakfast time wide-eyed signalmen brought a series of signals to the wardroom, beginning with *Exeter*'s message sent at 08:55, 'All guns out of action'.[10] Featherstone recalled: 'At first we thought that [Harwood] was conducting an exercise ... but it did not take long for the penny to drop and the only thing to do was to get there – and quick'.[11] After five days alongside, *Cumberland* had not completed provisioning and she was still encumbered with 107 German prisoners of war from *Ussukuma*, when at 09:45 (local time, one hour behind the Plate) on 13 December Fallowfield gave the order to prepare for sea. By 11:36 Fallowfield knew from Harwood's general warning to merchant shipping, first sent at 08:05, that there was a German pocket battleship off the Plate. Meanwhile, Harwood had sent three signals to *Cumberland* telling her the whereabouts of a pocket battleship and at 09:42 he sent an order, 'Close Plate at full speed'. Only at 20:42 that evening did Harwood receive *Cumberland*'s message timed at 11:01: 'sailed from Stanley 11:00 Wed 13 December. Proceeding to Plate area at 20 knots.'[12] Featherstone and his people in the engine and boiler rooms worked hard to connect up all *Cumberland*'s machinery,[13] and at 14:00, and in spite of fog which occasionally reduced visibility to half a mile, Fallowfield was able to order an increase in speed to 24 knots, and at 14:53 to 30 knots.

The remains of the day

Meanwhile, off the Plate, the chase settled down, with the two British light cruisers following *Graf Spee* at a respectful distance. She was evidently making for the Plate and *Ajax* and *Achilles* followed from one ship on either quarter. Harwood recalled: 'Right, I thought, we have fired 75% of our ammunition and have not sunk her. I must get within closer range, and that I can only do at night. I must haul off and wait'.[14]

Several times *Graf Spee* turned to fire at her tormentors. At 10:05 when *Achilles* got too close, *Graf Spee* fired two three-gun salvoes of 11in shell at her from 23,000yds. Harwood recalled: 'The first was very short, but the second fell close alongside. She appeared to await for the first salvo to fall before firing the second. *Achilles* turned away at full speed under smoke and resumed shadowing at longer range.'

Shortly after 11:00 a merchant ship, stopped and blowing off steam, was sighted close to *Graf Spee*, from whom a few minutes later *Ajax* and *Achilles* received a wireless signal: 'Please rescue lifeboats of English steamer.' Neither cruiser replied to this message, which was evidently a ruse with the object of delaying and evading the shadowing cruisers. The merchantman was the British *Shakespeare*, and as the British cruisers swept by, Harwood could see that all her boats were stowed, and in reply to a signal she reported that she did not need any assistance.

At 11:05 Harwood received *Exeter*'s signal reporting that her turrets were out of action, that she was flooded up to No. 14 bulkhead, but could still do 18 knots. He ordered her to the Falklands. His order stood even when he heard that one gun of 'Y'-turret could be fired in local control.

The afternoon passed quietly, until at 15:43 when 'There was an anxious period – but fortunately our anxiety was unfounded – *Achilles* reported a strange ship ... which she thought might be an 8in cruiser'.[15] To *Achilles*' signal for an enemy in sight, Harwood asked, 'What is it?' 'Suspect 8in cruiser, am confirming,' replied *Achilles*, but then signalled: 'False alarm.' She had identified the approaching ship as the British motor-vessel, *Delane*, 6,054 tons, of the Lamport and Holt Line. The peculiar appearance of this ship, whose funnel was streamlined into the bridge superstructure, gave her at long range a close resemblance to a German cruiser of the *Blücher* class.

Thereafter, the shadowing of *Graf Spee* continued without incident until 19:15 when she altered course and at 26,000yds fired two 11in salvoes at *Ajax*, who turned away under cover of smoke. *Achilles* also turned away on sighting the gun flashes, but quickly resumed her westerly course. These were the first shells fired by the enemy for more than nine hours.

By now it was clear to Harwood that *Graf Spee* intended to enter the estuary of the River Plate, which she had been steering towards for more than twelve hours. As Harwood well knew, the entrance to Montevideo on the northern side of the Plate lay between Lobos Island to the east and a sixteen-mile-long shallow bank called English Bank. Harwood saw the possibility that the German ship might attempt to evade the British by doubling round English Bank, and so ordered *Achilles*: 'If enemy passes west of Lobos *Achilles* is to follow him. *Ajax* will proceed south of English Bank in case she doubles out. Be careful you are not caught at dawn up sun as even if he anchors he may come to sea at anytime. He is not to be relied on to respect territorial waters.'

Graf Spee made a considerable alteration of course to the north-westward at 19:42 and, expecting her to open fire, *Achilles* made rapid changes of course but nothing happened and she soon resumed shadowing, urged on by Harwood who signalled, 'As you get near territorial waters take advantage of them to close up to enemy'. As dusk gathered, *Achilles* speeded up to pass between Lobos Island and the mainland.

Eventually, at 20:30 Harwood signalled to *Achilles*: 'I am leaving him to you this side. Make frequent enemy reports', and he ordered *Ajax* to turn west and to pass south of English Bank. Sunset at 20:48 silhouetted the German against the western sky, as *Achilles* altered course to the northwest to keep the advantage of the afterglow while she remained under cover of the land. A few minutes later, now under cover of dusk, *Graf Spee* altered course and fired three 11in salvoes at a range of 22,000yds. The first two fell short and the third dropped close astern, all being accurate for line. *Achilles* replied with five salvoes of 6in shell while turning away at full speed and making smoke. This brief exchange was seen from Punta del Este, the seaside resort of Montevideo, by many people who would later think that this brief exchange was the main action. Between 21:32 and 21:43 *Graf Spee* fired three more single salvoes, all of which fell short, but this time *Achilles* did not return fire since the flashes of her guns in the twilight would have given away her position. They were the last shots fired by *Graf Spee*. Since 19:40, when she headed for the River Plate, she had fired ten 11in salvoes, five of them from one turret only. They did not deter *Achilles*, who by 22:00 had closed in to 10,000yds. She could now estimate the enemy's course as taking him north of English Bank and reported this to Harwood. It was becoming increasingly difficult to see the enemy, but *Achilles* manoeuvred to silhouette *Graf Spee* against the lights of Montevideo.

Graf Spee anchored in Montevideo roads shortly after midnight. Harwood's appreciation was short and simple:

> My chief pre-occupation at this time was how long *Graf Spee* intended to stay there. The primary necessity was to keep to seaward of *Graf Spee* if she came to sea again, and at the same time to avoid being caught against the dawn light. At 23:50 I ordered *Ajax* and *Achilles* to withdraw from the Plate, *Achilles* to patrol the area from the Uruguayan coast to a line 120 degrees from English Bank and *Ajax* the southern area, both ships to move back into the Plate in their respective sectors after dawn.

Langsdorff had made two tactical blunders. First, he had closed on sighting the British ships, splitting his main armament, and bringing all three ships into effective gun range, so removing for them the most difficult problem of gaining range in the face of *Graf Spee*'s longer-range and heavier 11in guns. Secondly, he had failed to take advantage of his opportunity to finish off either *Exeter* or the ships of the 1st Division. In Harwood's opinion, Langsdorff had displayed little offensive spirit and instead 'retired between the two [*Ajax* and *Achilles*] and allowed himself to be fired at from both flanks.' *Graf Spee*'s gunfire was accurate, she showed a remarkably high degree of manoeuvrability and she was well-handled, and her smokescreens were good, but Harwood was impressed that in the British ships, by 'the adequacy of our peace-training. Little that had not been practised occurred, particularly among the repair parties ... [and] *Graf Spee* was heavily handled by the gunfire of the 1st Division and by that of *Exeter*.' Thereafter the German had turned away under cover of smoke and showed little interest in fighting.

So ended the day-long chase during which a modern pocket battleship, after putting *Exeter* out of action and partly disabling *Ajax* during the early part of the battle had refused to fight at close quarters and had fled to a neutral harbour. Throughout the day and the hours of darkness, *Exeter*, *Ajax* and *Achilles*, by their discipline, their fighting energy, their readiness to take risk and punishment, the competence and team-play of their captains, their self-assurance and confidence, all under the leadership of Henry Harwood, had gained a victory in one of the most brilliant cruiser actions in the long annals of the Royal Navy.

9
'My Object: Destruction'

It was an anxious night and day which followed: two small cruisers, one of them badly damaged and both low on fuel and ammunition, stood between the enemy and the open sea. The River Plate estuary is 120 miles wide between Lobos Island to the northeast and Cape San Antonio in the southwest, and there were three wide, deep-water channels which *Graf Spee* could take, the northernmost running between English Bank and Cumberland Shoal; the second between English Bank and Rouen Bank; and the third between Rouen Bank and Cape San Antonio.

Harwood had already, at 13:47 on 13 December, in the midst of the chase, asked McCall, the British naval attaché in Buenos Aires for surveillance to be organised and 'stressed the need for negative reports from the areas in which the enemy had not been sighted.' McCall was quick to respond and as Harwood withdrew for the night, he signalled at 23:05 that arrangements were in place for this to be done by tug and by plane. Next day, the indefatigable Lloyd Hirst arranged to sail a yacht from Buenos Aires to the outer end of the Whistle Buoy channel in order to indicate by a prearranged system of coloured rockets which way *Graf Spee* might be headed.[1]

The diplomatic battle

From the moment that *Graf Spee* anchored, there was a spate of Nazi propaganda which tried to gloss over the ignominy of her defeat and flight. In Montevideo, a considerable political and diplomatic struggle broke out, though Harwood played no direct part. *Graf Spee*'s wounded were landed and, in accordance with international law, her prisoners, the masters and fifty-four members of the crews of British ships sunk by her were released. Negotiations centred on the restoration of *Graf Spee*'s seagoing efficiency. A German shipping surveyor from Buenos Aires and the ship's senior engineer officer assessed the period required for repairs as not less than fourteen days, which time the German ambassador requested of the Uruguayans. On the grounds that *Graf Spee* had successfully steamed 300 miles since the battle, Millington-Drake, hoping to force a situation that would result in *Graf Spee* being interned, tried to insist upon time only to refuel, twenty-four hours.

Alberto Guani, the Uruguayan foreign minister, led the negotiations on behalf of his government, in the context of existing international law and of the Panama Declaration which had been agreed only weeks before. Under the latter, signed by the USA and twenty other American states, belligerent submarines were banned from entering their ports, subversive activities within their countries were condemned, and a maritime security zone, the so-called neutrality zone, was established extending 300 nautical miles on both sides of the American continent. Under international law, the warships of belligerent states were allowed only sufficient time in harbour to make themselves seaworthy, as distinct from battleworthy.

Initially, Guani granted a stay of forty-eight hours, while a Uruguayan technical commission, headed by José Varela, was sent on board to assess the damage to *Graf Spee*. Though Varela was denied access to *Graf Spee*'s engine room, he reported seventy-two hours would be sufficient to restore her seagoing capability, and on the morning of Friday, 15 December the President of Uruguay, Alfredo Baldomir, signed an order that *Graf Spee* should leave the port on Sunday evening, 17 December.

Thursday, 14 December

The next four days and nights were full of anxiety, as Captain Parry recalled:[2]

> Fortunately, the American broadcast service kept our enemy in a blaze of publicity; but naturally we had to remain ready for immediate action for it was always possible that he might slink out unmolested. This entailed keeping all hands at their stations all night and very little sleep could be got by those of us who might be faced with a quick decision. The first twenty-four hours was perhaps

> the most critical ... During this trying time the splendid spirit of the ship's company was most inspiring. If anyone's spirits had been inclined to droop they could not have failed to be revived by the strains of Maori music and songs, or the shouts of merriment which came from the various quarters.

As *Ajax* and *Achilles* kept watch over as wide an area of the Plate estuary as possible, Captain McCall flew to Montevideo, leaving naval affairs in Argentina in the safe hands of Harwood's friend, the assistant naval attaché, Lloyd Hirst. McCall and Lieutenant-Commander H D Johnston, the intelligence officer of the British consulate's Shipping Advisory Department in Montevideo, would keep Harwood informed of the latest news of *Graf Spee*.

Harwood's quickest source of information about what was happening in Montevideo harbour was the American journalist Mike Fowler, who had set up his watch on the Montevideo seafront and gave a minute-by-minute commentary of events:

> The tireless voice went on and on, vivid, resourceful and penetrating until it seemed as if the whole world were listening to Mike's words. Admiral Harwood certainly was ... In a matter of seconds Mike's voice bounced round the world and came back to every man in the three British ships ... the voice was hypnotic, It was impossible not to listen to it.[3]

However, Harwood's pre-war investment in the Uruguayans and in the British community in Uruguay also paid off and gave him access to deeper sources of intelligence, largely due to the foresight of the ambassador, Eugen Millington-Drake, the British consulate, and the 'Consular Shipping Advisory Department', formed in September 1939 from retired and reserve officers living in South America, who occupied the top floors of an office block in downtown old Montevideo, overlooking the harbour. John Garland, the local representative of Marconi's, had an office there too, as technical adviser on wireless matters to the consulate. On a hilltop outside Montevideo, Cerrito Radio was South America's most modern wireless station, which broadcast on fixed schedules to shipping, especially whalers in the South Atlantic, to the Falklands and to London: Cerrito station had been the first to receive and re-broadcast news of the battle.[4] Now Garland, with the enthusiastic help of a Uruguayan telegraphist, set up a receiving station which could pick up signals from ships and repeat them via Cerrito. Garland recruited British officers, released from imprisonment onboard *Graf Spee* on her arrival in a neutral harbour, to help man his station, and through goodwill and a certain amount of palm-greasing, Cerrito's on-air periods were increased to every two hours.

Meanwhile, the Admiralty in London informed Harwood of reinforcements: Force K, consisting of the carrier *Ark Royal* and the battlecruiser *Renown*, and the cruisers *Neptune*, *Dorsetshire* and *Shropshire*, and three destroyers, were all on their way, though none would reach him for at least five days.

Nevertheless, when the War Cabinet met in London that morning there was some satisfaction. Winston Churchill, once more the First Lord of the Admiralty, told the War Cabinet that 'a naval action had taken place on the previous day between three British cruisers and the German pocket battleship *Admiral Graf Spee* ... It now turned out that it was this vessel, and not the *Admiral Scheer* as had been thought, which had been in the South Atlantic', and he gave the bare bones of the action. He contrasted the offensive spirit shown by Harwood 'with the lack of enterprise shown in somewhat similar circumstances at the beginning of the last war when the German *Goeben* was allowed to escape'.[5] The War Cabinet was unanimous that Harwood had fought a very gallant and brilliant action. The First Sea Lord, who was also at the meeting, 'observed that the Admiralty had estimated that the German raider in the South Atlantic had sunk six [*sic* – actually nine] British ships'. The War Cabinet took note and expressed their high appreciation of a very gallant action.[6]

On the late evening of 14 December, the unexpectedly early arrival off the Plate of *Cumberland*, who had been keeping wireless silence during a passage of 1,000 miles in one and a half days from the Falklands, received a laconic greeting from Harwood: 'Very pleased to see you'. Her arrival shifted the balance of forces slightly in Harwood's favour. He was now able to have all three deep-water channels patrolled, *Cumberland* covering the central passage and well placed to reinforce either *Achilles* to the north or *Ajax* to the south.

Friday, 15 December

The next morning, Harwood later told an interviewer:

> Naturally, I was not averse to letting the German know that reinforcements had arrived. HMS *Cumberland* was ordered to steam up and down outside the estuary in daylight, and we even considered painting one side dark grey and the other light grey, so that when she turned out of sight of land and ran back, our reinforcements might seem even greater than they were.[7]

More practically, Harwood was also able to begin refuelling his ships from the tanker *Olynthus* at anchor in Samborombón Bay, albeit in weather so bad that the securing hawsers parted.

At 11:35 Harwood issued his orders for the day:

> My object Destruction. Necessitates concentrating our forces. Increased risk of enemy escape accepted. *Achilles* is now to watch North of English Bank and *Cumberland* to West of English Bank, latter showing herself off Montevideo in daylight. If enemy leaves before 21:00 [ie darkness], ships in touch shadow at maximum range. All units concentrate on shadower. If enemy has not left by 21:00, leave patrol positions and concentrate in position 090 degrees San Antonio 15 miles by 0030; *Ajax* will probably join *Cumberland* on her way south. If enemy leaves Montevideo after sunset, *Cumberland* is at once to fly off one aircraft to locate and shadow enemy, if necessary landing in a lee risking internment and trying to find a British ship in the morning. If plan miscarries, adopt Plan B, all units concentrate in position 36 degrees South, 52 degrees West at 0600 [to eastward of the Plate].

Harwood also repeated his ZMM order of 12 December, substituting *Cumberland*'s name for *Exeter*'s in the original. When word went round, a wag is supposed to have quipped, 'Yes, but whose destruction?'[8]

Johnston in Montevideo was keeping Harwood well-informed, and when he heard that *Graf Spee* had landed a funeral party and had sought and been granted an extension of her stay up to seventy-two hours in order to make herself seaworthy, Harwood began to realise that the German had been damaged by sixty to seventy hits, far more extensively than he had thought likely. Ashore, Millington-Drake's negotiating tactics changed: instead of insisting upon a minimum twenty-four hours for *Graf Spee* to sail or to accept the risk of internment, Harwood by signal now told him he wanted *Graf Spee* to stay longer to give time for more reinforcements to arrive. Under international law, an enemy warship could not leave harbour until twenty-four hours after a merchant ship of the opposing side had sailed, so the team in the Consular Shipping Advisory Department arranged for the British merchantman *Ashworth* to sail at 19:00. Temporarily British and German aims, whether *Graf Spee* stayed or not, coincided. Harwood understood this but he felt 'no security' that the German would not break out at any moment.

Saturday, 16 December

Following his plan, Harwood's three ships rendezvoused fifteen miles east of Cape San Antonio at 00:30 on 16 December, steamed north to close the River Plate at dawn, and *Ajax* flew off her aircraft for a reconnaissance of Montevideo roads, with instructions not to fly over territorial waters. The aircraft returned at 08:30 to report that it had not been possible to see anything for poor visibility, but that it had been fired on near Whistle Buoy. To Harwood, this was evidence that *Graf Spee* was taking advantage of the morning mist to put to sea, and the British cruisers went to action stations, but shortly afterwards Johnston assured Harwood that the enemy remained at anchor.

Later that day, the Admiralty informed Harwood that he was free to engage *Graf Spee* anywhere outside the three-mile limit and need not respect Argentine and Uruguayan claims to the Plate estuary. Harwood decided to move his patrol into the area north and east of English Bank, as he considered that an engagement in the very restricted water just outside the three-mile limit off Montevideo was impracticable owing to lack of sea-room and the 'possibility of "overs" landing in Uruguayan territory and causing international complications.'

When Harwood learned during the day that *Graf Spee* had taken in provisions but was still making good action damage with assistance from the shore, and that it was thought unlikely that she would sail that night, he 'did not feel able to rely on such an optimistic report'. That afternoon at 16:15 he signalled his appreciation with the tactical dispositions to be made in the event of the *Graf Spee* sailing. Harwood's messages were characterised by their economy of words and their succinctness, and his appreciation was the longest signal which he sent at any stage of the campaign in the South Atlantic in 1939:

> My object. Destruction necessitates keeping my force together. My Appreciation. Rely on getting his time of sailing and initial course from shore organisation. For subsequent movements rely on *Cumberland*'s aircraft reconnaissance reports. Enemy courses of action (a) North of English Bank. (b) between English and Rouen Banks. (c) Between Rouen Bank and San Antonio. (d) Double back on any track. My courses of action. I rule out fighting him off Whistle Buoy as being politically impossible. Until the dawn phase I want to keep the advantage of light and from this it follows that I must keep to the East and move to intercept him from area to area depending on time and information. My Plan. To keep within reach of intercepting him North of English Bank moving south or doubling back as information comes in. Tactical. I must keep *Cumberland* so placed that she will not have her fire masked initially and therefore I will work in Divisions 8 cables apart with *Achilles* in close order astern of *Ajax*. After action commences, Divisions have complete freedom of action. *Cumberland*'s aircraft is to be flown off as soon as news is received of enemy's sailing.

British skulduggery

During that Saturday morning McCall chartered a tug to go out to *Ajax* to discuss affairs with Harwood, whom he found 'his usual forceful, charming and imperturbable self'. From Harwood McCall learned that *Ark Royal* had only just reached Rio, 1,000 miles away, and was unlikely to reach the Plate before Tuesday. Harwood stressed the importance of keeping *Graf Spee* in harbour, and he asked McCall to assure Millington-Drake that, although he had permission from the Admiralty to ignore Uruguayan claims to waters outside the three-mile limit, he would do his best to ensure that no overs fell on neutral territory.

The situation was tense. *Graf Spee* had announced her intention of complying with the order to sail by 20:00 next day, while Force K was still out of reach. After the British merchant ship *Dunster Grange* sailed that evening, thereby adding a further period of twenty-four hours before the *Graf Spee* could be permitted under international law to sail, the Uruguayans closed the port and refused to accept any more notifications of sailing by any ships which would further delay the departure next day of an unwelcome visitor. It was reported, however, that she had made rapid progress with her repairs and might leave harbour at any time.

That afternoon Rex Miller had his brainwave, and Lloyd Hirst, still in Buenos Aires, was instructed to put up a bluff with the Argentine Minister of the Navy. In his diplomatic hat as assistant naval attaché, Hirst called on Admiral Léon Scasso, well known for his Fascist leanings, and asked, in confidence, a number of technical questions about the facilities at Mar del Plata available for *Renown* and *Ark Royal* should they be needed in within a day or so. Was the entrance dredged deep enough for them to enter, were the tugs big enough, etc? Scasso replied that fortunately a senior officer from Mar del Plata was in the building and he was brought in to answer the questions. That evening the popular newspaper *Critica* reported that it had learned from well-informed sources that *Renown* and *Ark Royal* would be at Mar del Plata, 150 miles south of the Plate estuary, within forty-eight hours.[9]

The first rewards

Earlier in the day in London, Churchill had told the War Cabinet at its morning meeting that he 'proposed to make a recommendation forthwith to His Majesty for some recognition of the gallant action fought by Commodore Harwood and the Captains of the three ships under his command'.[10] Evidently Churchill acted with his usual energy and 'in the dog watches of this evening', Harwood received the Admiralty's signal informing him of the honours bestowed by HM the King: for Harwood there was a knighthood and promotion to rear-admiral to date from the day of the battle, and his captains in *Exeter*, *Ajax*, and *Achilles* were made Companions of the Most Honourable Order of the Bath. Knowing that Harwood's cabin had been blown apart, 'Order of the Bath?' one cheerful rating was overheard to say, 'and they ain't got a blinking bath between them!'[11]

Harwood wrote soberly: 'This was a most stimulating tonic to us all, and I took steps to pass it on to HM ships under my command, emphasising the share of all concerned in the honours their senior officers had received'. In a letter to Joan, written that evening as he waited for *Graf Spee* to come out, Harwood allowed himself to express more personal feelings:[12]

> I am very well indeed. I was not touched, or nearly so, and nobody near me got hit. Parts of it were nasty, damned nasty, but on the whole we were never very badly off in *Ajax*. Poor *Exeter* bought most of the troubles.
>
> And now the rewards, tremendous. Heaven only knows if I deserve such a thing. A KCB for a Captain is, I think, unique in the modern world. I can't resist addressing you on the envelope as Lady H. Just fancy. I don't think really that you are entitled to it until I am told I can assume the dignity of the Honour. But just the first time. I feel you know what it means to me to be able to feel that I have done this by merit, and not by order on a list, and have given you, my beloved wife who has so helped me, the honour of being Lady H. Call it what you like. It is wonderful for me to feel. And the boys too ... Oh Joan, if only this beastly war would stop now.
>
> Things are tricky at the moment as we don't know if he is coming out again. I have a most difficult problem to catch him again and if he escapes then all the good we have done will be upset; not all but a lot of it. The mouth of the Plate is so wide and there are so many ways out that it is very difficult. Probably another battle, who knows? I hope for the best. If Yes or No you will know long before you get this. If the worst happens you know I have you at the top of my thoughts and you have all my love. All my thanks for your help in life. I at least will have the satisfaction of leaving a name. It will help the boys, perhaps. Well, my beloved, no more. I will write much more later but this is a hurried line in case the worst happens.
>
> All my love. Ever Yr B. 6pm 17 Dec

The British cruisers spent the night of 16/17 December patrolling on a north and south line east of English Bank. *Achilles* refuelled next morning from *Olynthus* off Rouen Bank, with *Ajax* and *Cumberland* acting as lookouts while the operation was in progress. The squadron afterwards cruised southeast of English Bank ready to take up the same patrol as on the previous night.

The German dilemma

The dilemma for the Germans was that their Nazi mentality required them to present the battle as a triumph: ***Deutsches Nachrichtenbüro*** proclaimed a victorious naval battle against a numerically superior force in which *Graf Spee* had only been hit a few times, ***Exeter*** was crippled and a light cruiser had been forced to drop out of the battle, and the only reason that *Graf Spee* had entered Montevideo was to replace her food supplies which had been contaminated by British poisonous gas shells.[13] In reality, *Graf Spee* was more badly damaged than the Germans wanted to admit, yet more time for repairs would also allow more time for British reinforcements. Moreover, Langsdorff was convinced by British propaganda and by one of his own officers, his otherwise reliable gunnery officer Paul Ascher, who claimed he had seen the aircraft carrier ***Ark Royal*** on the horizon east of Montevideo. After the German ambassador had been informed that *Graf Spee* would be permitted a stay of seventy-two hours, and that any extension was not acceptable, Guani agreed to recommend to his government that the period should be timed to commence from the return ashore of Varela's technical commission. This would, in fact, allow the ship nearly ninety-six hours in harbour from the time of her arrival.

On the same day that Harwood signalled his appreciation to his squadron, Langsdorff signalled an appreciation of the situation to the German naval high command. Harwood's was determined and aggressive, whereas Langsdorff's was gloomy. Langsdorff felt safe while inside the three-mile limit that the British would not attack him, but his options were gradually being closed down; it was more an admission of defeat and an abdication:[14]

1. Strategic position off Montevideo. Besides the cruisers and destroyers ***Ark Royal*** and ***Renown***. Close blockade at night. Escape into open sea and break-through to home waters impossible.

2. Propose putting out as far as neutral boundary. If it is possible to fight our way through to Buenos Aires, using remain ammunition, this will be attempted.
3. If a break-through would result in certain destruction of *Graf Spee* without opportunity of damaging enemy, request decision on whether the ship should be scuttled in spite of insufficient depth in the estuary of la Plata, or whether internment is to be preferred.
4. Decision requested by radiogram.

In Germany, Grossadmiral Erich Raeder conferred with Hitler. Raeder could not recommend internment in Uruguay as this was 'unreliable as neutral and not able to defend her neutrality'. He preferred a breakthrough to Argentina 'which was stronger ... since this would permit us to retain greater freedom of action'. Hitler was opposed to internment 'since there was a possibility that *Graf Spee* might score a success against the British ships in a breakthrough'. Hitler approved Raeder's reply to Langsdorff:

1. Attempt by all methods to extend the time limit for your stay in neutral waters in order to retain freedom of action as long as possible.
2. With reference to No 2. Approved.
3. With reference to No 3. No internment in Uruguay. Attempt effective destruction if ship is scuttled.

Late in the afternoon of 16 December, while Langsdorff was discussing his options with his officers, the German ambassador called again on Guani. During a heated meeting, the ambassador requested an audience with the president, which Guani insisted could only be granted if the ambassador acknowledged the seventy-two-hour time limit: *Graf Spee* must put to sea by 18:45 on 17 December or be interned. This was defeat, naked and brutal, and to it was added the sting of a sense of disgrace.[15]

Out at sea, the three British cruisers patrolled on a north–south line five miles to the east of the English Bank. Harwood ordered *Olynthus* to be at Rouen Bank by 10:00 the next morning if *Graf Spee* had not broken out.

In *Ajax*, her captain had decided that the degree of readiness might be slightly relaxed to allow a proportion of the ship's company to sleep in their hammocks, but a few minutes later he received a unanimous request from all quarters that they would prefer to remain all night ready at their stations: 'such a gesture is unforgettable', he wrote.[16]

Harwood wrote in his despatch: 'I would like to place on record the fact that at this stage the most cheerful optimism pervaded all ships in spite of the fact that this was the fifth night of waiting for the enemy.'

Sunday, 17 December

In the forenoon Harwood ordered *Achilles* to refuel from *Olynthus* while *Ajax* and *Cumberland* covered her. He was unperturbed when Johnston from his lookout over Montevideo reported that *Graf Spee* had landed all the welding apparatus which had been borrowed from the shore, and, expecting that she would break out at any moment, during the afternoon the squadron remained concentrated and cruised in company to the southeast of English Bank.

At 15:40 Harwood heard a signal that *Graf Spee* was transferring between 300 and 400 men to a German merchant ship *Tacoma*. At 17:20 a further report told him that over 700 men with their baggage and some provisions had now been transferred, and that there were indications that *Graf Spee* intended to scuttle herself. Shortly after this, *Graf Spee* was reported to be weighing anchor. Harwood immediately altered course to close the Whistle Buoy, at the entrance to the five-mile dredged channel leading into Montevideo, prepared for battle, and increased speed to 25 knots. *Ajax*'s aircraft was flown off with orders to report the position of *Graf Spee* and *Tacoma*.

Graf Spee left harbour at 18:15 and proceeded slowly westward, further into the Plate, followed by *Tacoma*, and at a distance by Harwood and his ships.

Unknown to Harwood, Langsdorff and a scuttling party were all that were left in Graf Spee. At 19:40 they too left in the ship's boats for *Tacoma*. Passing north of English Bank, the British cruisers were nearing Montevideo when at 20:45 *Ajax*'s aircraft signalled: '*Graf Spee* has blown herself up.' Harwood recalled:[17]

> There could be no doubt about it, and I passed the message on the loudspeaker system of the *Ajax*. The men were closed up at action stations, ready to pick up the battle where we had left off. For an appreciable space of time after the announcement, there was silence. Then, as it was fully understood, the cheers swelled up out of the ship, the sailors came up cheering until the whole deck was alive with them. I could see that the same thing was happening in the *Achilles* and I made a signal to that ship to 'Take station ahead of the Admiral'.

It was almost dark and *Ajax* was stopped to make-to her seaplane, and as *Achilles* swept past her the ships' companies cheered each other. All three cruisers then switched on their navigation lights and steamed past the Whistle Buoy about four miles off the flaming wreck. 'It was now dark,' wrote Harwood, 'and she was ablaze from end to end, flames reaching almost as high as the top of her control tower – a magnificent and most cheering sight.'

A fierce jet of flame leaped up from the doomed ship, followed by a dense cloud of smoke and the loud rumble of an explosion. Then a gigantic ball of flame burst aft as a second great explosion took place. There ensued a long succession of explosions accompanied by leaping flames and a great pillar of brown smoke rising against the red evening sky. Her destruction in the shallow waters of the Plate estuary was watched by tens of thousands of awed spectators crowded on the roofs of Montevideo and along the seafront, while radio broadcasts and press cables flashed their graphic stories round the world.

Fires continued to burn in *Graf Spee* for six days.

10

The Spoils of War

Harwood's next letter to Joan reveals how much his previous letter had been a farewell, and the disparity in force between his ships and *Graf Spee*, should Langsdorff have chosen to fight it out at point-blank range in the Plate estuary:[1]

> All over – what a relief – I wrote you a letter on that last night as we were waiting – pessimistic and sentimental. I nearly tore it up but haven't so you will see my attitude of that most trying time – I hope I shall never be in such a position again. Showered with honours before the job was done, faced with a most difficult problem to intercept her if she broke out, there are so many ways out to a wide mouthed river – Then on intercepting a point blank range battle – Oh, Joan – No wonder I was worried – As sunset came on we went to action stations & got ready – I had in my usual optimistic way always thought she would intern herself, but really could not believe my own luck.
>
> Suddenly out of the blue came a signal – '*Graf Spee* is transferring men to *Tacoma*'. Strange, my optimism returned but caution prevailed – next, '3 to 400 men being transferred'. Next '700 men' – What was up – It must be true – A long pause – From the BBC, 'she has sailed' – new anxiety – where gone – BBC, 'Gone up river towards BA'
>
> A trap I thought – Long pause going back again – *Tacoma* sailed – Then a report of smoke – vertical smoke looked like her fore structure – Increase speed, back to action stations – Smoke got no nearer. I sent the aircraft up – No report for an interminable time – Suddenly from the aircraft – 'she has blown herself up!'
>
> What a relief, cheers from all the quarters – the men poured up on deck. I looked at the *Achilles* – Her upper deck & turrets were black

> with men – I told her to take station ahead & as she passed – her New Zealanders & ours cheered & cheered & cheered
>
> I stood on the bridge and wore my Admiral's uniform for the 1st time – We all cheered. Like armistice night. Oh what a relief, Joan – Our victory was complete – I then realised the magnitude of what we had done – Later I went onboard *Achilles* & spoke to them & got a wonderful reception.
>
> It's all too extraordinary ... Frightened by two little 6" & one 8" [cruisers] ... We steamed passed Montevideo that night and watched her burn – a marvellous sight – Just TOO wonderful – All love – More later.

Harwood went on to tell Joan about the messages of congratulations which had begun to flood in from around the world and across the spectrum of Harwood friendships and acquaintances and the many people he had influenced, not least those who he had met in his three years as Commodore, South Atlantic.

Nelsonic comparisons

Harwood was a junior commodore on a remote foreign station and his was not a household name when the Battle of the River Plate took place. One exception who did know him was Professor Sir Geoffrey Callender, who had met Harwood at Greenwich over two periods, in early 1922 and again in 1934, and now was the first director of the newly founded National Maritime Museum. Callender had been impressed by Harwood's intellect and leadership and now, even before the victory was complete, he wrote:[2]

> The country already rings with your praises and all thirsty souls are drinking your health ... I am positively basking in the reflected glory of my friendship with you and wherever I appear I am mobbed by an unruly crowd with the cry 'Here's the fellow who knows Harwood personally and can tell us all about him ... I whisper "The first time I met Harwood I said to myself 'Nelson is come again!'" In sober earnest, your victory ... seems worthy to compare with the more delectable passages of Cochrane upon the same coast.

During the battle Churchill had apparently paced the war room, at some stage crying: 'Call him off, call him off! I don't want another Coronel'. The speed of wireless communications would not have allowed the timely arrival of such an order, but asked what he would have done if he had received such an order, Harwood was adamant that he would, like Nelson at Copenhagen in 1801, have 'Gone on!'[3]

Inevitably, there were other classical and Nelsonic comparisons. Admiral Sir Frederick Dreyer, whose son was serving in *Ajax*, wrote: '*Ajax* what an appropriate name! He was a brave fellow and when in a battle of the gods a thunderbolt was thrown at him he defied the lightning, just as you and your merry men defied the 11in salvoes. Well done indeed'.[4] 'Riddles' Ridley, one of the Hot Toddy Club, wrote:

> My Dear Bobby. Thank you for the greatest thrill of our lives. There has been nothing like it since Nelson's days ... there was a magnificently trained squadron, a complete understanding of the Admiral's intentions and the mind of a cunning old fox! ... It might amuse you to know that our password for tonight is 'Commodore Harwood'. The duty officer, who chooses it, is a soldier – such is fame, Bobby![5]

And from half-remembered history lessons, old admirals recalled their Nelson-era quotations, Admiral Sir Andrew Cunningham writing:

> My dear Harwood. For a week or so before the news reached us, my thoughts had been much the same as Old Jervis' before St Vincent and I was feeling most strongly that an early success was a vital necessity for the Empire and our Service – and lo, you produced it! You have done us all so much good and you and your lads have set a wonderful example and a high standard to the whole Service.[6]

Admiral Sir William Goodenough, a firebrand of the First World War, wrote enviously:

> Dear Harwood, You can imagine that every drop of my light cruiser blood and every beat of my light cruiser heart is with you at this moment. You have made history as surely as did Troubridge when Lord Nelson said 'Look at Troubridge. He carries his ships into

> action as if the eyes of all England were on him and I wish to God they were'. I won't spoil it by saying anything myself. God bless you.[7]

The redoubtable Admiral Sir Walter Cowan, even more of a firebrand than Goodenough, expressed his envy:

> This is something which others could only dream about. I have been entranced by your victory and the spirit and tactics of it. It was always my dream in the last war when I had a light cruiser squadron to have the chance of teasing the heavier armed ship into distraction and defeat and you have done it with faultless brilliance and most dauntless courage.[8]

However, when newspapers wrongfully circulated reports that Harwood had hoisted Nelson's signal 'England Expects', Harwood was cross: 'I did not hoist Nelson's signal. That was rubbish. I would not dare to do such a presumptuous thing. Nelson is a person apart and enshrined in history. It would be vandalism and cheap to be so presumptuous,' adding humorously, 'Apart from that, I never had time to get anything out even if I had wished to'.[9]

Churchill's interest

There was a reminder in the letters which poured in that events had been closely watched in the Admiralty, Captain Hallett, who had been Harwood's captain in *Southampton* and Captain of the Fleet in *Queen Elizabeth*, telling Harwood:

> My dear Bobby. Well done, old boy. A truly magnificent success. The whole country is thrilled by your most gallant action. It was most exciting up here getting all your messages as they arrived. Mr Churchill, 1st Sea Lord, and all the outfit were down in the War Room discussing the action as your news came in and everyone was full of praise for your gallantry and clever handling of the situation ... It was grand that your great success was so quickly recognised.[10]

On the night of the scuttling, Churchill and his wife were hosting dinner for the Digbys in the First Lord of the Admiralty's flat above

Admiralty Arch: the Churchills' son Randolph had in October married the Digbys' daughter Pamela (later Pamela Harriman). Her brother, Edward, recalled that before dinner a naval officer had appeared with a signal from the British ambassador in Montevideo saying that *Graf Spee* had raised steam and was leaving harbour, and Churchill had kept his guests until 03:00 when the signal arrived saying that *Graf Spee* had scuttled.[11]

The family and the Hot Toddy Club

At home, Joan, living at Broadwater in Sussex with her mother, was subjected to two days of intense pressure from newspaper reporters and photographers. The *Daily Express* asked her for an hour by hour diary of everything she did in the day. Even Henry and Stephen, who were at boarding school in Sussex, were not exempt. The headmaster, Major Charles Jennings, a man of small stature but immense personality, refused to produce them but allowed the press to photograph both boys displaying the name Harwood on their suitcases as they left school for the Christmas holidays. Joan was presented with a copy of the newsreel films of the battle which were widely shown to publicise the important naval victory.

In sending his congratulations, 'Wickie' Wickham, whose son was serving in *Exeter*, wished he had been able to support Joan more: 'I only wish I'd been a bit nearer Joan when she was badgered by the Press. I might have been able to help her a bit'.[12] However, another member of the Hot Toddy Club, Maitland-Dougall, was able to comfort Joan that 'the Club [The United Service Club or 'the Senior' – now the home of the Institute of Directors] almost cheered the roof off when the news came through.'[13]

From Australia, the fifth member of the Hot Toddy Club, 'Crack' Crace, who now commanded the Australian Squadron, sent his congratulations:[14]

> My dear Bobby,
>
> A thousand congratulations on your magnificent action which resulted in the final destruction of *Graf Spee*. I can imagine that you have spent many weary weeks searching for her and regarded her as your particular spoil. It is magnificent and must be a great

> satisfaction to you that you brought her to action with such a fine result. She was a big mouthful for your force to tackle ...
>
> I think it splendid that battle honours were announced so quickly and I send you every congratulation there is on being promoted and being made a KCB. It is simply magnificent and everyone will be so very pleased that your fine action has been recognised so quickly and appropriately. How proud Joan will be and all your friends.
>
> This letter is quite inadequate to express all I want to say, Old Man, but you know how frightfully pleased I am and how much I congratulate you.
>
> All the best. Yours Crack

Other messages poured from around the world, from North and South America, and from the Empire, not least one from a former student of Harwood's at the War College, Vice-Admiral Everard Hardman-Jones, who recalled Harwood's lessons on how to deal with a pocket battleship: 'My dear Harwood. My most sincere congratulations on an achievement which will stand out among the many gallant actions in our naval history. I remember well your offensive spirit, when I was a student under you at the War Course and may I say that I was not surprised when you put it into practice.'[15]

The battle summary

Harwood's action report, amounting to some 200 pages, took some weeks to compile but was ready by 30 December when he sent a copy to the Commander-in-Chief, South America, and a day later a duplicate, with the photographs of *Exeter*'s damage, direct to the Admiralty. His sixteen-page formal letter covered reports from his individual captains, a summary of lessons learnt during the action and photographs of the damage to *Exeter*. In their turn, his captains included many appendices on, for example, bridge and control officers' narratives, gunnery, aircraft, torpedo, engineering, communications, damage, repair parties, casualties and track charts.[16] The Admiralty's copy arrived in London on 31 January, but even before he had studied this, Pound had sent a personal letter to Harwood, handwritten in the First Sea Lord's green ink:[17]

Dear Bobby,

You can have no doubt in your own mind about what we feel here and your determined and courageous handling of the *Graf Spee*. I do not mind telling you that when we got the news of the first sighting I thought the Huns had all the luck as the first contact of one of his Pocket Battleships was being made in that area in which we had the weakest hunting unit ... I think the way in which your ships went for her bald headed must have had a great moral effect and largely influenced the *Spee*'s subsequent unintelligible actions. She must have realised that *Exeter* had only one gun in action when she dropped out of the fight and why the *Spee* did not turn on her and finish her off I cannot imagine.

Even if all our ships had been sunk you would have done the right thing. As things turned out I am delighted you did not have *Cumberland* with you – so even had you sunk the *Spee* it would not have been so glorious an affair.

Your action had a great effect in two ways. Firstly it has set a standard for this war; a matter of great importance. Secondly it has reversed the finding of the Troubridge court martial and shows how wrong that was ... Little did we think when we were shipmates so many years ago in the Mediterranean what Fate had in store for us. But Fate has been kinder to you even than to me because you have been allowed to command a British force in a successful action at sea. That can never be my lot ...

Yours ever
Dudley Pound

This gave Harwood the opportunity to set out a definitive account of his strategy and tactics in the hunt for *Graf Spee* and of the battle:[18]

My Dear First Sea Lord,

...

Looking back on the episode in retrospect it seems to me that the whole affair followed exactly a few well known principles:

Concentration. I got in all I could and left *Cumberland*, who had to self-refit, at short notice on two shafts. It was pure luck that the point I chose to proceed to, which was where my plot showed the greatest number of British ships, was also the one he went to.

Plan of Battle. This I issued as soon as they joined me. From this we just slid into action. Attack from divergent bearings, flank marking and concentration by the 6in cruisers were obviously desirable with 3 ships and a main armament of 8 x 6in guns. The immediate offensive was the only way in which to get quickly into range and reduce the advantage of his 11in fire though it necessitated taking the chance of getting the aircraft off. *Ajax* got hers off but *Exeter*'s was damaged before she could do so. Actually *Graf Spee* helped me by closing us which was stupid of him. I think there must be some truth in the report that he took us for *Exeter* and 2 destroyers. *Exeter* with her larger silhouette and tall masts must stand out in comparison with the *Ajax*'s and their low main topmasts.

Mutual Support. By coming at us he put us all within range when we opened fire and I think we must have given him a lot in this early phase and this caused him to turn away and make smoke. From then on the crux of the situation was to keep up pressure on both flanks. I pushed the 1st Division [*Ajax* and *Achilles*] in as fast as I could and *Exeter*, to Bell's great credit, kept her position and went on firing. I expected him to turn on *Exeter* but I think we countered this by our close action which kept him well occupied. I then waited for him to turn on 1st Division and as soon as he did so we gave him a broadside of torpedoes. This he evidently saw as he again turned away at once. When I saw *Exeter* dropping back I realised we would have to get out fairly soon and I was afraid then that he would turn on *Exeter*. But he had had a lot of punishment, particularly from *Achilles* who still had her 4 turrets left, and I am thankful to say he was happy to go on running for the Plate.

Resolute Offensive against a Raider. This principle was well put in your signal and is absolutely true. It leads me to the reasons why *Graf Spee* did not come out. We know her galleys, bakery, flour store, wash places and distillers were all damaged and he would have had great difficulty in the maintenance of his crew. I would put his ammunition expenditure at about 80 rounds per gun. How much did she have left? Entirely enough, I should have thought, to have risked a break out. But she was a compromise in construction and even on a nominal 10,000 tons she must have been short somewhere. They say her engine bed plates were cracked; possibly, but she went in at 20–22 knots. The morale of her crew had cracked; possibly, but if so it serves the Captain right because he lied to his crew by telling them nobody would dare to attack him except the Battlecruisers. His fire control tower was certainly hit but against this he did wonderful shooting at us at 13 miles while [we were] shadowing. There is now a rumour that his fore turret was jammed. This is possible as when he fired his last salvoes at *Achilles* he altered course round before firing.

To sum it all up, it is just the old principle of damaging a raider thousands of miles from his base, making him use up all his ammunition, upsetting his maintenance services and giving him severe damage to repair which can only be done in harbour. As soon as I got *Cumberland* I trailed her in front of him and the BBC broadcasts with threats of *Duquesne*, *Barham* etc. undoubtedly played a part in upsetting his morale. He was a poor fish not to try and break out. I gave him a 50% chance of escaping unseen. There are many ways out of the Plate and a very wide mouth to the River.

In one or two letters I have received I notice a tendency to class this action as a justification for the small ship school. This will need very careful handling if the tail is not to wag the dog. There are two distinct problems: one to cripple a raider, the other to sink an enemy ship. Crippling, Yes. But we were never in sight of sinking him and I do not think the 6in gun could ever do so. We had one or two thrills when we saw him list over but we soon realised that it was only due to his turning under full wheel. From what I hear, except for a few waterline hits, all probably from the *Exeter*, I do not believe that any of the 6in actually pierced his armoured deck. (We know there is one gallant 6in proj[ectile] still in his side, all through except for its last two inches. I think that must have been one of the close range ones). I had a long yarn with the Uruguayan Commander [Varela] who was on the damage commission. He told me that though his route along the main deck was carefully selected and he was shown a lot of damage he saw nothing which had pierced the armoured deck. The 8in, of course, present a very different problem. I was very relieved when *Cumberland* arrived. I was sad, however, when I realised *Cumberland*'s torpedoes had been removed. In the break out phase torpedoes would have had to play a big part ...

Very many thanks for your letter and for all that is being done for us at sea under your direction. Please remember me to Lady Pound and I hope she is as cheerful as ever.

Yours Very Sincerely,

Bobby

Langsdorff's suicide

There were no honours for the defeated. Langsdorff and his surviving ship's company arrived in Buenos Aires in tugs on the afternoon of 18 December. There, when the German ambassador told Langsdorff that he and his crew would be interned, rather than treated as shipwrecked seamen, Langsdorff shot himself in his hotel bedroom, lying on a German naval ensign. In a letter on 19 December to the ambassador he rehearsed the arguments for his decision to scuttle *Graf Spee*:[19]

> I am still convinced that under the circumstances, this decision was the only one left, once I had taken my ship into the trap of Montevideo. For with the ammunition remaining, any attempt to fight my way back to open and deep water was bound to fail ... It was clear to me that this decision might be consciously or unwittingly misconstrued by persons ignorant of my motives, as being attributable entirely or partly to personal considerations. Therefore I decided from the beginning to accept the consequences involved in this decision. For a captain with a sense of honour, it goes without saying that his personal fate cannot be separated from that of his ship ... After to-day's decision of the Argentine Government, I can do no more for my ship's company. Neither shall I any longer be able to take an active part in the present struggle of my country. I can now only prove by my death that the fighting services of the Third Reich are ready to die for the honour of the flag. I alone bear the responsibility for scuttling the pocket battleship *Admiral Graf Spee*. I am happy to pay with my life for any reflection on the honour of the flag. I shall face my fate with firm faith in the cause and the future of the nation and of my Führer ...

No copy of Langsdorff's letter had reached Berlin by the time of the last meeting of the year between Hitler and Raeder, on 30 December 1939. Raeder bemoaned the loss of the strategic effect of *Graf Spee* (and *Deutschland*, which had returned to Germany from the North Atlantic), and exculpated himself that no surface forces would be ready until the second half of January. He excused Langsdorff, saying that 'on account of insufficient details, no final judgement could be made concerning tactical conduct during the battle' and that 'the use of the remaining ammunition for effective destruction of the ship was justified'. Hitler sourly reiterated his view that *Exeter* should have been completely destroyed.[20] It was left to McCall, British naval attaché in Buenos Aires, to pay the tribute that Langsdorff was 'obviously a man of very high character and he was proud of the fact that he had not been the cause of a single death as the result of any of his various captures' of merchant vessels.

Harwood's comment on Langsdorff's death was 'and now the Captain has shot himself – poor man – a bad solution'.[21]

FAR LEFT: Captain Thomas Harwood who commanded the 56-gun *St Andrew*, flagship of Admiral Sir John Kempthorne, at the Battle of Solebay in 1672.

LEFT: Few pictures of Harwood in his early career exist, but this one shows him as a lieutenant in HMS *Bramble*.

BELOW: Harwood had an opportunity to study the damage caused by the Japanese to the Russian fleet at Port Arthur in 1904, and kept these photographs.

LEFT: The Hot Toddy Club: Wickham, Harwood and Maitland-Dougall studied each evening onboard the hulk HMS *Vernon*.

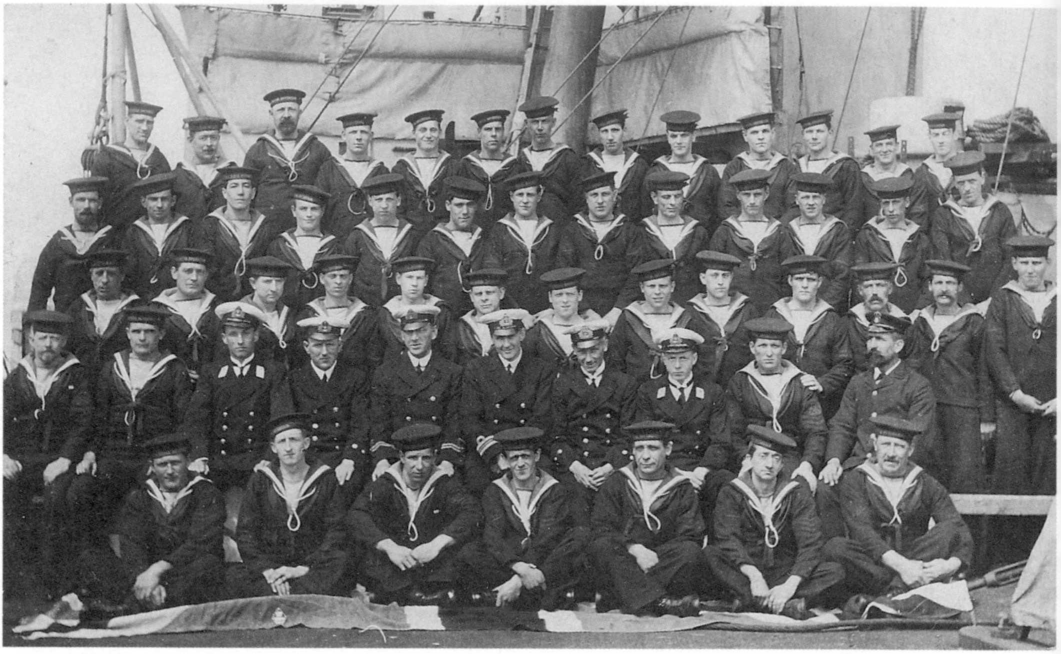

ABOVE: Harwood's first professional job as a torpedo officer was in HMS *Sutlej*, seen here with the men of his department.

BELOW: *Sutlej*'s weaponry included a picket boat which could be used to fire torpedoes.

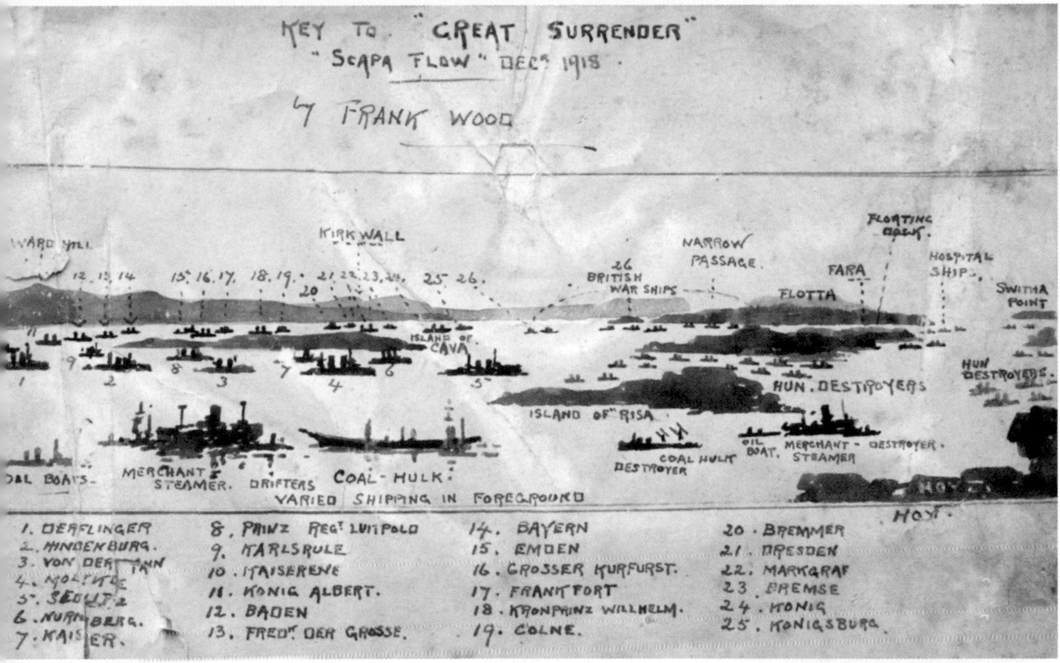

ABOVE: 'The Great Surrender, December 1918': Harwood witnessed the surrender of the German High Seas Fleet and kept this sketch by John Wood of where the ships anchored in Scapa Flow.

RIGHT: Joan Chard, seen here in 1923 as 'Jessica', had a brief career as an actress, in the days when she was chaperoned by her mother, before becoming engaged to Henry Harwood.

BELOW: Harwood went on two pilgrimages to Rome, this one to meet Pope Pius XI in 1932.

TOP: Receiving the cup after HMS *London*'s success in the fleet pulling regatta in 1933.

LEFT: As a means to maintain morale, Harwood liked to keep the ship's sports trophy cupboard well-stocked.

BELOW: The Naval War College staff and students in 1934 – apparently the only record of who they were. Harwood stands at the centre.

TOP: HMS *Exeter* at full power in 1932.

ABOVE: HMS *Exeter* alongside at Montevideo.

RIGHT: A smiling, confident Harwood as Commodore, South America.

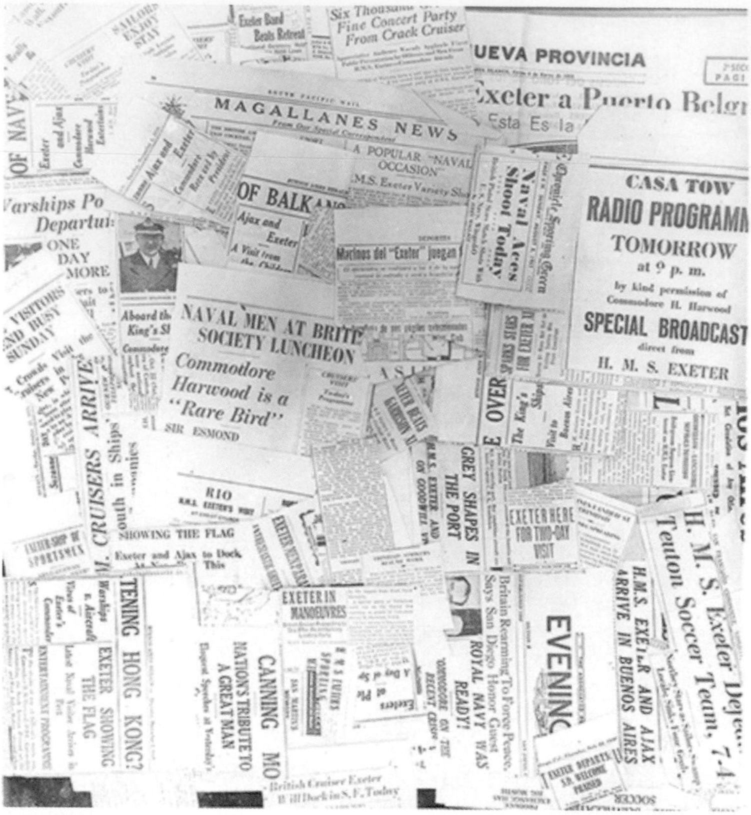

ABOVE: A high value was set on diplomacy and Harwood ensured that his ships were seldom out of the English- and Spanish-language newspapers of South America.

BELOW: Among many diplomatic functions was dinner with the President of Argentina in 1937.

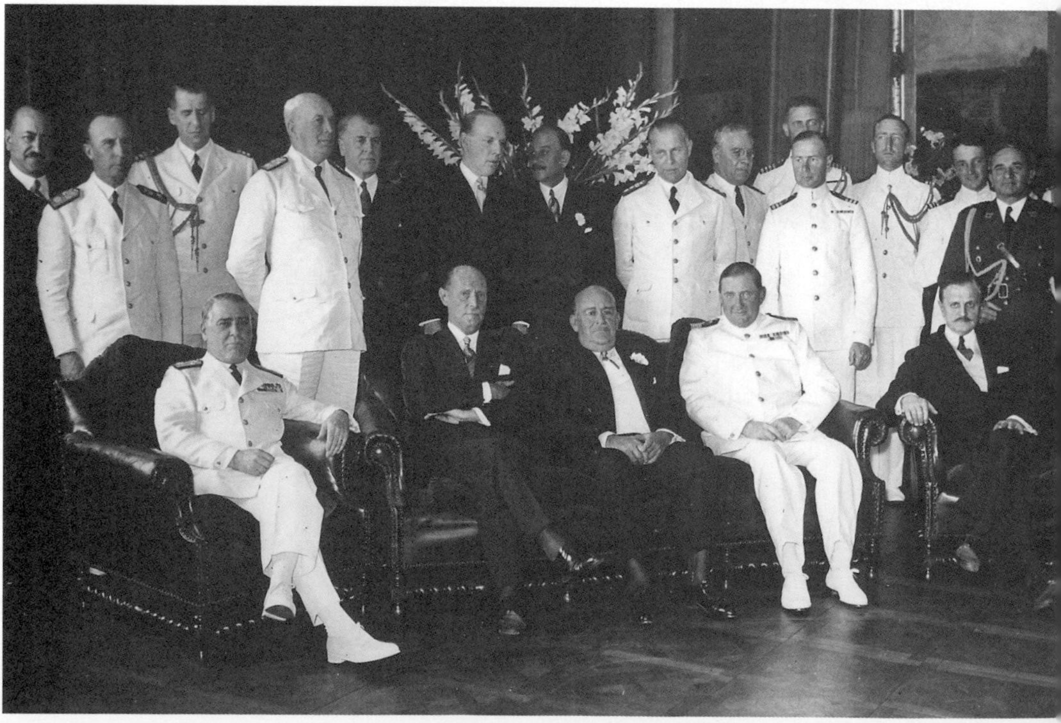

ABOVE: Hardly less formal than official functions, a dance for the Anglo community at Punta Arenas, Chile.

LEFT AND BELOW: Two scenes from the earthquake at Concepción. Harwood landed his sailors and marines to help in disaster relief.

ABOVE AND BELOW: HMS *Exeter* transits the Panama Canal before meeting the windjammer *Padua* off the tip of South America.

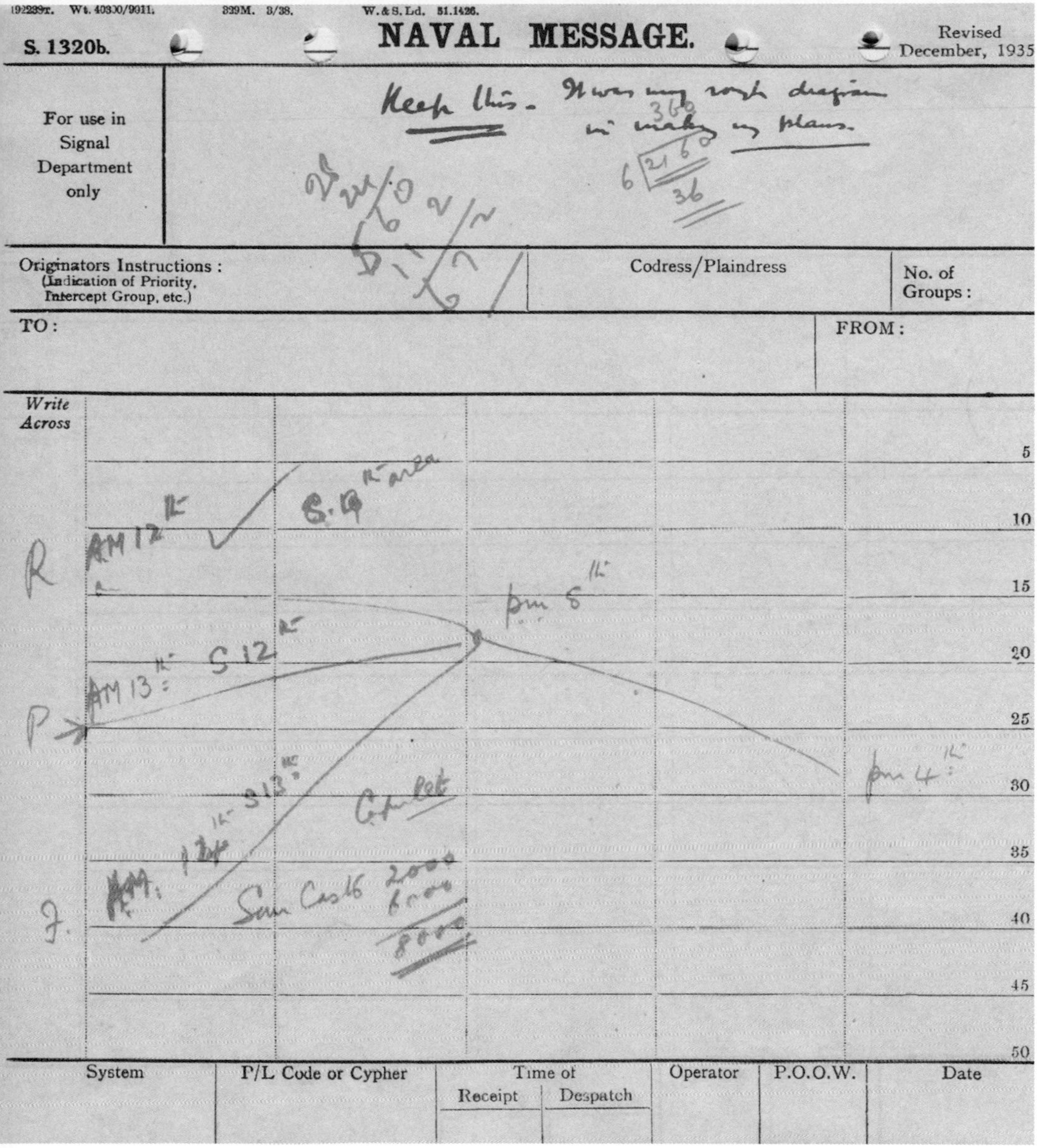

The famous doodle where Harwood estimated *Graf Spee*'s track, and as a result reckoned that she would go to the Plate.

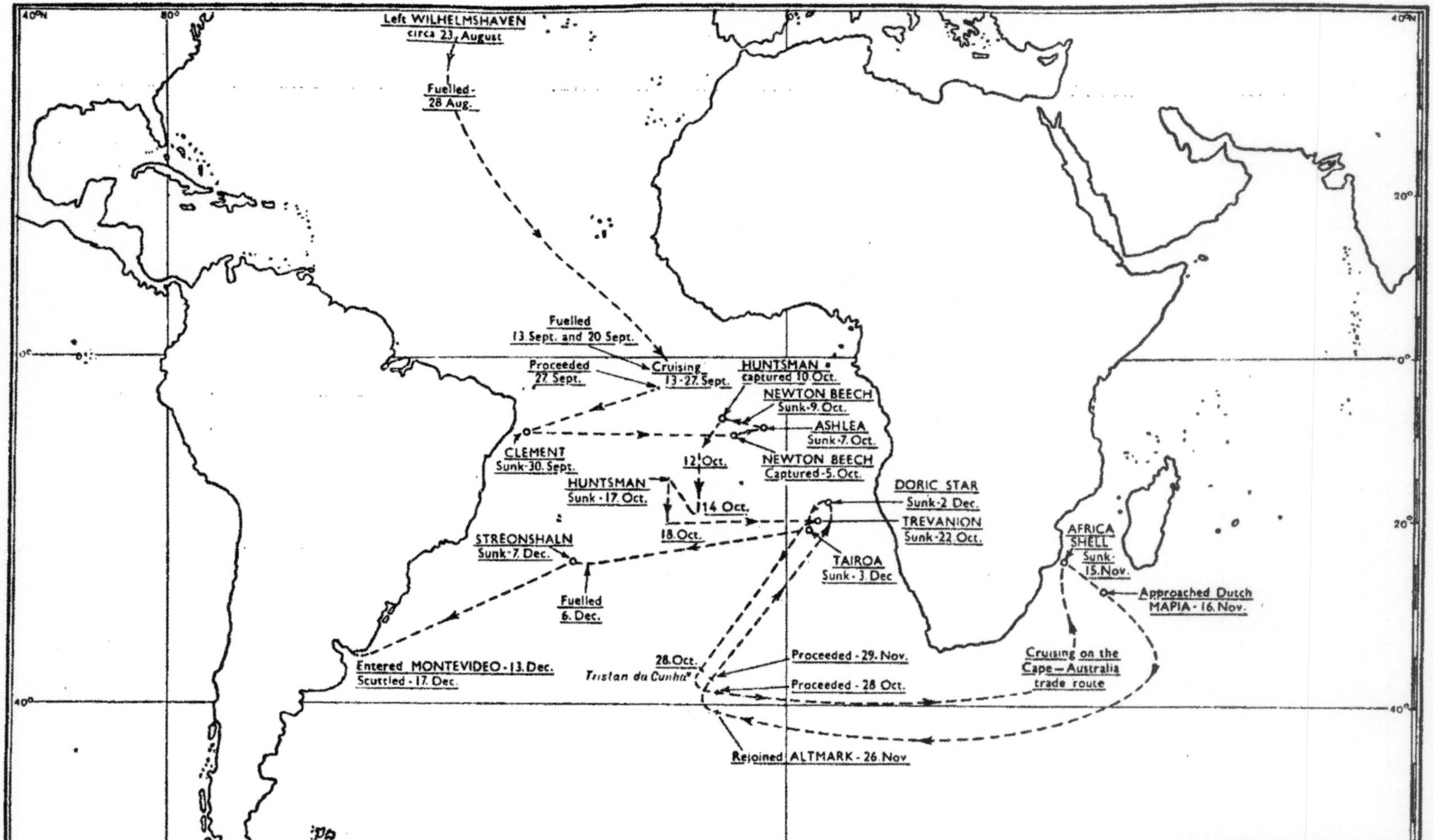
Left WILHELMSHAVEN
circa 23 August
Fuelled - 28 Aug.
Fuelled
13 Sept. and 20 Sept.
Cruising
13-27 Sept.
Proceeded
27 Sept.
HUNTSMAN
captured 10 Oct.
NEWTON BEECH
Sunk - 9 Oct.
ASHLEA
Sunk - 7 Oct.
NEWTON BEECH
Captured - 5 Oct.
CLEMENT
Sunk - 30 Sept.
12 Oct.
HUNTSMAN
Sunk - 17 Oct.
14 Oct.
18 Oct.
DORIC STAR
Sunk - 2 Dec.
TREVANION
Sunk - 22 Oct.
TAIROA
Sunk - 3 Dec
STREONSHALN
Sunk - 7 Dec.
Fuelled
6 Dec.
AFRICA SHELL
Sunk - 15 Nov.
Approached Dutch
MAPIA - 16 Nov.
Cruising on the
Cape – Australia
trade route
Entered MONTEVIDEO - 13 Dec.
Scuttled - 17 Dec.
28 Oct.
Tristan da Cunha
Proceeded - 29 Nov.
Proceeded - 28 Oct.
Rejoined ALTMARK - 26 Nov.
40°N
80°
40°
20°
0°
60°
100°
N.I.D. March 1940

THE CRUISE OF 'ADMIRAL GRAF SPEE', 1939

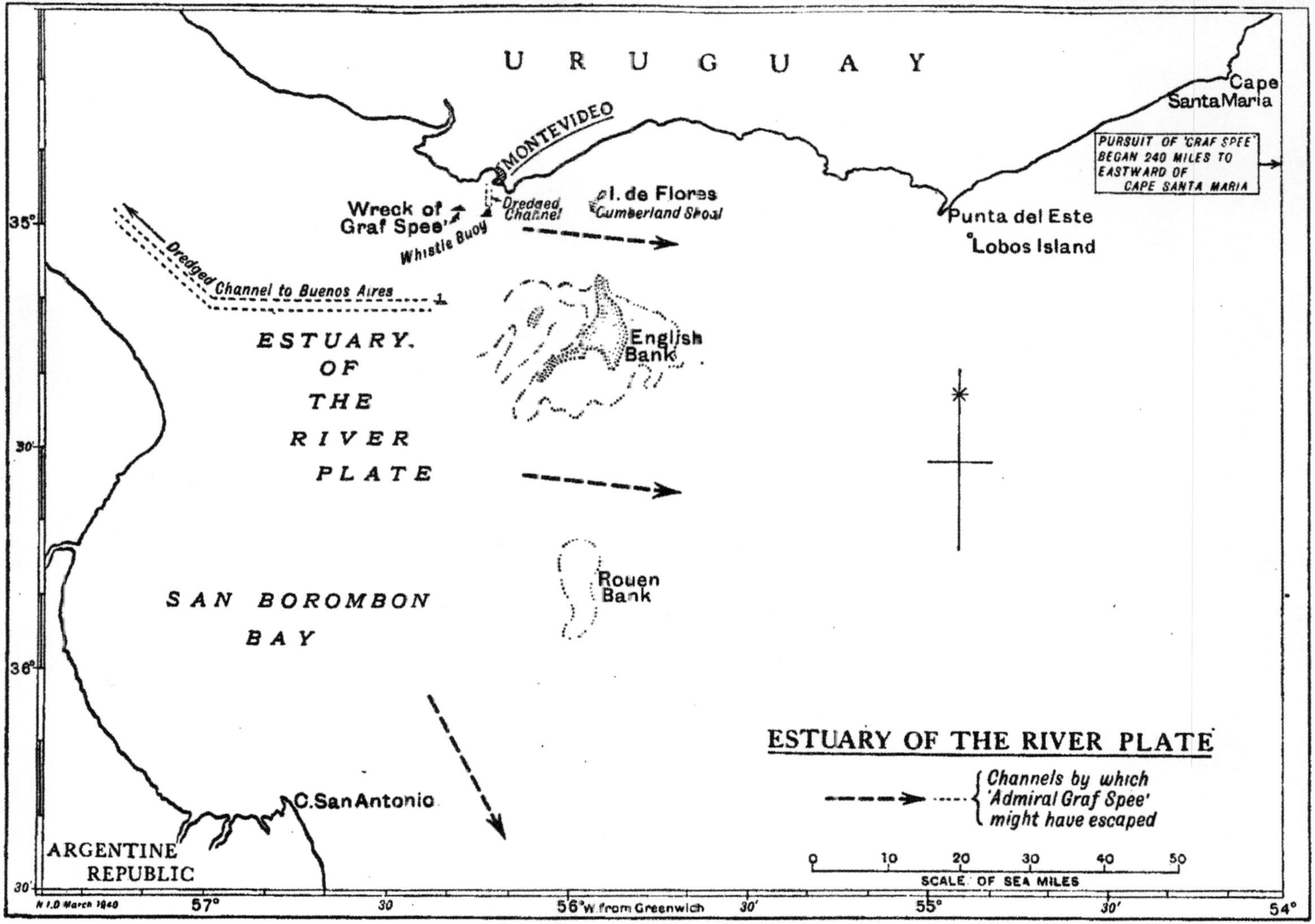
URUGUAY
Cape Santa Maria
PURSUIT OF 'GRAF SPEE' BEGAN 240 MILES TO EASTWARD OF CAPE SANTA MARIA
MONTEVIDEO
Wreck of Graf Spee'
Whistle Buoy
Dredged Channel
I. de Flores
Cumberland Shoal
Punta del Este
Lobos Island
Dredged Channel to Buenos Aires
ESTUARY OF THE RIVER PLATE
English Bank
Rouen Bank
SAN BOROMBON BAY
C. San Antonio
ARGENTINE REPUBLIC
ESTUARY OF THE RIVER PLATE
Channels by which 'Admiral Graf Spee' might have escaped
0 10 20 30 40 50
SCALE OF SEA MILES
35°
30'
36°
30'
N I.D March 1940
57°
30
56° W. from Greenwich
30'
55°
30'
54°

Dr Guani, Foreign Minister of Uruguay.

Mr (later Sir Eugen) Millington-Drake, British Minister in Uruguay.

Rex Miller, head of SIS in South America.

Captain (later Admiral) Henry McCall.

Lloyd Hirst, from the SIS, South America.

Captain Frederick Bell, commander of HMS *Exeter*.

Captain Parry, commander of HMS *Achilles*, New Zealand division.

Captain Charles Woodhouse, commander of HMS *Ajax*.

HMNZS *Achilles*,which was patrolling peacefully in the Pacific before the outbreak of war.

One of a set of photographs taken from HMS *Achilles* during the Battle of the River Plate and annotated on the reverse by Harwood: 'Situation at 0734 when *Ajax* altered course to the southward to avoid torpedoes and ordered *Achilles* to pass under *Ajax*'s stern'.

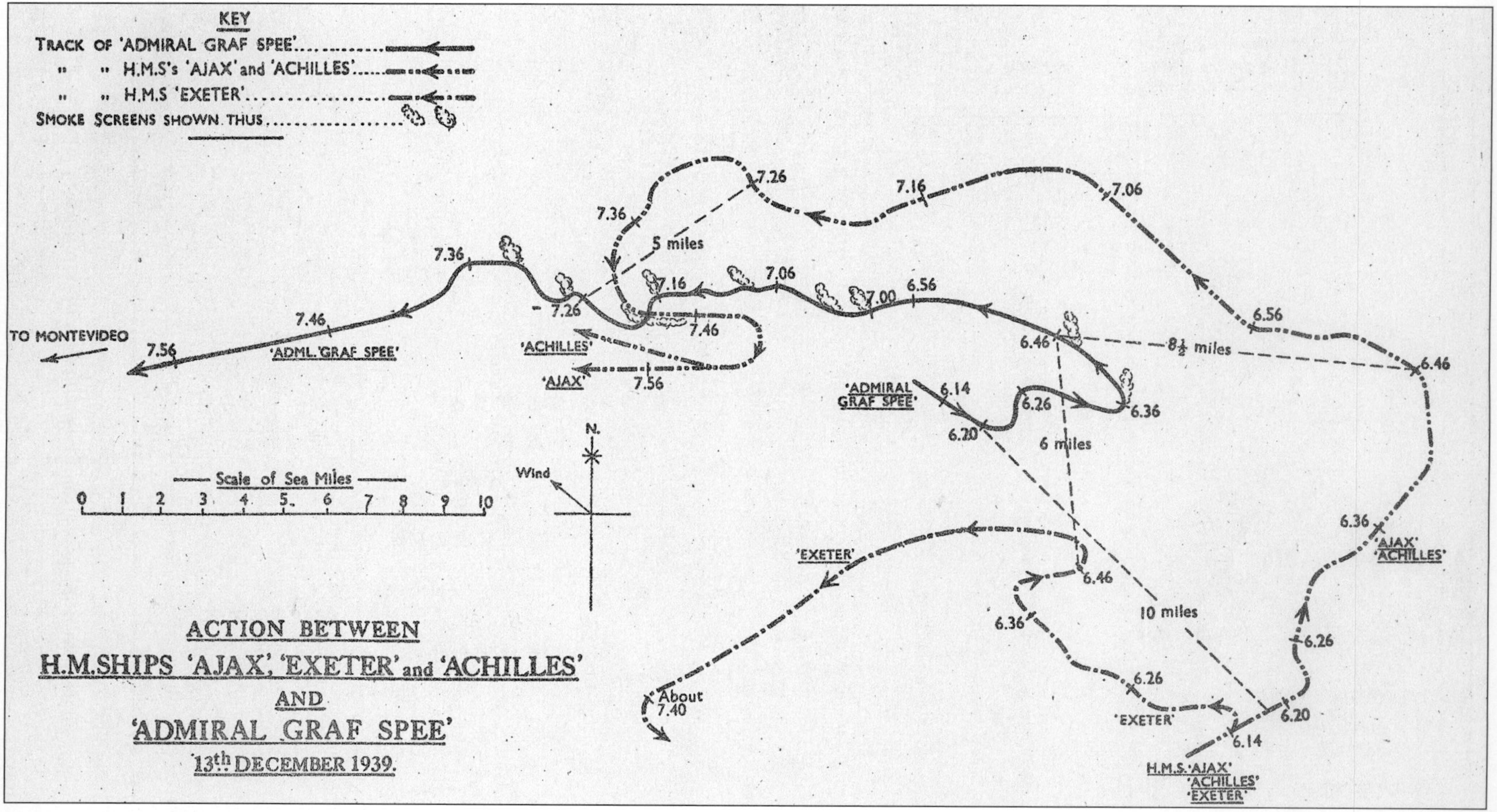

ACTION BETWEEN
H.M.SHIPS 'AJAX', 'EXETER' and 'ACHILLES'
AND
'ADMIRAL GRAF SPEE'
13th DECEMBER 1939.

A Spanish-language newspaper reacts to German propaganda by explaining how the British could have used mustard (*mostaza*) gas.

The damage to HMS *Exeter*'s forward turrets during the battle.

HMS *Exeter*'s homecoming with her temporary repairs disguising the damage.

An annotated drawing of the damage to *Graf Spee* which Harwood sent home to his sons.

ABOVE LEFT: Harwood acknowledging the crowd at Montevideo, January 1940.

ABOVE RIGHT: *Picture Post* depict the victorious sailors of HMS *Exeter* on its front cover.

RIGHT: The victors march by Nelson's column. *(Courtesy of Patrick Cogswell)*

LEFT: High expectations were placed on Harwood when he was sent to the Mediterranean. The text of the press cutting promises that 'the RAF will help you to the limit and beyond' – a promise which was not fulfilled.

LEFT: Harwood and some of his staff *(left to right)*: FPLO, SONP, E Tetlow, Harwood, Larry Allen, George Palmer, John Hexon, J Turner, D Prosser.

LEFT: Inspecting operations to clear Benghazi of obstructions left by the Germans and Italians.

The Royal Navy unloading stores for the 8th Army.

Acting Admiral Sir Henry Harwood, Commander-in-Chief, Mediterranean.

Admiral Sir Dudley Pound, First Sea Lord. (© National Maritime Museum, Greenwich, London)

Air Chief Marshal Arthur Tedder, Air Officer Commanding-in-Chief, Middle East Forces.

FAR LEFT: Admiral Philip Vian, seagoing commander Operation Vigorous.

LEFT: Lieutenant General Bernard Montgomery, 8th Army Commander.

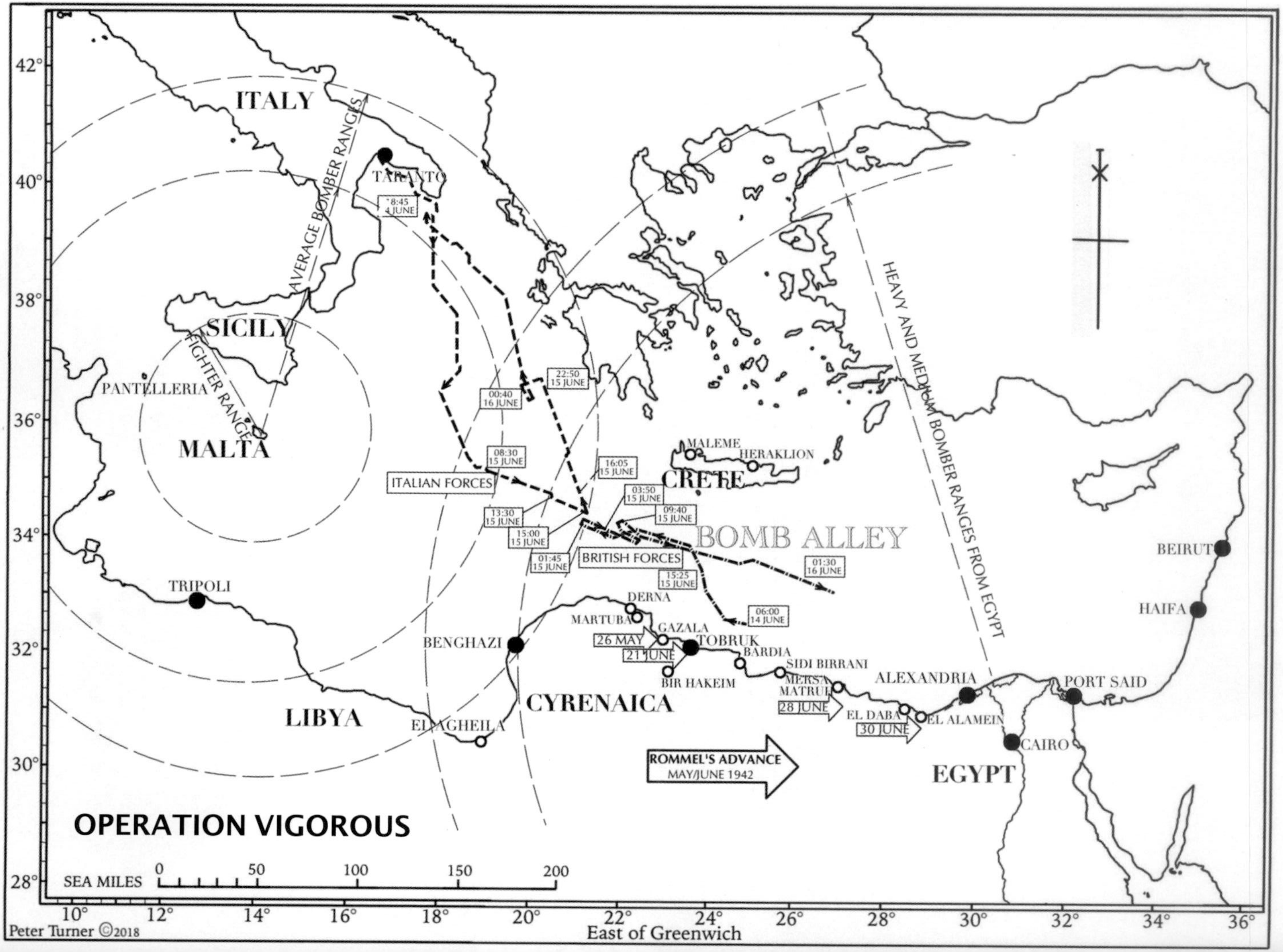
OPERATION VIGOROUS
ITALY
TARANTO
8:45 4 JUNE
AVERAGE BOMBER RANGES
SICILY
FIGHTER RANGE
PANTELLERIA
MALTA
TRIPOLI
LIBYA
EL AGHEILA
BENGHAZI
CYRENAICA
ITALIAN FORCES
08:30 15 JUNE
00:40 16 JUNE
22:50 15 JUNE
13:30 15 JUNE
15:00 15 JUNE
01:45 15 JUNE
16:05 15 JUNE
03:50 15 JUNE
09:40 15 JUNE
BRITISH FORCES
15:25 15 JUNE
06:00 14 JUNE
01:30 16 JUNE
BOMB ALLEY
CRETE
MALEME
HERAKLION
DERNA
MARTUBA
GAZALA
TOBRUK
26 MAY
21 JUNE
BIR HAKEIM
BARDIA
SIDI BIRRANI
MERSA MATRUH
28 JUNE
EL DABA
30 JUNE
EL ALAMEIN
ALEXANDRIA
CAIRO
EGYPT
PORT SAID
HAIFA
BEIRUT
HEAVY AND MEDIUM BOMBER RANGES FROM EGYPT
ROMMEL'S ADVANCE
MAY/JUNE 1942
SEA MILES
0
50
100
150
200
42°
40°
38°
36°
34°
32°
30°
28°
10°
12°
14°
16°
18°
20°
22°
24°
26°
28°
30°
32°
34°
36°
East of Greenwich
Peter Turner ©2018

Harwood looks askance at a scruffily dressed Churchill during a change of Army command in the Middle East: back row, Tedder (who denied him support), Alexander (who is about to relieve Auchinleck), Harwood, Casey (who would let Harwood down); front row, Smuts, Churchill, and Auchinleck and Wavell (who are about to swap jobs).

LEFT: Casey, who took chocolates home for Joan, but let Harwood down.

BELOW: French Admiral Godfroy looking in the opposite direction to everyone else.

LEFT: Bobby and Joan share a joke outside their house at Melsetter in Orkney.

ABOVE: Montgomery's visit to the Harwoods in 1944 passed off without rancour.

BELOW AND OPPOSITE TOP: One of Harwood's duties was to hand over HMS *Royal Sovereign* to the Soviet Union; Joan also attended the ceremony.

ELOW: Among his many civic duties after the war, Harwood, at the Dorchester, presented HMS *Ajax*'s ›ell to the Uruguayan government.

Formerly in the Chalk Walk at Greenwich and now in the Captain's flat at Dartmouth, this was one of a set of portraits of successful British naval commanders of the Second World War painted by Oswald Birley.

11
The Propaganda War

When it was proposed that *Ajax* and *Achilles* should pay visits to Montevideo and Buenos Aires, the Uruguayan authorities feared that pro-British demonstrations might get out of hand, while in Buenos Aires the British ambassador did not want to embarrass the government whilst it dealt with over a thousand German internees. Instead, *Cumberland* was left on patrol off the Plate while *Ajax* and *Achilles* went into Samborombón Bay on 18 December to refuel from the tanker *Olynthus*. Harwood boarded *Achilles* that evening to address the ship's company, praising them for their part in the battle. Both ships arrived in the Falkland Islands on 21 December, where they discharged several seriously wounded ratings to hospital ashore to join a number of casualties from *Exeter*. The staff of the hospital at Port Stanley were reinforced from the British hospital in Buenos Aires, where the British community paid for hospital equipment for 100 men and despatched it to the Falkland Islands. This equipment, a radiologist and fourteen nurses, all of whom gave up their own work at short notice, sailed in the steamer *Lafonia*.[1] Many of the lesser injured were cared for by Falkland islanders in their homes.

On Christmas Eve *Cumberland* arrived in Port Stanley, with another heavy cruiser *Dorsetshire*, which had sailed from Simonstown on 13 December. Christmas Day was observed by all five cruisers in traditional Navy custom. On Boxing Day there was a dance ashore in aid of the dependants of those killed and everyone contributed one day's pay. Harwood's Christmas message to his ships was:

Christmas comes but once a year
And with it brings good cheer
Let's hope that's all it brings
And not the *Admiral Scheer*.

There were few ship repair facilities in the Falklands but when it was suggested that *Exeter* should be abandoned, Churchill insisted that she be brought home in triumph. Consideration was given to using iron plates taken from ss *Great Britain*, then a hulk in Sparrow Cove. Instead, welding gear and sheet steel were ordered from Buenos Aires, which were also brought in *Lafonia* and transferred to *Exeter* alongside in Port Stanley by pack mule. Great ingenuity was exercised in making *Exeter* fit for sea and the ship's ordnance department even made 'Y'-turret operational and all remaining ammunition was transferred to 'Y'-magazine.[2]

Ajax *visits Montevideo,* Achilles *visits Buenos Aires*

After sharing evenly their remaining 6in ammunition stocks, *Ajax* and *Achilles* sailed from Port Stanley on 30 December for visits to the River Plate capitals. Harwood's forty-eight-hour visit to Montevideo began on 3 January 1940 and was vividly described in a letter to Joan: 'Montevideo was a most hectic time ... on arrival the jetty black with people, who broke through the police and cheered quite wildly,' though unfortunately, 'I waved in reply and got photographed with my hand up which looks like a Mussolini salute.' He continued:[3]

> British people, the Press & others poured on board. I gave the press a written statement – a copy of which I sent you – and showed them my damaged sleeping cabin nothing left of it, holes everywhere, all chest of drawers, bed and wardrobe smashed to pieces. Large holes in the deck above and below. Padded up with mats etc. They were very impressed. Then my calls. As I passed through the streets & was recognised we were cheered & waved at – Bravos etc – Quite impressive as it was entirely spontaneous. At each official call there was a crowd waiting, much noise, many handshakes etc. – all from Uruguayans.

After lunch at the embassy Harwood enjoyed a round of golf and after a reception at the embassy he escaped for a quiet dinner with Lloyd Hirst. That evening he visited the casino where:

> The German Minister was at the same table and he watched me losing my money with great satisfaction. I then backed No 13, the date of the battle, and told some of my Uruguayan friends what I was doing. This got passed around and up turned 13 accompanied by loud applause from everybody except the German Minister who departed looking like a thunder cloud. Another victory over the Germans by the democratic countries![4]

Achilles' visit to Buenos Aires was also warmly received, but more restrained diplomatically. Ashore, despite misgivings expressed by some, McCall reported that the fellowship of the sea prevailed and that British and German sailors had met and drunk each other's health.

Harwood in the New Zealand Achilles

When the two cruisers rendezvoused in the Plate estuary, Harwood and his staff transferred to *Achilles*. *Ajax* then searched unsuccessfully for the German blockade-runner *Rio Grande* before a visit to Rio and a triumphal return to Plymouth on 31 January 1940. *Cumberland* had by then gone to the Cape area in exchange for *Dorsetshire* and *Shropshire*, which had been sent to escort the patched-up *Exeter* home. Harwood had only four weeks to get to know his New Zealanders. In a message to the New Zealand Naval Board, repeated in his despatch to the Admiralty, Harwood told them that he was 'deeply conscious of the honour and pleasure of taking one of His Majesty's ships of the New Zealand Squadron into action. The *Achilles* was handled perfectly and fought magnificently by her captain, officers and ship's company.' In his despatch he said he fully concurred with the remark of Captain Parry that 'New Zealand has every reason to be proud of her seamen during their baptism of fire.'

Achilles also needed a refit: during the six months since she had left Auckland in August 1939, she had steamed over 50,000 miles and spent 168 days at sea and only ten days in harbour. Leave had been given to the ship's company on nineteen occasions, mostly for brief periods while in harbour for only a few hours. Harwood proposed to the Admiralty in London that *Achilles* should be refitted in New Zealand instead of Malta as had been planned, and when on 28 January Harwood's flag was struck in *Achilles*, the ship's company cheered him and serenaded him with 'For He's a Jolly Good Fellow' and 'Now is the Hour', the Maori farewell song. 'During the short time his flag was flying at our masthead, he endeared himself to us all,' recorded Captain Parry:

> It was, therefore, very gratifying that, when he left us, he signalled: 'My best wishes to you all. I have enjoyed flying my flag in your very happy ship.' Besides the debt we all owe him for his unforgettable example and leadership in the Battle of the River Plate, we are also more than grateful to him for forwarding a proposal that we should refit at Auckland instead of an Imperial dockyard.[5]

Achilles arrived in Auckland to her own very special welcome when more than 100,000 New Zealanders greeted the ship's company, led by Captain Parry, as they marched from the wharf to attend the civic reception and luncheon at the town hall.

HMS Hawkins *and the changed threat*

The threat from pocket battleships had been removed, but the Germans were soon expected to deploy as commerce raiders a fleet of disguised, armed merchant ships, following their First World War strategy – which Raeder had codified in the 1920s. 'So much for the *Spee*,' Harwood had commented in a letter to Pound, 'we are all well out here and waiting for the raiders. I can't understand why they have not yet arrived.' To meet this threat, and to hunt down German merchant ships in South American ports, including those which might be used as blockade-runners to smuggle raw materials back to Germany, the British deployed their own armed merchant cruisers (AMCs). In the South Atlantic Harwood was given as flagship the elderly cruiser HMS *Hawkins*, which had been rearmed after demilitarisation under the Washington Treaty, while his other ships were replaced by two AMCs, the Cunard liner *Alcantara* and the Furness liner *Queen of Bermuda*. Both about 22,000 tons, they mounted eight 6in guns with rudimentary fire-control, but, of course, no armour: their high fuel capacity gave them long range, ideal in the South Atlantic where, as warships, they were restricted to occasional refuelling visits in neutral ports or the long haul to the

Falklands for fuel. Harwood implemented a simple planning policy: visits to Simonstown once every six months for dockyard maintenance and four days' self-maintenance in the Falklands every three months.

One of *Hawkins*'s former commanding officers was Tom Phillips, now the Vice Chief of Naval Staff, who had the opportunity to write:[6]

> My dear Bobby ... It cheered us all up so much and I feel has vindicated the Navy from the *Goeben* incident of the last war which I have always thought was a great blot on our name; not that one man should make a mistake as Troubridge did, but that his peers should acquit him. And now you have shown that those days of counting tons and guns are over and the Service is back in the old spirit in which the Empire was built in which we do not always ask for bigger and better ships to beat the enemy with but win our battles because we have better men and better training ... Hope you like my old ship you now have your flag in *Hawkins*. We saved up her 7.5's [guns] for the express purpose of putting them back if a war came ... You have brought great credit to our old term!

Hawkins was an obsolescent cruiser of 9,800 tons armed with seven 7.5in guns in single mountings, very much in contrast to the modern, efficient ships Harwood was used to. One consolation was the commodious quarters which had been designed for a commander-in-chief. Harwood wrote to Joan:

> Well, words fail me! Ex-Reserve Fleet. Filthy. Most lovely suite of cabins and nicely got up too. In 1928 she was flagship in China and later flagship in East Indies. As a result the Admiral's accommodation is really perfect. On two floors with a stair case. The only trouble is that except for one desk it is so ornamental that it only holds half a desk's contents. There is no cupboard for any of my toys.[7]

Another consolation was that John Donnelly, Harwood's coxswain, was now an Acting Chief Petty Officer: 'Donnelly, works hard and is a great stand by. Between you and me he is one of my best shipmates. I talk a lot to him. He is a nice man. Terribly proud of us all. Do anything for me and is most thoughtful.'[8] But what Harwood really wanted was his missing mail from Joan or better still to be home with her: 'Damn this war. I want to come home and see you and be with you.'[9]

The Wakama *incident*

However, Harwood, in *Hawkins*, had to make a succession of visits. One of the first was to Rio de Janeiro where a number of German merchant ships were sheltering. The British accused one of these, *Wakama*, of using her wireless to aid German naval operations by reporting British ship movements, and she was ordered to sail by the Brazilian authorities. Harwood was due to visit Rio in *Hawkins* but did not want to arrive with 'blood on his hands', so he ordered *Dorsetshire*, which was escorting the badly damaged *Exeter* homewards, to investigate. Outside territorial waters, on 11 February, *Wakama* was spotted by an aircraft from *Dorsetshire*, whereupon the German promptly scuttled herself. When *Dorsetshire* arrived she rescued ten officers and thirty-five crewmen and shelled *Wakama* to prevent her from being a navigational hazard. The Brazilian authorities now complained to the British about a breach of the neutrality zone, which had been declared by the American nations, but not recognised by the belligerents. In Rio, Harwood's visit coincided with a meeting of the Neutrality Committee, and in his calls on Brazilian naval officers he referred to the growing number of unprovoked German attacks on merchant ships and argued that British warships were protecting local trade. Harwood, ever the diplomat, argued for a sympathetic interpretation of the neutrality laws, and this was sufficient to restore calm.[10]

More visits

A flood of congratulatory messages reached Harwood, yet still some letters from Joan were missing. Slowly the significance of his victory began to sink in: 'I am astounded at the fuss made over our battle. I can see it now. It came completely out of the blue as a surprise to everybody and a tremendous relief to the Admiralty.'[11] However, after three years on the South America Station, Harwood was well-known and well-liked, and his victory had gained him enormous prestige. He was a valuable diplomatic asset in South America, while in Britain, despite his promotion, no vacancy existed into which a new rear-admiral could be shifted. Yet he longed for home: 'I suppose I am here for the duration of the war. May God end this stupidity quickly.'[12]

In March *Hawkins* was in the Falklands, and in April at Montevideo again. There he received a visit from two Argentine naval officers who had visited *Graf Spee* accompanied by Paul Ascher, her gunnery officer. They gave him a copy of the report and photographs that they had prepared for the Argentine admiralty, which they had been instructed to pass on. This gave details of the various shell hits they had been shown and commented on the fusing and bursting effects of the British shells. They said that Ascher had openly criticised his captain for making him shift target eight times during the action and had said that there was a considerable difference of opinion between Langsdorff and his officers about the decision to enter Montevideo.

There was another visit too, to Buenos Aires in April for a busy, forty-eight-hour call, when he told Joan that he was out of training for such a hectic time. Notable among Harwood's calls was one on Cardinal Santiago Luis Copello, a deeply conservative priest (and later a supporter of the dictator Perón) who, contrary to reports, Harwood found 'perfectly charming', perhaps because, 'My Spanish that morning was brilliant'.[13]

At the end of May, there were fears of a pro-German coup in Uruguay mounted from Brazil, which Eugen Millington-Drake doubted the country's capability to resist, and on 3 June Harwood paid a brief visit to Montevideo to discuss the political situation with the ambassador and the assistant naval attaché in Rio. The attaché reported that there was no firm evidence, only rumours that Germans in Brazil were also planning to invade Guiana using German ships in Brazilian ports. He thought that Brazilian resolve needed to be bolstered and on 27 June Harwood was back in Rio in *Hawkins*. In July, after a brief visit to the Falklands, *Hawkins* was again in Montevideo, less than three months since her previous visit and, presumably, at the request of the Uruguayan government.

Alcantara *footnote*

Harwood's time on the South America Station ended as it had begun, brilliantly moving his ships like chess pieces across the South

Atlantic.[14] On 17 July 1940 he had sailed from Montevideo after a twenty-four-hour visit to patrol the Plate, when he heard via the Admiralty that direction-finding (D/F) had placed an enemy raider west of the Cape Verde islands. Combined with other intelligence, this suggested that a surface raider was moving south into the Atlantic, and Harwood ordered *Alcantara* to patrol off Pernambuco while *Hawkins* moved up to patrol off Rio. On 20 July he moved *Alcantara* to search Trindade Island and then to patrol 250 miles off the Brazilian coast. After refuelling from the tanker *Arndale*, she resumed patrolling on a line from Rio to the Plate.

When Harwood learned that a U-boat had sunk a Norwegian ship near the Cape Verde islands, and that three ships were overdue at Freetown, he correctly deduced that the raider was in his area. Yet again he had been prescient, for at 10:00 on 28 July *Alcantara* sighted masts over the horizon and as she turned to intercept, the unknown ship manoeuvred suspiciously. At the end of a chase of several hours, at 14:00 *Thor*, a German raider, hoisted her colours and turned to open fire at 16,000yds, 2,000yds more than *Alcantara*'s maximum range. *Alcantara* closed the range and also turned, to bring her own broadside to bear, but the German gunners, with the afternoon sun behind them, had an advantage over the British, and scored three hits (out of 284 shots) causing flooding and reducing *Alcantara*'s speed. *Thor* too was hit, and she withdrew behind a thick smokescreen. *Alcantara*, holed and listing, limped to Rio (where she was eventually refitted as a troopship): she had done everything she could to force the action and it was the fortune of war that an unlucky shot had enabled *Thor* to escape.

This was not quite the stuff of the Battle of the River Plate, but it was a suitably warlike note for Harwood to bow out on, for he had heard about his relief. He had spent 296 days at sea and just thirty-eight days in harbour since the war began, but on 4 September he and his staff, Weekes, his secretary, John Donnelly, his coxswain, and Petty Officer Steward Joseph Pantoll, embarked in a merchant steamer at Montevideo.

Reaction in London

Harwood's report of the Battle of the River Plate was seized upon by

Churchill as First Lord of the Admiralty, who wanted an official Admiralty narrative to be rushed out, while Pound, the First Sea Lord, wanted the narrative to be extended to include *Cumberland* and the 'bad English and faulty typing' to be corrected. The editors noted that the various despatches from the captains of ships did not agree 'and in such cases Harwood's original despatch would be taken as correct'. The Stationery Office wanted to publish the narrative as a stand-alone pamphlet and reckoned that it would be a 'best seller' at twopence a copy, while the Ministry of Information wanted thirty copies for translation into other languages and urged the simultaneous release of the Admiralty narrative at home and overseas. And then Churchill announced that he required that an advance copy 'should be sent to President Roosevelt to be in his hands prior to release' in April 1940.[15]

Also, early in 1940 Lord Strabolgi was able to write a book, copiously illustrated with photographs, evidently from official sources and with official backing. Strabolgi's work was largely propaganda, but contains, uniquely, transcripts of contemporary broadcasts by the BBC and by the German broadcasting service. Harwood had read Strabolgi's book before the end of May, when he told Joan it was 'merely a series of extracts from reports, papers and cuttings etc.'[16] Two other books in 1940 were by men who had been captured by *Graf Spee*: one by a seaman, Tom Foley, who had been captured in *Doric Star* and released when the supply ship *Altmark* was boarded on her way to Germany,[17] the other by Captain Patrick Dove of *Africa Shell* who was a prisoner in *Graf Spee* for several weeks after his capture off the east coast of Africa, and who was released in Montevideo when *Graf Spee* entered neutral waters.[18] Harwood dismissed Dove as a blowhard.[19] Nevertheless, when a film with a star-studded cast was produced by Michael Powell and Emeric Pressburger in 1955/56, it was largely based, not on Harwood's despatch, but upon Patrick Dove and his relationship with Langsdorff.[20]

The Admiralty also wanted wide circulation of the full report with its technical annexes to all commanders-in-chief and to flag officers and to attachés abroad. Harwood's original despatch, with its faults, was made into a Confidential Book, before any analysis had been completed, so that the Navy could absorb the practical lessons as soon as possible.[21] This was all done so quickly that before the end of June

Harwood had received his copies of the Admiralty official despatch, via his mother, which was, he thought, 'better than all the books written ... is well done and while it cuts out much confidential stuff it presents a very accurate and complete picture.' He also had the full report via official channels.[22]

Fly in the ointment

It will be recalled that on 5 October 1939, a vital clue as to *Graf Spee*'s whereabouts had been missed.[23] Captain Walter Fallowfield in *Cumberland* had received a signal from the British merchantman *Martand*,[24] reporting that she had just received a distress message from an unknown ship which was being attacked by a raider in position 9° 20' South 6° 19' West. However, Fallowfield decided neither to investigate nor to report the message. Not even on 9 October when he met Harwood at sea in *Exeter*, nor on 14 October when he called on Harwood at anchor in Samborombón Bay, did Fallowfield think to mention the message. However, he did include it in his report of proceedings for the month of October, which Harwood received on 7 December and forwarded without comment on 12 December to the Admiralty in London and to Lyon, his commander-in-chief.

Lyon did not receive Fallowfield's report until 21 January, when he became incensed, immediately signalling Fallowfield that the ship which had sent the distress message was 'now known to have been the British ship *Newton Beech*. This is the first information that I have received of any raider report having been made by *Newton Beech* and if it had reported to me immediately it might have resulted in *Graf Spee*'s career being cut short considerably earlier.' Fallowfield was ordered to forward his reasons in writing.[25] Lyon told the Admiralty:

> Force K did not arrive at Freetown and Force H at Simonstown until 12 October, but had I known that *Graf Spee* was operating on the Cape route, I should have immediately ordered a sweep by both Forces K and H on the Cape route instead of ordering Force K to keep towards Pernambuco, and there is little doubt that *Graf Spee* and also *Altmark* would have been destroyed before *Trevanion* was sunk on 22 October.

Lyon also wrote privately to Pound's chief of staff:

> The only echo of *Graf Spee* which is concerning me is Fallowfield's amazing omission to pass on to me or anyone else that a raider report had been intercepted on 5 October on the Cape Route ... it is maddening to think that if that report had been received ... not only *Graf Spee* but also *Altmark* might have been rounded up between 14 October (when Force K went off on their first hunt) and 22 October when the *Trevanion* was sunk.

Fallowfield's reasons, signalled from Simonstown on 22 January, were weak: when he received *Martand*'s message, the raider's position was 900 miles away; he thought other ships would have passed on the message or that a shore station would have picked it up; that the preservation of wireless silence in order not to give away his own position was important; and that when he met Harwood four days later that it was not of sufficient importance after an interval of several days. Lyon was furious, telling the Admiralty by signal on 13 February: 'If I had appropriate officers available I should bring Captain Fallowfield to trial by court martial for grave neglect of duty. I recommend for Their Lordships' approval that he shall be relieved of his command at the earliest possible moment'. In the Admiralty a court martial was ruled out on the grounds of inconvenience, but it was recommended that Fallowfield should receive 'an expression of severe displeasure because he should have broken wireless silence and should have realised from the lack of instructions that Harwood had not received the same report; he had gravely neglected his duty by not telling Harwood on 9 October, and that he should have immediately altered course towards the enemy.' However, when the papers reached Pound, he characteristically prevaricated, ruling that in view of Fallowfield's subsequent action in December in leaving the Falklands on his own initiative 'as soon as he knew that *Graf Spee* had been sighted', that no further action would be taken and 'the matter is to be considered closed'. Nevertheless, Fallowfield received no further promotion and ended the war and his career in command of the reserve fleet in the Clyde.

Reception in London

Ajax reached Plymouth on 31 January, was joined by the patched-up *Exeter* on 15 February and was greeted by Churchill, the First Lord, and Pound, the First Sea Lord. On 23 February 760 officers and men of both ships, and six of the Merchant Navy captains who had been prisoners on board *Graf Spee*, marched from Waterloo station to Horse Guards where they were inspected by King George VI, who took their salute at a march-past and conferred decorations. They then marched to the London Guildhall, cheered all the way by assembled crowds, for a lunch given by the Lord Mayor. In *Hawkins* Harwood sat glued to his wireless to hear the BBC describe events.

During the lunch, Churchill made one of his stirring speeches, recorded in newsreel film of the time, saying that 'this brilliant sea fight which Admiral Harwood conceived and you executed will take its place in our naval annals and in a dark cold winter it warmed the cockles of the British hearts.' Both Captains Woodhouse and Bell paid tribute to Harwood, and Bell stressed that his *Exeter* had been trained by Harwood for three years before the battle. Churchill and Pound both sent Harwood appreciative signals about the event, while Harwood wrote that he was astounded at the fuss made but now realised the importance of the psychological effect it had on the Empire. Joan and the families of the ships' companies were sent invitations to the ceremonies. Joan left her own account of the march through London:

> I and the Captains' wives assembled at the Admiralty. The Queen came and spoke to us (and to the relatives of those who had fallen in the battle). We followed the Ships' Companies as they marched to the Guildhall. As we reached the City the crowds pressed in on our cars. Winston and the officers lunched in the Hall. The women sat in a sort of balcony. I sat next to Mrs Churchill. Then back to the Admiralty. The Horse Guards Parade was full of cheering crowds. Winston took me by the arm, led me to the window overlooking the crowds, and said 'Look ...!'

For the next few months, concerned about his family's welfare and finances and informed by letters, Harwood followed the progress of the war in the North Atlantic, in Norway and in the Blitzkrieg against Western Europe, until on 30 September he arrived at Liverpool in the Blue Funnel liner ***Empire Star,*** to be met by Joan. Lord Halifax, the Foreign Secretary, took the unusual step of writing formally to A V Alexander,[26] who had replaced Churchill as First Lord of the Admiralty, desiring him to 'take this opportunity to convey to the Lords Commissioners his deep appreciation of the services rendered by Admiral Harwood during the period of his command of the South American Division of the America and West Indies Squadron and in particular to the cause of British prestige in Latin America, where he has been deservedly popular.'[27]

The summer school holidays had just finished and the Harwoods had planned to go straight across to see their second son, Stephen, at Ampleforth. However, a royal command awaited Harwood to go at once to Buckingham Palace where he had a private audience lasting an hour. The King bestowed the accolade of knighthood, chatted informally about the battle and proudly showed the recent bomb damage to the palace. Only then were the Harwoods allowed to enjoy a few brief weeks of family life.

12
The Admiralty

Winston Churchill had become Prime Minster in May 1940 and the Labour politician and Member of Parliament, A V Alexander succeeded him as First Lord of the Admiralty, an office which he would hold for the next five years. Prime Minister Churchill, however, having appointed himself as his own Minister of Defence, continued to interfere in the internal affairs of the RAF, the Army, and of the Royal Navy, which he knew especially well.

One of the reasons why Harwood might have been left so long on the South American coast after his unexpected promotion is that neither Churchill nor Alexander nor Pound could agree what his next appointment should be. An undated note in Churchill's hand on 10 Downing Street notepaper indicates his wish that Harwood should go in October 1940 as second in command to Vice-Admiral Sir Tom Phillips as Commander-in-Chief, Home Fleet. Other Churchillian plotting included Vice-Admiral Jack Tovey to command Force H based at Gibraltar, and Vice-Admiral Sir Max Horton to become Vice Chief of Naval Staff (VCNS). Admirals Geoffrey Blake and Dudley North were to be placed on 'the beach'.[1]

Alexander evidently consulted Pound and on 30 September, the day that Harwood arrived in Liverpool, Alexander made his own proposals to Churchill: Phillips to be second in command of the Mediterranean Fleet, and Vice-Admiral Lancelot Holland to be VCNS; 'other appointments would fall into place.' Alexander mused whether Tovey or A B Cunningham should be the next First Sea Lord, but he finished his note: 'Pound has been discussing with me privately the position of Harwood and I was pleasantly surprised to hear that he would like to have him as ACNS! I like the sound of that.'[2] This also suited Churchill, who 'had an adulation for Harwood after the Plate Battle and wanted to make him ACNS and bring him on to high command' wrote Blake, who may have felt aggrieved that Harwood was about to supersede him.[3]

The prequel

Churchill had also been First Lord of the Admiralty in August 1914 when the German battlecruiser ***Goeben*** and the light cruiser ***Breslau*** bombarded Philippeville in French North Africa, and then steamed northabout Sicily to Messina to coal. On 4 August two British battlecruisers intercepted and shadowed the Germans along the north coast of Sicily, but losing contact during the night, went on to guard the northern exit from the Messina straits, leaving the cruiser ***Gloucester*** to cover the southern exit. The Germans left Messina on the afternoon of 6 August and were shadowed eastward by ***Gloucester***.

Rear-Admiral Ernest Troubridge, who with four armoured cruisers was guarding the southern end of the Adriatic to bottle up the Austrian fleet, set course to intercept the German squadron. Troubridge's orders were to 'husband his forces and avoid being brought to action by a superior force', and he was persuaded that the modern ***Goeben*** represented a superior force who could use her superior speed and gun range to pick off his ships one by one. That ***Goeben*** could only concentrate her main armament on one target at a time does not appear to have been considered, and Troubridge broke off the chase. Only later did Troubridge learn that in outrunning the British battlecruisers ***Goeben*** had damaged her boilers and her speed was much reduced. ***Goeben*** and ***Breslau*** reached Istanbul unmolested, where their arrival brought Turkey into the war against Britain and France, and led eventually to the fiasco of the Dardanelles. Troubridge was court-martialled and acquitted, leaving many, including Churchill and Pound, with many other officers in the Grand Fleet, smouldering under the shame of this failure.

The Battle of Cape Spartivento

On 17 November 1940, during Operation White, a mission to fly aircraft reinforcements from the carrier ***Argus*** into Malta, ferried aircraft were launched too soon, several ran out of fuel, and ditched at sea. Ten days later during Operation Collar, the co-ordinated movement of a number of ships from the Mediterranean Fleet based at

Alexandria and the smaller Force H based at Gibraltar, a night action took place against Italian battleships and cruisers off Cape Spartivento, Sardinia. Aircraft from the carrier HMS *Ark Royal* attacked the Italian battleship *Vittorio Veneto* and, despite having superior force, the Italians withdrew. The charge against Troubridge had been that he 'forbore to pursue an enemy then flying', and now in 1940 Churchill, and Pound, thought that Vice-Admiral Sir James Somerville commanding Force H had also failed to pursue an enemy.

The British public and politicians, not least Churchill, expected victories like Harwood's at the Plate and Cunningham's in the Western Mediterranean. When Pound told Cunningham that 'Troubridge's failure to bring the *Goeben* to action set a very low standard in the conduct of naval operations', both men understood the reference to events in 1914. Pound continued: 'Harwood's conduct of affairs at the Plate and your conduct of operations in the Mediterranean put it back on a high plane again, and I can't afford that anything should again lower it.'[4] Churchill was particularly outraged, thinking that Somerville should have pursued the Italians, and 'Ginger' Boyle, Admiral of the Fleet the Earl of Cork and Orrery, was sent to Gibraltar to conduct an inquiry. Without waiting for the result, Alexander wrote suggesting names as different as Admiral Sir George Lyon (newly returned from the South Atlantic), Rear-Admiral Ronald Hallifax, and, as an afterthought, Vice-Admiral 'Jock' Whitworth to relieve Somerville. Churchill countered: 'But why could we not give Harwood his chance here?'[5] The Prime Minister's proposal was taken seriously, and Harwood and his secretary, Victor Weekes, 'were all set up to go to the Med but it was a secret.'[6]

Alexander and Pound exchanged further notes: Churchill feared that Cork's inquiry would last for weeks, Pound thought it would report soon and if it 'reports, as I think it must, that Somerville's judgement was at fault', he made a plan for Harwood to 'go in a destroyer or flying boat' and to take over from Somerville on 10 December.[7]

Few of these appointment occurred as Churchill, Alexander or Pound envisaged them, and after Cork found, to Churchill's chagrin, that Somerville had acted appropriately, Somerville remained in command of Force H. Tovey took over from Charles Forbes as

Commander-in-chief, Home Fleet on 2 December, and on the same day Harwood relieved Blake to become Assistant Chief of Naval Staff (Foreign). With Harwood's appointment came a seat on the Board of Admiralty.

Religion

Harwood was a Roman Catholic in the Royal Navy at a time when 'to be Roman Catholic in the Service gave you another kind of oddness, since the King's Regulations and Admiralty Instructions laid down a strictly observed freedom to worship as your conscience dictated. Roman Catholics were always fallen out earlier from divisions or otherwise finding themselves in the limelight.'[8] He did not wear his religion on his sleeve, but he had led two pilgrimages to Rome, his Catholicism had aided his diplomacy in South America, where he had charmed the hard-line, right-wing Cardinal Copello, while his career had been watched by Catholics in England, among them Arthur Hinsley, the liberal Cardinal-Archbishop of Westminster. When Hinsley wrote to him after the Battle of the River Plate, it was not to offer congratulations on his victory, but on his 'deserved promotion, following on your long and distinguished service.' Hinsley added that he would be honoured if, when Harwood was in London, he would bring Joan and the boys for a visit.[9]

In the privacy of his letters to his wife, Harwood had told Joan that the reversals in war in 1940 had tested and weakened his faith,[10] but now Harwood became the first Roman Catholic since the Glorious Revolution some 250 years before to sit on the Board of Admiralty.

Underground at the Admiralty

Whitehall Wireless, the main hub of the Admiralty's worldwide communications, the Operational Intelligence Centre (OIC) and other offices had moved into the hastily-constructed, ill-ventilated and semi-underground Citadel besides the Admiralty building, at the end of the Mall. The hours were long and Harwood kept a room at the nearby United Services Club in Pall Mall, though nightly air raids throughout the winter of 1940/41 gave him little rest. If there were no emergencies, Harwood was able to get away to Goring for a twenty-four break most weeks, being driven in an official car, where his garden at

White Cottage became a major source of delight and relaxation. Once he arranged a happy reunion of the Hot Toddy Club.

The Admiralty was both an administrative and an operational authority. Under the First Sea Lord, Pound and the other Sea Lords ran the Royal Navy. Pound was also Chief of Naval Staff and under him were Phillips, as Vice Chief of Naval Staff with a Deputy and three Assistant Chiefs: (Home), (Trade) and Harwood as (Foreign) each responsible for the planning and conduct of operations within their spheres. Phillips was one of Harwood's term at the naval college and they had worked together on the Commander-in-Chief, Mediterranean's staff in 1925/26, where Harwood had not been Phillips's greatest admirer. Harwood had also twice before worked for Pound, in the interwar years in the plans division of the Admiralty and again as one of his staff officers in the Mediterranean Fleet. Pound and Harwood quickly fell into their previous relationship, albeit now at the highest level within the Navy. Both would be accused of being mere staff officers to Churchill, who, though no longer First Lord of the Admiralty, meddled in the detailed affairs of the Navy.

Harwood was also responsible for mining and local defence. Under the latter rubric, policy for the Mobile Naval Base Defence Organisation (MNBDO), which he had seen exercised in the 1930s when he was on the staff of the Commander-in-Chief, Mediterranean, fell to Harwood. The MNBDO was mainly manned by Royal Marines and Harwood wrote a prophetic paper in which he noted the varied roles which they fulfilled and commented that in many cases it was actually the Army who assumed responsibility for the defence of naval bases. He recommended that the Royal Marines should expand their landing units and concentrate especially on beach landing.[11]

He also drew up for Churchill and for Pound a wide range of policy papers, covering relations with the USA and with France, the deployment of ships to and operations in the Far East, and inter-service co-operation, especially with the RAF.

Operation Workshop

One of Harwood's first tasks, within a few days of taking office, was to confront Admiral of the Fleet Sir Roger Keyes, who was the Director of Combined Operations. Keyes had conceived a plan, Operation

Workshop, using 2,500 commandos to seize Pantelleria, an island midway between Malta, Sicily and North Africa. Workshop appealed to the ever aggressive and thrusting Churchill, and this enthused him and Keyes against the chiefs of staff and the joint planning staff, who doubted the strategic value of Pantelleria, even if the plan was sound tactically.

Nevertheless, on 4 December 1940 Pound sent Harwood to discuss the shipping requirements of Workshop, when Keyes confided to his dairy: 'Harwood who had grown very fat since I had last seen him – his appearance and his look-out was profoundly disturbing to me'. Harwood had little else to contribute other than to repeat what he had rapidly learned from the naval staff. The operation was wrong strategically and the commandos should be directed against the Italian army in Libya. Even if captured, Pantelleria could not be garrisoned, no air defence could be provided, and there were no aircraft available to be based there, and that the capture could not be exploited. A frustrated Keyes appealed personally to Harwood: 'I told him it shocked me to think that Harwood of the River Plate could be so blind to the possibilities of offensive action against Italy'.

Meanwhile, Pound assured Keyes that he was 'all out to help'. A few days later Harwood phoned Keyes to tell him that he could have four destroyers and some transports, and on 15 December Harwood and Keyes lunched together, when Keyes asked him to consider the possibility of executing Workshop in the next moonless period at the end of the month. Keyes wrote: 'I think Harwood was impressed with the force of my arguments, and he promised to study the possibility of providing an escort for my small force if it should be decided to strike this month'.[12] Harwood duly prepared a long staff paper which discussed the political and strategic effect of the capture of Pantelleria, the forces available and the tactical plan.[13]

However, Pound was being duplicitous, for he had already told Cunningham on 12 December that 'I did all I could to stop Keyes, and can't do more, as of course Churchill is in a strong position being a self-appointed Minister of Defence'.[14] Whether Churchill would have overruled the chiefs of staff and ordered Workshop to proceed is not known: with the entry of the Germans into the war in the Mediterranean, the strategic situation so changed that Workshop was postponed and then forgotten.

The Far East

Starting in July 1941, five months before the Japanese attack on Pearl Harbor and Singapore, Harwood wrote a series of papers on the Far East. In his first, prophetic paper he foresaw the coming war, and the need to hold a line from Trincomalee through Sumatra and Java to Port Darwin. He did not anticipate the scale of Japanese aggression to come on 7 December 1941, but he did suggest that Singapore was insecure and that the fleet 'along the line which we have already agreed' should be based on 'one of the Indian Ocean bases with its light forces thrown forward on to the line of the islands'. There were two assumptions: either that America had joined the war, or that she still remained neutral. Harwood copied this paper to Phillips, who was the commander-in-chief designate of the Eastern Fleet.[15]

By August, Harwood was clearer in his views: the battlecruiser *Repulse*, at least one other capital ship and the carrier *Eagle* should be sent to reinforce the Far East and to deter the Japanese, but they should only go as far as one of the secret anchorages 'W' or 'T'.[16] In October he recommended to the new VCNS, Vice-Admiral Henry Moore, that a battleship force of four ships should be sent to Singapore, to have the maximum deterrent effect and a fighting value. Harwood now anticipated that the Japanese 'might realize what we are doing and strike before we are ready ... no further time should be wasted.'[17] Four days later he found himself arguing against sending the new *Prince of Wales* and discussing which 'R'-class battleships were ready to be sent to the east. He recommended that *Rodney*, *Royal Sovereign*, *Revenge* and *Repulse* should proceed to Trincomalee, but that 'we could accept a certain delay in sending reinforcements'.[18] However, two days later the situation in the Far East had deteriorated so much that *Prince of Wales* was ordered to join *Repulse*, who was already at Colombo.

The pace of events accelerated. Harwood's next paper was written after the loss of *Repulse* and *Prince of Wales* and the Fall of Singapore. He acknowledged how bitter the Australians and the Dutch were, and the urgent need to reconstitute the Eastern Fleet.[19] In an undated draft, he rued that 'we have now, at considerable cost, got the measure of [the Japanese] and indeed it is a higher measure than that displayed by either the Germans or the Italians'. Again, Harwood advocated adequate fighter protection for the fleet, specifically that twin-engined, long-range fighters 'should be stationed in various areas of the world to protect the fleet from shore-based aircraft' and that 'every battleship or pair of battleships must have an attendant carrier to provide fighter protection'.[20]

On 16 February Harwood, while counting the Allied losses in the East, was already devising a three-phase strategy to defeat Japan. First, hold a line across the Indian Ocean, and the coastline of Australia, by reinforcing Ceylon; secondly, bomb Japan from the sea, and attack the Marshall Islands and the Carolines; and, thirdly, move to a general offensive against Japan. He saw this third phase being led by the USA.[21] Harwood's thoughts were even clearer a month later when he set out for Pound how the Japanese, gorged by conquests, would pursue the war. The danger he thought, agreeing with a message from General Smuts, was that the Japanese, whose best defence was attack, would interrupt British convoys in the western Indian Ocean bound for Suez and the Middle East.[22] He also wrote a paper urging that the USA should be encouraged to take to the offensive.[23]

Seizing the Atlantic islands

Other concerns in 1942 were whether Spain would join the war on the side of the Axis powers, whether Spain would invade Portugal, and whether Gibraltar might become untenable, and would U-boats be based in the Azores, the Canaries and Cape Verde islands. Plans were drawn up to forestall such possibilities. Operation Puma foresaw the capture of the Canaries, where Force H might be based if it were ousted from Gibraltar, and Cape Verde islands. Other operations, Thruster, Baseball and Springboard, foresaw the Portuguese islands being handed over to the British for protection. Harwood recommended that the Azores were important to the defence of convoys in the Atlantic but that the capture of the Canaries was only important in order to deny its use to the enemy.[24]

Celebrity

During his time as ACNS(F) Harwood played his part in many official and social occasions. On the first anniversary of the Battle of the River Plate, Admiral Sir William Goodenough, who had commanded the light cruisers in the previous war, hosted a lunch for Harwood at Quaglino's. He was lunched at *The Times* in January 1941, and he was guest of honour at a lunch given by the RNVR Club, where the menu card bore a copy of Norman Wilkinson's painting *River Plate Action*: the fare was pea soup, chicken pie, and plum duff, followed by the wartime luxury of coffee. In March 1941 Harwood and Joan dined with Prince Bernhardt of the Netherlands at the Bell Inn at Purley, near Reading, when the Prince was supposed to be incognito and the women were instructed not to curtsey, but most of them did. In July they attended a sherry party for South American naval missions at the Ritz hosted by Hugh Dalton, the Minister of Economic Warfare in Churchill's Cabinet. In October 1941 they lunched at the RAC Club with Philip Clarke, now a captain, who had been his second in command in *Exeter*. Clarke had with him some USN officers who were being secretly trained in convoy work. As neutrals they were supposed to wear plain clothes, and when the film actor Robert Montgomery appeared in uniform, he was sent away to change.

When the Millington-Drakes returned to London from Montevideo, they hosted several parties to which the Harwoods were invited. At one of these Joan sat next to General de Gaulle who, she said, never smiled, but she had had a long talk with de Gaulle's wife, Yvonne. Joan, whose French was competent and well-accented, and Yvonne talked about family matters: Yvonne explained that she tried to keep a low profile because so few other of the Free French wives were in England.

In November the Harwoods dined with Lord and Lady Iliffe at their home, Yattendon Court, near Goring, when the Willingdons, whom Harwood had met in South America in 1939, were also guests. In January 1941 Lord Iliffe and Harwood jointly received two ambulances from Uruguay as a memorial to the fallen in the Battle of the River Plate. In August 1941 Harwood presented the sword-belt of honour at the passing-out parade of Royal Armoured Corps cadets at Sandhurst, the first naval officer to do so. Harwood also spoke to the British Sailors' Society at their Trafalgar night dinner and he opened the roof gardens at Derry and Toms department store, in Kensington High Street. Few invitations were refused, but in March 1942, when a German squadron including the German capital ships *Gneisenau* and *Scharnhorst* made a daring dash up-Channel from Brest, Harwood was obliged to cancel an engagement to open the city of Exeter's Warship Week.

Few personal letters have survived from this period, but there is one account of Harwood as ACNS(F) which comes from an unusual source: Major-General John Kennedy, who had been Harwood's opposite number in the War Office wrote:

> Harwood's work at the Admiralty had often brought me into touch with him. I admired him very much for his solidity and stolidity, and his comments on Churchill's interventions in Admiralty affairs were always amusing. We had a farewell lunch together and he said he had handed over to his successor at the Admiralty with the words 'The chief feature of my period of office has been a steady and continuous deterioration in the situation.'

More flag plotting

By the spring of 1942 Cunningham had been Commander-in-Chief, Mediterranean for almost three years, and Churchill wanted him to go to Washington, to head the British Admiralty Delegation. When Cunningham heard this, he wrote on 15 March to Pound:

> Your signal re Washington came rather as a surprise, although it had been my intention to write to you at the end of this month ... and tell you that, though I was perfectly fit and ready to go on if desired, if you felt that a change was desirable to make it without considering me. I was perfectly ready to go. As you say, there is now no fleet to go to sea in, but counting heads this is still the largest command. The personnel numbers over 25,000!!![25]

Churchill wanted a fighting admiral to replace Cunningham and his eye fell on Harwood, who had been at the Admiralty just sixteen months. On 1 April 1942 Harwood was offered Cunningham's command and a double-jump promotion from rear-admiral to acting-admiral. He did not feel entirely fit after many stressful months working and sleeping in the ill-ventilated, underground Citadel, but he felt confident about his future and he prepared himself for what could be another long separation from his family. In early April Cunningham departed from Alexandria in great secrecy, leaving Acting-Admiral Sir Henry Pridham-Wippell temporarily in command, while Harwood was relieved by Rear-Admiral H B Rawlings on 8 April 1942 and was able to enjoy a few, rare weeks of leave. He flew out via Lisbon and West Africa using a passport in his mother's maiden name, Ullathorne: though his appointment as Commander-in-Chief, Mediterranean was dated 22 April 1942, he did not take over from Pridham-Wippell until 20 May.

Cunningham had other ideas about how the Mediterranean command should be organised, and when he heard who his relief was he wrote to Pound expressing his doubts. He was concerned that a number of vice-admirals had been passed over and he doubted whether Harwood was the right man for the job: 'I pointed out that his principal job would be working in with the two other CinCs and keeping up the morale of the sailors. An outstanding commander at sea was wasted. I don't think I ever had an answer.' When Cunningham met Pound, 'I had a two hours interview with D P [Dudley Pound] and told him just what I thought about Harwood's appointment. I shook him very badly, I could see that, but it was too late'. Later he met Harwood, telling Edelsten, who was chief of staff in the Mediterranean, 'I gave [Harwood] about 3 hours on the Middle East – he is able enough I think'.[26]

Harwood, accompanied by Joan, took his leave of the Prime Minister at Chequers, she confiding in her diary: 'When Churchill said goodbye to Bobby when he went as C in C Med he told him to hit the Germans hard – I forget exact words – adding "none knows better than you how to do it" and his eyes filled with tears as he said it.'[27]

13
Mediterranean Command

Harwood's appointment as Commander-in-Chief, Mediterranean was a surprise to many. While he had displayed great fighting qualities, tactical insight, and offensive spirit at the Battle of the River Plate, his appointment gave him a double-step promotion to acting-admiral and some doubted whether his experience as ACNS(F) was sufficient to equip him as one of the triumvirate of commanders-in-chief in the Middle East. He would need to win the confidence of his peers in the other two services, to understand their own particular problems, and to convince them of the importance of the Navy's needs. He had tactical skills aplenty, but he would now need to show strategic insight, and to stand up to bullying from the Prime Minister.[1] The auguries were not good.

The lowest ebb

The fortune of the Mediterranean Fleet was at its lowest ebb, and the mastery which Cunningham had won in 1940 and 1941 was now in jeopardy. The Mediterranean Fleet had not conducted a convoy to Malta since Operation MG1 in March 1942, when the three merchant ships which reached Malta had been sunk in harbour before their cargoes could be unloaded. Even this result had only been possible because Admiral Vian, in command of the convoy's escort, had at the Second Battle of Sirte brilliantly held off a superior Italian force led by the battleship *Littorio*.

By the summer of 1942 a rejuvenated Regia Marina consisted of four battleships, nine cruisers, and fifty-five destroyers and torpedo boats, while the Mediterranean Fleet had only four cruisers and fifteen destroyers.[2] There were two British battleships, *Valiant* and *Queen Elizabeth*, at Alexandria, but these had been seriously damaged by an underwater attack by Italian frogmen in December 1941 and still awaited completion of repairs. Without either of these ships Harwood had no proper flagship, and little prospect of going to sea to fight a battle.

Communications by wireless, or radio as it was now coming to be called, had barely improved since the beginning of the war, and were unsuitable to the control of fleets from headquarters ashore. Several hours could still lapse between the transmission of a wireless message and its reception, and longer for a reply to be received. The British did have the advantage that they could read Italian communications, sent using adapted versions of a commercially available Swedish encryption machine C38m,[3] but the Axis powers were also reading British Naval Cypher No 3 with ease.[4]

References are rare, though in a letter written in Harwood's time at the Admiralty, Pound did refer to 'Intelligence X' and to 'Intelligence Y', which were Bletchley Park and the all-important intercept, direction-finding and listening stations of the Y-service,[5] and it is not known for certain whether Harwood as ACNS(F) knew about Ultra, the distribution intelligence gleaned from decoding enemy signals at Bletchley Park, or Station X. Intelligence derived from Ultra was strictly limited to a few officers in each command, but almost certainly as Commander-in-Chief, Mediterranean, Harwood would have been a recipient of Ultra. He was, however, inexperienced in its tactical use.

Relationship with Cairo

A besetting problem for Harwood was that his naval headquarters were at Alexandria, while the land and air headquarters were 100 miles away in Cairo. His predecessor, Cunningham, had insisted on remaining with his fleet instead of basing himself in Cairo, and this had caused persistent friction, not least with Oliver Lyttleton, the Minister of State for the Middle East, who was a close confidant of Churchill; later Lyttleton was replaced by another Churchill confidant, the Australian Richard Casey. Although the geographical boundaries of their respective commands differed, Cunningham, the General Officer C-in-C, Middle East Forces, General Sir Archibald Wavell, and the Air Officer Commander-in-Chief, Middle East, Air Marshal Sir Arthur Longmore had constituted themselves into a formal committee in September 1940 and conducted their affairs satisfactorily. They met together as the Commanders-in-Chief Committee or with the Minister of State as the Middle East Defence Committee.

Cunningham made weekly visits to Cairo, an additional naval chief of staff was appointed in Cairo, and there was adequate naval representation on a joint planning committee (JPC).[6] Relations with the RAF deteriorated when Longmore, who was formerly a Royal Naval Air Service pilot and sympathetic to the Navy's needs, was relieved by Air Marshal Sir Arthur Tedder, 'who firmly believed in the theory that air superiority must be won before close support at sea or on land could be offered, and he was the judge of where and when that support could best be offered'. This inevitably set Tedder at odds with the naval and army commanders. Arrangements in Cairo became further strained when General Sir Claude Auchinleck succeeded Wavell in July 1941:[7] Cunningham found Auchinleck 'undoubtedly a fine man but narrow viewed in comparison with his predecessor'.[8] Cunningham wrote of his last few months as Commander-in-Chief, Mediterranean:[9]

> Politico-strategic problems have occupied much of the C-in-C's time, but as I see it, one of his most difficult jobs is keeping up the morale of the sailors – the seagoing ones – in present circumstances. It is not easy to sit in an armchair and send ships out while knowing the time they are going to have until they return to harbour. If one went oneself it would make all the difference. In the circumstances I should feel happier if someone more experienced and better known to the personnel was to relieve me. Pridham-Wippell will certainly be able to carry on for the time. With my strong staff team behind him he won't go far wrong.

Cunningham's strong staff, which included several officers who would reach flag rank, was led by none other than John Edelsten, Harwood's long-standing friend with whom he had frequently served, and who was now a rear-admiral. As though to forestall problems, even before Harwood's appointment was publicly announced, London declared that it was not practicable for Harwood to function permanently from Cairo, but he would spend considerable time there and would need suitable office accommodation near the army and air headquarters. It was promised that Harwood would discuss 'arrangements for delegation of joint responsibility during his occasional periods at sea'.[10]

201 (Naval Co-operation) Group

Harwood had formed his views of the need for air cover in the Mediterranean in the 1930s. As ACNS(F) in July 1941 he had, in an answer on behalf of the chiefs of staff to a 'prayer' by Churchill about cutting German supply lines to North Africa, discussed the development of German dive-bombing tactics, the need to fit ships with large numbers of short-range anti-aircraft weapons, and how fighter aircraft could be used to break up enemy air attacks into flights of twos and threes. Otherwise, the Navy must accept restrictions on its operations in areas where the enemy could concentrate his dive-bombers:[11]

> The Chiefs of Staff do not consider that the Eastern Mediterranean Fleet [*sic*] can proceed from Alexandria through the Crete–Cyrenaica gap ['bomb alley'] to operate in the Central Mediterranean until they can be adequately supported by long and short range fighters. To do this they are of the opinion that it is necessary to regain the Cyrenaican coast, at least sufficiently far to enable us to operate from the Derna aerodromes. The Chiefs of Staff desire to stress the very urgent need for an adequate force of long and short range fighters to be stationed in the Middle East so as to ensure that a fighter umbrella can always be maintained over the fleet when it operates within dive bomber range.

Cunningham had pressed for an air organisation in the Mediterranean rather like Coastal Command at home, where aircraft came under naval command and were 'fully trained and accustomed to working over the sea, a highly specialised function.'[12] The eventual decision to set up 201 (Naval Co-operation) Group, a force of long-range fighters and bombers drawn from the Fleet Air Arm and the RAF, had been hard won in October 1941, while Harwood was still ACNS(F). The final agreement being reached between the Chief of the Air Staff (CAS) and the Chief of the Naval Staff (CNS) at Chequers: at the first CAS could not even agree that the words 'naval co-operation' should be in its title, and he held out for the right of the Air Officer Commanding-in-Chief, Tedder, to choose to allocate or to withdraw aircraft from the group; CNS retained a single sentence that Fleet Air Arm units might be withdrawn if 'required for service afloat.'[13] Given his views about the indivisibility of air power, Tedder resisted the creation of 201 Group, and in December 1941 Cunningham had had to signal formally requesting that it be brought up to strength, and that any further aircraft sent out from England for naval co-operation purposes 'may now join the group'.[14]

It was fortunate that the commanding officer of the group was a former Royal Naval Air Service 'ace', Air Vice Marshal Leonard Slatter, whom Harwood thought was excellent. 'We work in adjacent houses and have a combined war room. Slatter attends my staff meeting every day ... All our reconnaissances are worked out together. I know his strikes and he knows all about the submarines ... they do not however own any fighters except the Beaufighters, but over that question they act as our agents and get out the air plans for convoys etc', Harwood wrote to Pound in November 1942. Nevertheless there was a hint of dysfunctionality, Harwood continued his letter, 'Cairo [ie Tedder] are jealous and run the heavy bombers and interfere as much as they [can] with 201's sea strikes.' Nevertheless, Harwood thought that there was 'a good balance on the whole by having a 3-service committee in Cairo who decided on the best targets for the day and sent out the signal to co-ordinate 201, Malta and the heavy bombers.'[15]

Nevertheless, the Navy was persistently denied the air cover it needed. On 10 May 1942, just ten days before Harwood became commander-in-chief, the very situation which he had repeatedly warned against came about. The 14th Destroyer Flotilla, consisting of *Jackal*, *Jervis*, *Kipling* and *Lively* under the command of Captain A L Poland, had sailed from Alexandria to intercept an Italian convoy off Benghazi carrying troops, weapons and supplies from Italy to North Africa, Operation MG2. The destroyers were sighted by German reconnaissance planes on the afternoon of 11 May and, as surprise had been lost, the destroyers reversed course. Before dark they were found by two waves of German bombers, which sank *Lively* and *Kipling*, and severely damaged *Jackal*. *Jackal* was abandoned and sunk next morning by *Jervis*, who returned alone to Alexandria laden with 650 survivors. The record shows that the RAF's fighter cover was feeble, the fighters were on the wrong radio frequency and so could not be directed from the ships, and the RAF's claims of enemy aircraft shot down or damaged were exaggerated. Harwood decided that Poland's actions were worthy of the highest traditions of the Navy, that his feat of saving so many of the crews was magnificent, and that Poland had displayed fine seamanship and a complete disregard of danger. Tedder was defensive about the loss of ships and lives, carefully absolving himself in a 'private and personal signal' to CAS, not only of responsibility, but of all knowledge of the operation. Among the excuses he gave was that air cover had not been provided because it would have drawn attention to the operation and that the aircraft were needed on the next day.[16] However, Harwood was hoping to develop a better relationship with the RAF and decided against a board of inquiry into the loss of the three ships.[17]

Sub-surface and in the air

A little-sung success of Harwood's time were his submarines which, when surface convoys could not get through, were partly stripped of their armament and batteries to run desperately needed supplies and equipment to a beleaguered Malta. Submarines also carried out minelaying operations and in Operation Vigorous would be deployed in a moving screen to cover the convoy. Submarines were effective in shelling troop and supply trains running down the coast of southern Italy where the railway ran conveniently close to the sea, and sometimes demolition parties were landed to blow up trains in tunnels. After the daring and very successful attack on Alexandria harbour in 1941 by Italian chariots, two-man torpedoes with detachable warheads, some British submarines were adapted to launch this type of weapon. A successful chariot attack was made on shipping in Palermo and Harwood used chariots to attempt to sink blockships being prepared in Tripoli.

There were three submarine squadrons under Harwood's command in the Mediterranean, the 'Fighting Tenth' based at Malta, the 1st at Alexandria and the 8th at Gibraltar, which included Dutch, Greek and one Yugoslav boat, which operated against Axis shipping. The submarines' main task was to prevent enemy troops and supplies reaching North Africa by sea, and the availability of Malta as a base was key to this task. Enemy convoys to North Africa were frequently known about through signals intelligence, but there was a rule, in order to protect this source of information, that they could not be attacked unless they had been 'spotted' by more conventional means. Within a few days of taking office at the end of May 1942, Harwood pointed out that in the previous six weeks, twenty-six convoys had passed east of Malta, but only nine had been reported by Allied aircraft and only five had been intercepted: 'Even when air reconnaissance [was] available position errors prevent contact being made in about 50% of cases'.[18]

When in early 1942 Axis air attacks became so fierce that submarines in the harbour were forced to submerge by day, only surfacing at night for work to be carried out, and there was also a danger of being trapped inside the harbour by mining, the Fighting Tenth was obliged to leave Malta. In July they were able to return, but for several weeks during their absence Axis supplies flowed freely, enabling Rommel to build up reserves for his Gazala offensive on 26 May. When the submarines returned, the Axis lost between a quarter and a half of its supplies and the German high command would attribute Rommel's defeat at El Alamein and his failure to hold Tunisia to the attrition of his logistics by submarines.

These successes became a cause of friction, and Harwood complained to Tedder about the RAF putting out often inflated and unproven claims for its success, while Harwood's submarines had to wait until they returned from patrols of several weeks and their reports were exhaustively compared with intelligence. This gave the impression that the RAF were sinking all Rommel's supply ships with occasional help from the submarines, while in fact the submarines were sinking more than the air. Harwood welcomed the high honours given to the air for their work, but would very much liked to have seen the captains of the 1st and 10th Squadrons given something for the grand work of their submarines. Harwood told Pound: 'I found rather sadly a tendency to underrate the work done by our submarines. The RAF get their story out the same night. We are not able to put out the submarine story until 2 or 3 weeks after ... and the prevailing idea is that the RAF have sunk all Rommel's supply ships.' Harwood was disgusted to find the RAF producing their own, ie made-up, figures.[19]

Much of the same obfuscation applied to the Fleet Air Arm. RAF publicity about 201 (Naval Co-operation) Group overlooked the fact that Fleet Air Arm squadrons were a significant component, that 826 Naval Air Squadron had played a role in developing 'pathfinder' flare-dropping tactics, or the FAA role in Operation Chocolate, a daring raid behind enemy lines in July 1942, and in the Battle of El Alamein.[20] The same muddying of information applied to the role of 828 and 830 Naval Air Squadrons flying Swordfish and Albacore torpedo-bombers from Malta. The issue came to a head when RAF publicity claimed that Tedder was 'the man who must stop Rommel's supplies' and how 'our bombers battered the convoy and its escorts', referring to an incident on 23 January 1942 when Lieutenant-Commander Frank Hopkins of 826 NAS was awarded the DSO for sinking the 14,000-ton troopship *Victoria*.[21] On this occasion only a handful of bombers from two squadrons of the RAF had found the target, but RAF publicity promptly claimed that they had sunk a *20,000*-ton [*sic*] troopship plus 'two merchant ships, a cruiser and a destroyer damaged and a battleship hit by a torpedo'. From Malta, Captain 'Shrimp' Simpson of the Fighting Tenth protested about this. Simpson was concerned about the effect of misinformation on the British public, that the Navy and the Army would resent these overblown claims, and that such misleading reports would be the basis of post-war policy. Harwood forwarded this to Tedder with the mild-mannered observation that this was 'modern sensational journalese' and suggesting that honest argument should be supported by facts. He concluded, 'Let's discuss it next time we meet.' Tedder scrawled across Harwood's letter 'Worth keeping as an example of naval hysteria when it is criticised.'[22] This was the tenor of relations between the Navy and the RAF.

14
Operation Vigorous

Harwood inherited Operation Vigorous when it was already in an advanced stage of planning, although he must have seen something of its beginnings while still in London. On 20 April Lieutenant-General Sir William Dobbie, governor of Malta, had signalled that the situation on the besieged island was 'so grave that it is my duty to restate it in the clearest possible terms', and that the decision not to run a convoy to Malta in May 'materially reduces our chances of survival not because of any failure of morale or fighting efficiency but because it is impossible to carry on without food and ammunition'. After listing the island's needs, Dobbie concluded his message stating that it was a question of survival, and drastic action was needed now if Malta was to be held.[1] The Defence Committee replied in Churchillian tones that 'you must hold out ... until mid-June'.[2]

In the Indian Ocean, Somerville, who now commanded the British Eastern Fleet, was tasked with Operation Ironclad, the capture of Madagascar. In London the chiefs of staff hoped that 'should the decision be made to make a dart into the Mediterranean and see [a] convoy through in style, Admiral Somerville should proceed with all three aircraft carriers and *Warspite* and ancillaries through the Canal.'[3] A ten-ship convoy for Malta was being prepared, but without reinforcement from the Eastern Fleet, the interim commander-in-chief Pridham-Wippell signalled on 7 May, 'the Commander-in-chief Mediterranean has not, repeat not, sufficient fleet destroyers ... to provide adequate antisubmarine and close antiaircraft escort to such a large convoy.'[4]

The developing plans, drawn up by Edelsten, envisaged the Mediterranean Fleet (Plan Julius) and the Eastern Fleet (Plan Brutus) escorting separate parts of a convoy from the Eastern Mediterranean toward Malta.[5] Meanwhile, Ironclad was taking longer than anticipated, and in London Churchill interfered in planning to object to plans for aircraft carriers and the battleship *Warspite* to cover the convoy from the east: 'considering the capital risk involved ... we must make sure that there is absolutely no other alternative.'[6] So on 15 May complex plans for air support to two Malta convoys, one from the east and one from the west, were formulated and next day a submarine plan was set out.[7] Some thought had been given in London to sending the escort carrier *Archer* to reinforce the Mediterranean Fleet,[8] and in Edelsten's plan, recognising that on D+4 shore-based fighter cover would not be available, he 'hoped to bridge the gap with [ten Grumman] Martlets flying from *Archer*.'

Edelsten's plan highlighted other weaknesses in what was to be called Operation Vigorous. There was a shortage of anti-aircraft guns, particularly of 20mm Oerlikon: there were none at Alexandria; one store-ship had delivered two guns instead of the expected seventeen and another had delivered fourteen guns but without their mountings; twelve guns had been lost in ships sunk in Operation MG2; and the battleship *Queen Elizabeth* had been stripped of all her Oerlikons to arm the anti-aircraft cruiser *Coventry*.[9] Experience during Operation MG1, the March westbound convoy, had shown how much ammunition would be fired off, and so Edelsten estimated that there would only be one-fifteenth of the ammunition needed by the destroyers after they arrived in Malta: 'It must be accepted that they may be delayed at Malta through lack of ammunition ... until further supplies are unloaded from the convoy'. Besides the general shortage of anti-aircraft guns and ammunition, there was only sufficient fuel on the island for one cruiser, *Coventry* and for the nine Hunt-class destroyers.[10]

One of the last signals which Cunningham had sent before relinquishing command of the Mediterranean was about his serious concerns regarding running the next convoy to Malta. He thought that a convoy would be intercepted 'sooner or later but I trust our good fortune in getting away with it is fully realized and that this success will not lead to the idea that the problem is not difficult.' The enemy have had a full dress rehearsal 'and will next time ensure a force of such strength that our light escort forces will not be able to play the same game with comparative impunity.' More destroyers were needed and more fighters in Malta. He noted that while a convoy from

Gibraltar would withdraw away from air attack, a convoy from Alexandria would have to pass twice through 'bomb alley', 'the gauntlet of the narrows between Crete and Cyrenaica.' Losses must be expected and the price would be high.[11]

Harwood takes command

On 20 May, the very day that Harwood took command, Plan Brutus, the participation of the Eastern Fleet in the convoy from Alexandria, was cancelled. Harwood was on his own. Reviewing the forces available to him he signalled Pound on 22 May:[12]

> I accompanied Pridham-Wippell to CsinC meeting in Cairo yesterday ... Experience of [Operation] MG2 which resulted in sinking of 3 and nearly 4 destroyers gives clear indication of what is to be expected ... and of very high efficiency of German aircraft attacks ... Quite frankly I do not see how under present conditions envisaged very serious loss to both convoys and supply can be avoided. The first hurdle is the air attack, and then that of Italian Fleet, and finally the return passage of Mediterranean Fleet. To reduce the threat to reasonable proportion a very heavy and sustained bombing offensive against aerodromes and the Italian Fleet would be required and also the maximum possible defensive air. Such forces I gather are not available ... convoy from the West [ie Gibraltar] has better chance particularly if we can keep present air bias toward East by using Eastern convoy as diversion.

Pound's reply later that night, signed by Harwood's successor as ACNS(F), was that 'it is intended to run both an Eastern convoy from Egypt and a Western convoy from Gibraltar in June.' A few minutes later these operations were named Vigorous and Harpoon.[13]

The strategic situation in the Western Desert was about to change: the Allies, British forces which encompassed men and women from Australia, India, New Zealand, South Africa and the United Kingdom, some Colonial troops, as well as Free French, Czechs, Greeks, Poles and Yugoslavs, were preparing an advance westwards from the Gazala front. However, on 23 May Pound warned Harwood that there were 'very definite indications of large scale enemy operations' and early in the afternoon of 26 May 1942 the armies of the Axis of Italy and Germany, led by Generaloberst Erwin Rommel, 'the Desert Fox', launched a pre-emptive attack. Settled Axis strategy in May was to recapture Tobruk and then to launch Operation Herkules, the invasion of Malta. Over the next few weeks Rommel would roll back the British Army almost to the gates of Cairo, and the loss of airfields along several hundred miles of coast from Tobruk to El Alamein would affect the outcome of Vigorous. Rommel's success changed Axis strategy, causing the German high command to delay landings on Malta.[14]

Meanwhile, Harwood asked that if he could not have the Eastern Fleet carriers and battleships, could he have a reinforcement of cruisers and destroyers? Rear-Admiral Phillip Vian would be in overall command of the escort,[15] but Harwood asked if Rear-Admiral William Tennant would command the Eastern Fleet cruisers.[16] In London it was thought that the land battle in the desert was going well for the British, and on 3 June Pound sent Harwood a personal signal:

> You are no doubt watching the situation in the Western Desert as if things go well and a rapid advance appears probable it might be advantageous to defer the sailing of the Eastern Malta convoy for some days even if it meant having a certain amount of moonlight. At the same time you will realise our anxiety to return the Eastern Fleet ships to their station.[17]

There were other considerations. At Malta, to prevent the port facilities from becoming congested, the Harpoon and Vigorous convoys were wanted on successive days. This suited the air planners: if the convoys were timed to arrive together, both would require long-range Beaufighter and short-range Spitfire protection over two widely dispersed forces on the same day. Instead it was proposed that on D+1 there would be Beaufighters over Vigorous, on D+2 there would be Spitfires over Vigorous and Beaufighters over Harpoon, and on D+3 when the ships of Harpoon were under the guns of Malta, there would be Beaufighters and Spitfires over Vigorous. There was a further complication: Harpoon could not sail any earlier and it could be delayed without missing the short, moonless nights of mid-June, so London gave Harwood further discretion to adjust the date of sailing of Vigorous.[18] London also acknowledged the risks: it was vital to the continued resistance of Malta that 'a high proportion the ships should get through', but 'because of our weakness in surface forces and in long range air striking forces to pass these convoys is extremely hazardous and we have the best reasons for believing that the enemy know about them and intend to stop them at all costs.'[19]

Meanwhile, with Harwood now firmly in command, the final plan emerged on 4 June in a 'most secret and personal' signal from the Commanders-in-Chief, Middle East in Cairo to the chiefs of staff in London. A diversionary convoy of four ships would sail forty-eight hours before Vigorous, would turn back after dark and enter Tobruk. Harwood hoped this would provoke the Regia Marina into sailing and 'run it out of fuel before the main convoy arrives'. He recognised that any plan needed air cover and that there was a growing risk that the landing grounds in North Africa might be overrun by an Axis advance: in this case, it would be essential to delay Vigorous 'although we could still sail part of it as a diversion to assist Harpoon.' If Harpoon were sailed and failed to arrive, it would then be necessary for the chiefs of staff in London 'to balance the probable loss of a substantial part of both the Mediterranean and Eastern [*sic*] Fleets against the possible improvement of the situation in Malta, and to say whether Vigorous should sail independently'. However, should the war situation in the Western Desert improve 'say within the next ten days as to deny the enemy the use of the Derna and Martuba airfields [west of Tobruk], we intend to delay Vigorous for a few days until this situation can be exploited but would still sail diversionary convoy to assist Harpoon'.[20] The response from London on 7 June was unequivocal:[21]

1. Malta cannot be allowed to surrender owing to lack of supplies without an effort being made to run the Eastern convoy.
2. An attempt must therefore be made to run the Eastern convoy.
3. It is accepted that heavy losses may be incurred. The day on which the convoy sails must be left to discretion of C in C Mediterranean as he will have better information regarding the military and air situation, the movements of enemy surface forces and the weather prospects than we have.

Operation Vigorous – the execution[22]

Harwood had reduced Vigorous to its principles. He intended Vigorous to arrive at Malta on 16 June, which would force the enemy to disperse his air and surface forces, while requiring minimum dispersion of friendly air assets. The Italians must either divide their surface forces to attack both convoys, Harpoon and Vigorous, or leave one convoy not attacked. Significantly, he added, 'Tedder agrees'.[23] Five days later he issued his executive order: 'Carry out Operation Vigorous ... Day One 12th June repeat 12th June'.[24]

Without capital ships and without carriers to provide the convoy's organic fighter protection, the surface forces assembled from the rump of the Mediterranean Fleet and elements of the Eastern Fleet comprised just eight cruisers, twenty-six destroyers, and a number of minor warships. Among the later was the elderly former battleship *Centurion*, a veteran of the Battle of Jutland, who between the wars had been converted to a wireless-controlled target ship: disguised as a Home Fleet battleship and using *Duke of York*'s call sign, she had little military value.[25]

A novel feature of Harwood's plan was that nine submarines should form a screen to the north of the convoy's route, moving westwards as the convoy steamed towards Malta.[26] Also, a series of raids by special forces was planned on Axis airbases in Cyrenaica and on Crete, in particular, where Junkers 88 twin-engined bombers were thought to operate.[27] However, there was not the 'very heavy and sustained bombing offensive against aerodromes and the Italian Fleet' Harwood had asked for, though six Liberator heavy bombers en route to India had been retained temporarily in Egypt to reinforce 'the long range air striking force'. Tedder came from Cairo to join Harwood at the headquarters of 201 (Naval Co-operation) Group in order to conduct the air movements.

On 10 June when the Commanders-in-Chief, Middle East jointly approved that Vigorous should go ahead, the Germans were about to win a decisive advantage at the Battle of Bir Hakeim, begin to encircle Tobruk and threaten the vital airfields at Sidi Barrani.[28]

Vigorous: 11–14 June

The four merchant ships of Convoy MW11C left Port Said on 11 June, escorted by *Coventry* and seven Hunt-class destroyers: they were to go west as far as the meridian of Tobruk, turn back at night, and meet the main convoy. This was a diversionary convoy which, it was hoped, would bring the enemy fleet south prematurely. The main body of seven ships, Convoys MW11A and MW11B, which had been loaded at different ports before gathering at Haifa and Port Said, sailed to rendezvous off Alexandria on 13 June, and Vian and his cruisers and destroyers sailed that evening to overtake the merchantmen off Tobruk. Even as the convoys and escorts sailed, the strategic situation in the Western Desert was collapsing, and Rommel's tanks were infesting the airfields which the RAF had planned to use. Harwood spelled out the air cover which would be lost on D+3 and D+4 of Vigorous if Sidi Barrani, east of Tobruk were overrun.[29]

Enemy aircraft quickly found the main convoy and damaged one ship, which was sent into Tobruk, another did not have the necessary speed (13 knots) and was sent back to Alexandria, but she was found and sunk by about forty German bombers. Also, on the evening of 13 June several MTBs, under tow of merchant ships, were damaged by the weather, the tows had to be slipped, and ***MTB 259*** was lost, though the remainder reached Alexandria.

On 12/13 June the Allied army lost a tank battle and some 200 tanks, and Rommel's army began to roll eastwards. Casey described it as 'a bad day.'[30]

At sea, throughout the night of 13/14 June enemy aircraft dropped flares continuously. Daylight came at 04:30 when fighters from the Western Desert broke up a strong formation of enemy bombers. A lull came in the fighting, but between 16:30 and 21:15 when the ships were well inside 'bomb alley', the gap between Cyrenaica and Crete, and outside the range of friendly fighters based in Egypt, some seventy aircraft attacked in waves of a dozen or so at a time: one merchantman was sunk and another damaged by bombs. But by 23:15 Vian learned that two Italian battleships and four cruisers had left Taranto and on present course would intercept him at 07:00 the next morning. During his last convoy, MG1, in March which had led to the Second Battle of Sirte, and in bad weather and long nights, Vian had held off an Italian battleship with skilful use of smokescreens and the threat of torpedo attack, but the fair weather and long days of June now favoured the

Italians and at 23:15 Vian asked Harwood by signal: 'Do you wish me to retire? Request immediate reply.'[31]

Vigorous: 15 June

An 'immediate reply' took over an hour to be sent: at 00:21 Harwood told Vian, 'Turn back along same track at 02:00 Beaufighters arranged', and ten minutes later Harwood sent 'Delay turn till 03:00'.[32] Unfortunately, this gave the Italian MTBs their chance and while the convoy was completing this difficult manoeuvre in the dark, the cruiser *Newcastle* and the destroyer *Hasty* were torpedoed.

At 03:25 Harwood signalled 'Torpedo bombing Wellingtons attacking during the night and Liberators and Beauforts about 0930/15. If attacks are successful intend forwarding convoy for Malta.'[33] At dawn on 15 June the Italian fleet, consisting of their two newest battleships, *Vittorio Veneto* and *Littorio*, two heavy and two light cruisers and about a dozen destroyers, was some 200 miles northwest of Vian. By 05:25 the risk of entering 'bomb alley' was judged greater than interception by the Italian fleet and Vian was ordered to turn to the northwestward. At 07:05 Harwood ordered, 'when over 100 miles from coast resume course for Malta', and the convoy again turned westwards. Harwood told Vian: 'Avoid contact until aircraft have attacked which should be by 10:30. If air attack fails every effort must be made to get convoy through to Malta by adopting an offensive attitude. Should this fail and convoy cornered it is to be sacrificed and you are to extricate your forces proceeding either to the east or to the west'.[34]

Between 09:00 and 10:00 the Italian fleet ran into Harwood's submarine lines, but just as the Italians made large alterations of course to avoid being bombed by the Liberator bombers and Beaufort torpedo-bombers. Consequently, only two submarines achieved firing solutions, but without success. At about the same time, Malta-based torpedo-bombers attacked the enemy and hit and disabled the heavy cruiser *Trento*.

With the Italian battleships only 150 miles away and still heading southwards, at 09:40 Harwood ordered Vian to turn east for the second time. When at 11:15 the airmen of the Liberators and Beauforts had returned to base where they made exaggerated claims for their success, at 11:51 Harwood ordered the convoy: 'Resume course for Malta. Beauforts claim torpedo hits on both battleships … a/c out of touch with enemy battlefleet at present. Believed one 8 inch cruiser also damaged and ships retired to northward. Further Beaufort attack may take place about 1430 if enemy is located.' He added that long-range Beaufighter protection would cease at 12:30 'for today owing to losses.'[35] Aerial reconnaissance, which had been intermittent and was barely more reliable than the bombers' claims, also ceased.[36]

As the fuel, ammunition and damage situation in Vian's force was not known, Harwood signalled at 12:45: 'I must leave the decision to you whether to comply with my 0705/15 or whether to again retire with hope of carrying out night destroyer attack if enemy stand on.' Vian received this message at 14:20 by which time the cruiser ***Birmingham***, ***Centurion***, and the destroyer ***Airedale*** had suffered severely in dive-bombing attacks, and another merchant ship, which could not keep up, was detached from the convoy, reducing its numbers from the original eleven to six.

When a reconnaissance aircraft found the Italians again at 15:15 they were only about 100 miles from the convoy, but at 16:05 the shadowing aircraft reported that they had turned for Taranto. At 16:15 Harwood signalled: 'Now is a golden opportunity to get convoy to Malta. Have Hunts [the destroyers], *Coventry* minesweepers and corvettes enough fuel and ammunition for one-way trip? If so, I would like to turn convoy now, cruisers and destroyers parting company after dark and returning to Alexandria.' Two hours later, having had no reply from Vian, Harwood modified his plan, intending to send to Malta only the four fastest merchant ships and adding the cruiser *Arethusa* and two destroyers to the escort. However, Harwood's first signal had arrived during a heavy air attack which started at 17.20: Vian later commented 'in the conditions existing at the time a general reversal of course was out of the question'. For about two hours some forty German and Italian aircraft carried out synchronised high-level and shallow dive-bombing and torpedo attacks, on a scale rather larger than the RAF had been able to stage earlier that morning on the Italian fleet. Fortunately, only the Australian destroyer ***Nestor*** was seriously damaged.

At 18:42 Vian answered Harwood's first signal reporting that his ships had less than 30 per cent of ammunition left and this was being used fast. Vian considered the ammunition to be insufficient for the passage to Malta 'and request your [Harwood's] decision'. This crossed with the second signal, and at 20:53 Harwood ordered Vian 'Return to Alexandria with your whole force.'

The balance sheet

While returning to Alexandria, on 16 June the cruiser *Hermione* was torpedoed by a U-boat, and the damaged *Nestor* had to be scuttled. Apart from the failure to revictual Malta (only two merchant ships of Harpoon made Grand Harbour), the Mediterranean Fleet lost a cruiser, three destroyers and two merchant ships, and three other cruisers; *Centurion*, a corvette and two merchant ships had been damaged. Considering that Vian's force and the convoy had been under incessant air attack for hours at a time, and on three occasions by scores of aircraft, it is surprising that the losses were not greater.

The Italians lost the cruiser *Trento*, the *coup de grâce* delivered by a British submarine, and the battleship *Littorio* had been slightly damaged by a Malta-based Wellington which scored a torpedo hit as she approached Taranto: otherwise, the Italian fleet returned unscathed. Vian's ships had shot down a score of the two hundred aircraft which attacked them, and the RAF suffered considerable losses while shooting down other enemy aircraft. By contrast, the SAS raid on the Axis airbase at Heraklion destroyed twenty-two aircraft including seventeen serviceable Ju 88s and blew up an ammunition store.[37]

Nevertheless, the enemy's success was undeniable: the Vigorous convoy had failed to arrive in Malta, and no further convoys would sail from Egypt to Alexandria until November 1942. The primary cause of the failure was the deteriorating strategic situation in the Western Desert, for while the convoy was at sea fighting westwards, ashore the British Army was retreating eastwards and losing desert airfields. Secondly, aerial reconnaissance over the Eastern Mediterranean was deficient, and for long periods Harwood was without adequate information as to enemy whereabouts. Thirdly, in the words of Harwood's report, 'our air striking force had nothing like the weight required to stop a fast and powerful enemy force, and in no way compensated for our lack of heavy ships'.

Tedder's excuses

With enemy aircraft established in strength on both flanks of the convoy route, success or failure had been decided in the air. There had already been a sharp exchange between Pound, the Prime Minister, and Air Chief Marshal Sir Charles Portal, the Chief of the Air Staff (CAS), when, following the loss of three destroyers in mid-May, Pound had suggested that, unless the RAF could provide the same degree of skill as the Luftwaffe, 'the war in narrow waters such as the ... Mediterranean ... is going to continue to be a very one sided affair.'[38] Pound had also raised the organisation and training of the air force for naval operations in the chiefs of staff committee, and expressed surprise that the RAF was putting forward proposals for aircraft production without consulting the Navy.[39]

Now, in June 1942, even before the ships had returned to Alexandria, Tedder in a self-exculpatory, three-page signal to Portal, the Chief of the Air Staff, hastened to put his interpretation of Vigorous to his chief. Tedder adopted an ambivalent position: he claimed success for the air attacks on the Italian fleet, but blamed the lack of effect on the bombs, for not being big enough (the USAAF Liberators could not carry bombs larger than 500lb), and he blamed the torpedoes saying 'we are used to disappointment from our torpedoes'. This produced a polite but sharp exchange between Pound and Portal: Pound pointed out how successful a weapon the torpedo and its Duplex pistol was in naval hands, and concluded that Tedder's remark was a 'damaging indictment' of organisation and training in the RAF and its inability to use the torpedo properly. After an inquiry, Portal agreed at the end of August that 'a good deal' needed to be done to improve the RAF's methods and he asked for the Navy's help: it was not until long after Vigorous that there was any improvement in the RAF's use of aerial torpedoes and the Duplex pistol.

Tedder's other contradiction was that while he claimed his air plan had 'proved absolutely sound' and had located the Italian fleet, his aircraft had in fact lost the Italians on the night of 14 June and a radar search had failed to find the enemy or Vian's ships the next morning.

Tedder blamed 'less experienced individuals' among his own people, and he blamed Vian for 'a complete lack of information from our ships ... [Harwood] himself was gravely handicapped and blindfolded. Our fighters were completely ignorant of the position [and] movement of the convoy once it had departed from original programme'.[40]

This was the pot calling the kettle black, as extracts from 201 (Naval Co-operation) Group's own analysis showed:[41]

> Throughout the night the CinC Medn had a most difficult task deciding what action to take with the convoy on account of the meagre information provided by air reports ...
>
> The shortage of reconnaissance aircraft for daylight patrols was very evident ... no aircraft were left for shadowing.
>
> We were unable to keep the enemy under continuous observation once they were at sea owing to the long distance ... reports must be sent every 30 minutes whilst the aircraft is in touch otherwise the CinC of the Naval Forces has insufficient information on which to make his decisions ... striking forces and shadowers should report at once any results observed from attacks. This is of the greatest importance to CinC and was not done in this operation. Very few of the promised ASV [radar-fitted] Wellingtons arrived and those that did arrived so late that they could not be tested or got into operational condition, in consequence only 4 out of the seven available aircraft managed to operate. This failure had a very big bearing on the operation and caused our search to miss the enemy ...

Significantly, Tedder did not make any excuse that Rommel's advance into Libya had deprived the RAF of the use of advanced airfields, or that the land battle had made heavy, competing demands on his aircraft, or that his fighters had flown many sorties to the limit of their endurance and thus their time over the convoy had been very short. However, it is hard to avoid the conclusion that Tedder and the RAF bore a large measure of the responsibility for the failure to relieve the siege of Malta in June 1942.

The blame game

It is too easy to say that Vigorous, and to a lesser extent Harpoon, failed because one man or another failed to do something or did it poorly.[42] Nevertheless, many have blamed Harwood for alleged faults during the mid-June convoy, and from these assertions have derived opinion about his conduct and character. Correlli Barnett's analysis that Harwood lacked the same 'sheer ruthless powers of leadership and the certainty of mind' of Cunningham, his predecessor, may be true,[43] but Richard Woodman has repeated Barnett's charge that Harwood dithered,[44] while Max Hastings has reduced this analysis to one unfair, journalistic sound-bite, dismissing Harwood as 'a notoriously stupid officer', a superficial judgement which is not supported by the facts surrounding Vigorous or by Harwood's record.[45]

This is to see Vigorous out of context, for Harwood was not criticised at the time. He, Pridham-Wippell and Cunningham had repeatedly warned of the risks and consequences before Vigorous was set in motion, and Harwood had repeated these warnings even as the military situation in the Western Desert was collapsing in early June. The risks were accepted by the Commanders-in-Chief, Middle East and by the chiefs of staff in London. Vigorous had strategic value if only as a diversion to split the Italian fleet and the Axis air forces and to divert them from an attack on the Harpoon convoy. It also distracted the Axis air forces from the land battle in North Africa. As the complex sea–land–air battle was played out in the Mediterranean and on the North African shore during June 1942, Axis strategy was put out of kilter by Rommel's unexpectedly easy victory over the British at the Gazala lines in the Western Desert. This led to a postponement of Herkules, the planned invasion of Malta, while Rommel rushed at Egypt. As it was, scores of airfields were lost, and the Allies' air plan, Tedder's plan, failed because his 'indivisible' air force was unable to support a simultaneous battle on two fronts, over the land and the sea. Equally, Rommel might have advanced further and sooner had his air support not been diverted to attack the convoys.

At sea, Vian's force was larger than that which had covered the March convoy, but the Italian fleet was larger again. Arguably too, the Regia Marina had evolved faster than the Royal Navy and by mid-1942 was on a par in skills with or even superior to its enemy.

Reconnaissance was significantly improved since the spring, air strikes were conducted at greater range, strength and determination, and sea–air co-operation was better – better certainly than the Allies.[46] Curiously, although the German and Italian air attacks were fearsome, losses of escorts and to the convoy were not as great as had been expected. Nevertheless, in a complex sea–air battle drawn out over several days and spread across the Eastern Mediterranean, Operation Vigorous, the larger of the two convoys, had been defeated, and of the seventeen merchant ships which sailed from east and west, only two arrived. The Regia Marina rightly claimed the mid-June convoy battles, *Battaglia di mezzo giugno*, as a victory.

A particular charge subsequently levied against Harwood by Barnett and even by O'Hara, whose analysis is considerably more sympathetic, concerns the reversals of course which he ordered. There were a similar number of changes of course by the Harpoon convoy, but Harpoon had more sea-room and more choices of headings to steer and, as Cunningham had pointed out, the option of steering towards the Tunisian coast and away from the air threat. There were no such options for Vigorous, which in order to keep away from enemy-held airfields to the north and south could only steer west or east. Once it had passed 'bomb alley', Harwood did well in ordering the convoy westwards while keeping it out of range of the Italian fleet. Also, Harpoon benefited from the protection provided by two aircraft carriers, even if these were old and small and able to fly at most only six Sea Hurricanes and four Fulmars. Over Harpoon, 'The results achieved by the small force of naval fighters [were] most outstanding' – made more remarkable because the carriers, *Argus* and *Eagle*, lacked modern fighter-direction systems.[47] Churchill himself had denied the loan of Eastern Fleet carriers to Vigorous, and for many hours there were no land-based fighters over Vigorous.

As Cunningham had pointed out, the enemy had had a dress rehearsal and was unlikely to make the same mistakes as in Operation MG1 and the Second Battle of Sirte, while the fair weather and the long days of midsummer favoured the Italians, and the British forces allocated to Vigorous were inadequate. But having so protested, Harwood had no option but to make the effort. He did not have the luck of his predecessor.

Vian's health

A curious feature of Vigorous was Vian's irresolution. He had already succeeded once against a superior Italian force and he had a detailed plan for meeting them again: the escort would divide into two large components, a striking force and a close escort for the convoy. The convoy would turn south and the striking force would move out in divisions to attack the enemy's main body. Vian was skilled, courageous and experienced, and a strong leader with a reputation for acting upon his initiative, yet twice during the battle for Vigorous he showed indecision, when he asked Harwood on 14 June 'Do you wish me to retire?' with its plaintive coda 'Request immediate reply', and again next day when, low on ammunition, he had asked for Harwood's decision whether he should press on towards Malta, even after having been told by Harwood that he had a golden opportunity to pass his convoy through to Malta.[48]

Later, Vian told the official historian that he lacked confidence in the plan for Vigorous, and lacked confidence in Harwood and in Harwood's ability to conduct the plan, which conduced to his own lack of confidence and 'its fatal corollary irresolution'. Vian added that no flag officer would ever have thought of not going through with a direct operational order from Cunningham, but that Cunningham would never have issued an order not capable of achievement with the forces allocated.[49]

Vigorous, Vian told Roskill in 1954:[50]

> Could have been a splendid operation had a battleship covering force been provided. Once Harwood accepted a weak, unescorted, air striking force as a substitute, we were sunk – or such was my opinion. This because it was not a practical proposition, bearing in mind that most cruisers and destroyers of the force had dual purpose guns, to fight a fleet action from dawn to dusk in a June day with these ships with the ammunition remaining after passage to the battle area without fighter escort. And save enough for the return passage. In the event, of course, neither reconnaissance nor striking force functioned; in such circumstances the very greatest confidence in the C-in-C would have been needed for me to have pressed on to the inevitable early encounter with the Italians.

Discussing Vigorous in 1956 Cunningham told Roskill:[51]

> I always knew that a mess had been made over that convoy from the east ... I never knew what a terrible mess it was. Why on earth didn't Harwood tell Vian to push right on instead of going backwards and forwards in bomb alley? In spite of the failure of the air striking force Vian with his seven cruisers could have held off the Italian Fleet and nothing worse could have happened than did happen. But as I read it Vian weakened a bit and did not have a real driving force behind him. I hope he would never have asked me what he was to do – he never did and always did himself precisely as I would have wished.

Cunningham discussed Vigorous with Vian and with Vian's former flag captain, Captain Guy Grantham. 'Vian,' wrote Cunningham, 'is afraid that too much odium is attached to Harwood over the mishandling [of Vigorous] and considers that some should sit on him.' Grantham was more pointed, telling Cunningham that 'the preparations, reconnaissance, striking force, timing etc. were badly arranged and that Vian was not fully informed of them'. Grantham blamed the RAF:

> Reconnaissance was quite hopeless. The Italian Fleet was sighted and then lost for long periods. The night before they turned back they had no idea where the Italian fleet was or Vian might have attacked it by night with all his light forces. The air striking force was just futile and made no impression on the Italian fleet as far as their movements were concerned.

Grantham was quite definite that had Harwood left them alone they would have gone straight on, and this was Cunningham's judgement too. Vian was less sure, reminding his old chief that, low on ammunition, they would have had fourteen hours of daylight in which to keep off the Italian fleet. Nevertheless, Cunningham wondered why Harwood had not ordered Vian to press on.[52]

Yet Harwood had given Vian discretion to press on, and he had told him that there was a golden opportunity to make for Malta with his fastest ships. The question must be, why did Vian, 'an officer possessing unusual qualities of leadership, determination, readiness to accept responsibility, physical courage and endurance',[53] not seize the opportunity as he had done on so many other occasions? A possible explanation for Vian's uncharacteristic behaviour only emerged in 2009: Vian was already showing signs of fatigue and he was ill. At Gibraltar in late 1942, a Surgeon Lieutenant Paul Houghton was consulted in secrecy by Vian, who was run-down and had been relieved of the command of his cruiser squadron. Houghton's examination revealed a large subcutaneous cyst under matted hair, which Vian had been hiding for some weeks and which had become infected. In Houghton's opinion, the cyst was life-threatening and was affecting both Vian's concentration and his decision-making. Houghton performed emergency surgery, dressed the wound, and, sworn to secrecy, made the admiral his private patient. Vian did not receive another appointment until New Year 1943, after he had recovered from a stay in the Royal Naval Hospital, Haslar, and a bout of malaria.[54]

On further reflection, Vian in his memoirs in 1960 thought that a more resolute commander than himself might have held on regardless, and that 'something might have got through'. However, he made no mention of his health, of cysts or of malaria, though he did quote the farewell signal in which Harwood noted that Vian's relief was solely due to the Admiralty's desire 'that you should not break down by unhealthy lack of rest ... and that after a rest your services may again be available.'[55]

Harwood's own analysis was that the failure to get the convoy through to Malta was the shortage of ammunition after two days of continuous air attack, rather than the presence of enemy surface forces. Ever the optimist, he told Pound:[56]

> Vigorous ... failed but it had many valuable points. Tedder came down and stayed with me for it and we worked and planned together and between us we did get the American Liberators, 2 lots of Beauforts and the submarines to attack more or less together. The results signalled were most hopeful and I thought for a bit we should have a clear run on, but it turned out the claims were false, the

> torpedo hits were presumably near misses with the Duplex pistols and the American Liberators did get some hits but did not do any harm, all they had were small bombs.

Pound, when he had read all the reports, decided that it was small comfort that Tedder had been induced to come down and co-operate with Harwood at his headquarters, but he wrote to A V Alexander, the First Lord, on 2 January 1943, 'This convoy had to be turned back owing to the opposition it encountered, but Admiral Harwood was in no way to blame.'

15
Withdrawal from Alexandria

Even while *Vigorous* was being defeated at sea, the Allied army was in retreat, falling back on its lines before the Delta. Ever since Rommel had opened an offensive at the end of May 1942, he had enjoyed a string of successes as he closed in on Tobruk. On 17 June all British merchant vessels were ordered to leave the port, and three days later Rommel's tanks broke through, reaching the harbour before demolitions were complete and some small ships had not sailed.

Shock news for Churchill

Churchill received this news on the morning of 21 June while he was at a meeting in Washington with President Roosevelt:[1]

> I went to see the President in his study. General Ismay came with me. Presently a telegram was put into the President's hands. He passed it to me without a word. It said, 'Tobruk has surrendered, with twenty-five thousand [actually 33,000] men taken prisoners'. This was so surprising that I could not believe it. I therefore asked Ismay to inquire of London by telephone. In few minutes he brought the following message, which had just arrived from Admiral Harwood at Alexandria: 'Tobruk has fallen, and situation deteriorated so much that there is possibility of heavy air attack on Alexandria in near future, and in view of approaching full moon period I am sending all Eastern fleet units south of the canal to await events. I hope to get HMS *Queen Elizabeth* out of dock towards the end of this week'. This was one of the heaviest blows I can recall during the war.

In England, Pound, the First Sea Lord, was warned to prepare for the loss of the Mediterranean Fleet's base at Alexandria, and in Egypt

Harwood put in hand plans, which had been drafted under Cunningham when he was commander-in-chief in April 1941, to move the fleet and to block the Suez Canal. Plans, the official historian wrote, which Cunningham 'had prepared to face the dire consequences of defeat on land, but this time the threat was far more serious'.

Churchill wrote to General Auchinleck, Commander-in-Chief, Middle East Forces, on 24 June:

> Please tell Harwood that I am rather worried about reports of undue despondency and alarm in Alexandria and the Navy hastening to evacuate to the Red Sea. Although various precautionary moves may be taken and *Queen Elizabeth* should be got out at the earliest, I trust a firm confident attitude will be maintained. The President's information from Rome is that Rommel expects to be delayed three or four weeks before he can mount a heavy attack on the Mersa Matruh position.[2]

Churchill was too late: the British Army had already retreated beyond Mersa Matruh, back towards the Delta, leaving the Egyptian frontier airfields to be occupied by the Germans and Alexandria in range of fighter-escorted bombers. Harwood's view was that by falling back from Mersa Matruh, Auchinleck had saved Egypt, remarking: 'somebody has to have 200 miles of waterless desert and it isn't going to be me!' He ordered the Army to fall back and not to try to stand at any of the prepared defences, only one division being used to fight a rear-guard action at Mersa Matruh and:

> Rommel was on it like a knife. It had colossal casualties and only just extricated its remnants. A very good example of what might have happened had other orders been given. At the Delta end everything was done to re-inforce the already existing defence line at El Alamein while Rommel advanced, largely on British stores and petrol that he had captured in Tobruk, but, as Auchinleck had foreseen, his lines of communication were so long and vulnerable that he could no longer press his offensive and the line held.[3]

An 'interesting' position

However, Harwood's position was unenviable: he called it 'interesting'. Alexandria was the main base of his fleet, or what was left of it: three cruisers and five destroyers. Alexandria also had all the stores and the technical schools for both the Mediterranean and the Eastern fleets, and housed a vital intelligence organisation, and the battleship *Queen Elizabeth* was still in dry-dock and in an unseaworthy condition. The Army recognised that the fleet base lay nearest the enemy,[4] and estimated that if the line at Alamein broke, Rommel would be at Alexandria in two days. 'Like so many difficult problems this was best solved by a principle,' said Harwood:

> The principle I took was that when the enemy could send over fighter-escorted divebombers ... we must evacuate the fleet, its stores, and in particular the intelligence organisation, to the Canal Zone and Palestine. Even then, the Germans nearly did for us on the night before the fleet and store ships sailed. The Germans mined the entrances but thanks to the admirable mine-spotting organisation and the minesweeping force they all got out including, very shortly afterwards, the *Queen Elizabeth*.[5]

So, on 27 June Harwood sent the battleship *Queen Elizabeth* to Port Sudan. The destroyer depot ship *Woolwich*, the fleet repair ship *Resource* and six destroyers were also sent south through the Canal, and the rest of the fleet was divided between Haifa in Palestine, Port Said and Beirut.[6] On the morning of 29 June Rommel reached the uncompleted British lines of defence at El Alamein, only sixty miles from Alexandria, where the sound of gunfire could be heard at night.

The President's information from Rome was wrong: far from needing three to four weeks to mount an attack on Mersa Matruh, with only a little more effort and resource, German tanks could break through into the Delta, and Alexandria, the most westerly of British bases, would be the first to fall. Signals intelligence told the British that Rommel intended to attack on 30 June. That day the heavily escorted and very valuable submarine depot ship *Medway*, which was being redeployed to Beirut to support the 1st Submarine Flotilla, was sunk by a U-boat off Port Said.

Operation Discretion

The 'worst possible case' scenario of British forces being driven out of the Delta had been considered a year before by the chiefs of staff committee under the pseudonym of 'WPC'.[7] Cunningham's plan, Operation Discretion, had assumed three weeks' warning, but now Harwood had just two days in which to save his fleet. He was troubled by the risks of leaving the decision until too late, and there was a second plan, Operation Hornblower, to use merchant ships to block the harbour and to demolish harbour installations. Harwood also had to consider what to do about the French Admiral Godfroy and his ships. The consul-general warned of the distressing effect on the British population of Cairo and Alexandria, and there was the disorganisation and loss of morale within the fleet to be considered. On the other hand it was unthinkable that the dockyard, with its equipment and stores, and many damaged warships should be allowed to fall into enemy hands. Also, there was the unpleasant feeling that '500 persons would have had to evacuate by roads, or rather road, which [were] chocked up with retreating soldiers'.[8] Harwood made the difficult decision and chose to put Discretion into effect.

Over the period 29 June to 1 July Harwood's staff left by rail for Port Said, the administrative staff to set up offices in the Marina Savoy Hotel and the operational staff to Villa Laurens to be near the makeshift headquarters of 201 (Naval Co-operation Group). The WRNS were evacuated further away, to Ismailia, in something of a party atmosphere.[9] The staff remained at short notice to move again, with much gear packed into lorries. All secret documents and papers not considered essential were destroyed. Preparations were also made for Hornblower, the demolition of facilities in Alexandria harbour, although explosives were not put into position so that British intentions should not be known to the Egyptians. Four damaged ships were chosen as blockships, eight retained to load naval, victualling, and armament stores, and all other ships in Alexandria were ordered to raise steam and leave.[10] Inevitably, there was confusion and there were mistakes. Two motor-torpedo boats were destroyed on the slips, and the White Ensign was still flying over the deserted naval camp at Sidi Bishr when looters entered. Harwood recalled:[11]

> It was a very difficult decision to take whether to leave Alexandria or not. Cunningham had got out a plan for the orderly withdrawal from Alex which was supposed to be done in three weeks. It had no circulation so as to avoid alarm and despondency and so when it was opened, we only had 48 hours to do three weeks work in. This caused great confusion and lots of bad things happened such as destroying pistons and smashing up of two MTBs which were on the slips.
>
> The real trouble came in a stupid way. I had decided to get out of Alexandria all the training classes and sent them off with *Scott* [a survey ship] to the Cape, there to form the balance into a defence force. The Drafting Officer, so as to speed up the training party, tried to hurry them up by saying Rommel was at the gates and they must hurry. This was of course, disastrous as it got passed far and wide and everybody who heard it believed it. The prisoners in the detention quarters were released for the defence of Dukeila aerodrome and so on ...
>
> I shifted my headquarters into the 201 Naval Co-operation Group and organised the operational staff there. This carried us out over the immediate issue and finally when all my party had thinned out I moved to Ismailia. This had many advantages as it put me nearer the Fleet, close to the many canal area activities and also closer to Cairo. In many ways though I wish we had not left here [Alexandria]. It is the story of being wise after one knows the answer. We had the guidance of Singapore to help us which clearly indicated not to leave it too late.

In Cairo there was a run on the banks, and the Director of Military Intelligence reported the smoke from the chimney of the British headquarters in Cairo as documents were burned, and 'bits of charred paper floating past.'[12] Foreign diplomatic posts and civilian organisations, including 1,500 non-essential personnel, were moved out and on 1 July the British minister burned his papers. Arrangements were made to move millions of pounds worth of gold from the Bank of Egypt.[13]

Rommel attacks

It was no idle threat: on 30 June Rommel considered whether to take Alexandria first or to mask Alexandria and drive direct to Cairo. Possession of El Daba airfield put the German bombers within ninety miles of the naval base. Only on 1 July did the British learn from further signals intelligence that the German tanks were temporarily stranded for lack of fuel, and that a sandstorm had delayed the move of the Luftwaffe to advanced bases. Meanwhile, intelligence reported that the Regia Marina was moving ships forward to bases in the Aegean and that troop convoys from Italy to Alexandria were being prepared, Mussolini arrived to lead the Axis parade into Cairo, and the Panzer army had ordered 10,000 copies of maps of the chief Egyptian cities.

On 2 and 3 July Rommel renewed his onslaught, while on 2 July Harwood's operational staff transferred by air and road to Ismailia, chosen for its closeness to and communications with general headquarters in Cairo, ships at Port Said, and 201 (Naval Co-operation) Group, which in its turn had been evacuated to Abu Sweir about twelve miles away. Harwood's intelligence staff were established at Port Said with 'C-in-C's office records of a most secret nature'.[14] On 3 July the Luftwaffe dropped mines in the Canal. It was not until 4 July that Rommel admitted that he must go onto the defensive for two weeks to allow for his logistics to catch up with his rapid advance, and it was the next day before signals intelligence of this German decision reached British authorities in the Middle East.[15] After several weeks of fierce fighting and continuous success, Rommel was finally held at El Alamein.

Harwood returned his headquarters to Alexandria on 8 August, while 201 (Naval Co-operation) Group headquarters did not return until 14 September. Only with hindsight, and the British victory at El Alamein at the end of October 1942, was the evacuation made to seem premature and unnecessary. Most of the naval stores were recovered, including many spare torpedoes from the sunken depot ship *Medway*: Hornblower had not been put fully into effect. General Bernard Montgomery, who took command of the Eighth Army on 13 August 1942, was especially critical, but he conveniently forgot that while it was not him but Auchinleck who had ordered the Army to stand at El Alamein, all three services had put in hand similar arrangements for a withdrawal from Cairo.[16]

Nevertheless, Harwood's decision was another titbit to feed the worm of distrust which was growing in the minds of Pound and of Churchill.

16
Operation Agreement

Auchinleck assumed personal command of the Eighth Army on 25 June 1942, leaving his chief of general staff, Lieutenant-General T W Corbett, as his deputy in Cairo for all matters except those of the highest strategic or political importance. As Auchinleck masterminded a fighting retreat to the lines at El Alamein, Harwood had asked whether there was anything that the Navy could do to help, and the reply he received was that 'any and every help' would be welcome. When finally in July Rommel was halted in his precipitate advance on the Delta, the Axis and the Allied armies still fought furiously for the next several weeks.

In London in July 1942 Churchill told A V Alexander that Harwood was 'doing very little in this fight, either in cutting off the enemy's supplies or actively bombarding the enemy bases', to which Alexander replied with a list of what Harwood had achieved,[1] while Harwood's relief as ACNS(F) told Pound in the plainest terms that the Mediterranean Fleet was reduced to a fleet-in-being to protect Egypt, Syria and Cyprus from sea invasion, its heavy casualities caused by helping the Army without efficient fighter cover, and to ask Harwood to bombard Tripoli was like asking the Home Fleet to bombard Cuxhaven.[2]

Harwood himself protested to Pound about the continuing failure of the RAF to provide air cover for the very operations which Churchill wanted. Tedder fought 'tooth and nail' against any proposals which Harwood made to send ships more than thirty-five miles to the westward of Alexandria. He objected to the blocking operation which Auchinleck had requested and Harwood had prepared against Mersa Matruh, and cruiser and destroyer bombardments of the coast 'were always opposed by the RAF on the grounds that if a ship got winged ... they would be faced with this big fighter battle which they could not afford. It was hard,' Harwood wrote, 'having to do nothing for so long except to play about in the Levant area,' adding, 'Out of the urge to do something emerged the plan for Tobruk where big risks were justified by big results.'[3]

Admiral H R Moore, Pound's Vice Chief of Naval Staff, took up the cudgel, urging Pound to raise the matter in the War Cabinet, writing that the time for 'more talk and compromises' had passed and that a showdown was a necessary: 'without doubt there would be an unholy row, but good might come of it.' Pound vacillated.[4]

Churchill in Cairo

Churchill himself arrived in Cairo on 3 August, accompanied by the Chief of the Imperial General Staff and others. Next day, after interviewing the principals individually, he met Casey and the commanders-in-chief,[5] and there can be little doubt that the stentorian language and the ambition of the subsequent plans for an attack on the German-held ports owed much to the Prime Minister.

Joint Planning Staff Paper No 106 of 6 August examined the possibility of an attack on Tobruk and Benghazi, and concluded that an attack 'during August might have a decisive effect on the enemy's maintenance if timed to coincide with an enemy offensive, which must, however, be followed by a counter offensive by us', and concluded that 'We must be prepared to accept the loss of all naval forces, together with the majority of the personnel taking part in the operation'.[6] On 7 August Auchinleck, who had returned to the front, through his deputy told the commanders-in-chief that this operation should be carried out in August if possible, since the Axis forces' situation was such that a serious interruption of their lines of communications might have immense results.[7] Next day Auchinleck himself signalled from the front:[8]

> I am in NO (R) NO doubt that it is essential (R) essential that these operations take place in August and that probable losses must (R) must be accepted in view of the advantages likely to result. I urge the Defence Committee to put preparations in hand at once for earliest execution projects. All possible aid will be given from here and plans are already in hand for increased assistance. Consider JPS

> paper fails altogether to appreciate tremendous moral and psychological value of proposals and most unaccountably neglects to take into account enemy's present state of mind. I consider Defence Committee should enjoin JPS to adopt a more vigorous and offensive habit of thought.

Before Churchill left for Moscow on 10 August, he had decided that 'a drastic and immediate change of command is needed in the high command', putting Lieutenant-General Bernard Montgomery in command of the Eighth Army on 12 August, and replacing Auchinleck as Commander-in-Chief, Middle East Forces by General Sir Harold Alexander on 15 August.[9] Meanwhile, though the plan for Operation Agreement was born in Cairo, the details were worked out in the naval headquarters at Alexandria. The naval force would be supported from seaward by the anti-aircraft cruiser *Coventry*, and three Hunt-class destroyers. A force of Royal Marines, embarked in the destroyers *Sikh* and *Zulu* and in twenty-one MTBs, would make a night landing at Tobruk, where seemingly well-authenticated intelligence indicated that enemy troops retired to camps outside the town at night and that all except anti-aircraft gun crews took shelter during air raids. The marines would meet up with the Long Range Desert Group (LRDG), a covert unit operating independently of the Eighth Army. The marines and the LRDG would join hands and capture enemy guns commanding the entrance to inlets north and south of Tobruk, and hold the port for twelve hours, long enough to destroy harbour installations, store dumps and shipping in the harbour.

Churchill was in Cairo on his return journey when there, at a meeting of the commanders-in-chief on 21 August, Operation Agreement was deferred until 3 September, when it was reviewed again. The fighting was in full swing at El Alamein, where Allied intelligence reckoned that Rommel had only two weeks' reserve of supplies. Although there was little hope of doing irreparable damage to Tobruk, the chiefs in committee still thought that a temporary dislocation of the enemy's supplies would prove disastrous to the Axis. Even if operations were unsuccessful they would undoubtedly have an effect on enemy morale and probably lead him to take precautions against a repetition, which would diminish the strength available for the defence of his positions in Egypt.

Tedder did not veto the plan, but he was disobliging: fighter cover was impossible throughout the proposed operation owing to the distance, and no other air support whatever could be provided except an attack by bombers to help in covering the approach. Harwood realised that the whole seaborne force, including the two destroyers he proposed to use, might well be lost, but he accepted the risk, and the chiefs decided that the effects of success would be great enough to justify the perils involved and orders were for Operation Agreement to be carried out on the night of 13/14 September when the moon would be right.[10]

Since Auchinleck had strongly advocated the raid on Tobruk, there had been a double change in the Army, and when the commanders-in-chief met to discuss Agreement for the last time, Montgomery had defeated Rommel's attempt to break through to Cairo, a defeat which owed much to the Axis armies' exhaustion. Thereafter the strategic and logistic situation began to swing in the Allies' favour. Although Agreement did not involve any units of the Eighth Army, a copy of the orders undoubtedly reached Montgomery's headquarters, but Montgomery, who anyway disliked operations by special forces outside his chain of command, would have nothing to do with it and viewed the operation with disfavour. Certainly, the naval liaison officer at Eighth Army headquarters, Commander T L Bratt, was not briefed: 'He was not put in the picture by the staff at Alexandria otherwise, he says, he was in a position to point out that during the delay in execution of the plan the Army's situation completely altered and in his opinion no longer justified so risky an operation.'[11] Neither at Eighth Army headquarters, nor in Alexandria, nor in Cairo over the next ten days did anyone re-evaluate the need for a seaborne attack on Tobruk.[12]

Notwithstanding the lack of communication within Allied headquarters, outside the headquarters the forthcoming attack appears to have been general knowledge.[13] The Germans may have had signal intelligence before the attack, and on the eve of the attack the RAF's bombing raid six hours beforehand only served to warn the German garrison commander.

Churchill's interest

Churchill, by his prompting from London in July and his meddling in Cairo in August, was deeply implicated in Operation Agreement, and he took a personal interest in its outcome, signalling Harwood: 'May all good fortune attend your efforts. Shall be glad if you will send me timely reports as you receive them.'[14]

On 12 September eighteen MTBs and three motor launches left Alexandria with 150 troops onboard; next day the destroyers *Sikh* and *Zulu* sailed with 350 marines embarked to meet the anti-aircraft cruiser *Coventry* and the ships of the 5th Destroyer Flotilla. The plan was to land the marines on the north side of Tobruk harbour, while the troops carried by the MTBs landed on the south side in support of the LRDG. At first the attack seemed to go well and Harwood replied to Churchill: 'First shore objective gained. Great hopes. Weather conditions for landing from destroyers good.'[15]

However, the RAF bombing on the evening of 13 September stirred the enemy, and though the LRDG gained possession of the gun positions to the south of Tobruk, only two of the twenty-one coastal craft got their troops ashore. The LRDG opened fire on the first MTBs, thinking they were German craft, deterring the remaining MTBs from entering the harbour. During the night the weather deteriorated, and in an attempt to expedite the northern landings, the destroyer *Sikh* came too close inshore and was heavily engaged by enemy shore batteries. Only half the marines got ashore from the destroyers and when *Sikh* entered harbour to land her marines, she was disabled by heavy fire from the defenders' guns. The destroyer *Zulu* tried to tow her out, but was ordered to retire. On the way home, *Coventry* was bombed, caught fire and was abandoned: extraordinarily, *Zulu* survived a day-long aerial attack, but was bombed and sunk by the last bomb of the last dive-bomber of the day. There was little gloss to be put on this catalogue of woe, and Harwood's signalled summary made poor reading:[16]

> The whole Tobruk plan was a mass of impertinences ... The stakes were very high, as a successful breaking up of Tobruk dumps and facilities would have had a big effect. Big risks were therefore deliberately taken. Timing of various events could not be ideal as

> L.R.D.G. (no publicity) had to seize Mersa Sciause to make operation practicable and latitude in time had to be allowed.
>
> I much regret the heavy losses with, as far as I can hear at present, few direct compensating gains but I feel it is better to have tried and failed than not to have tried at all.
>
> To our great surprise, the whole force reached Tobruk unreported by air. This is probably due to Germans using so much air to escort convoys.

His signalled summary of events went on to list in gory detail even minor failures during the operations, including broken signal glasses and a reference to the age of the commander of the inshore shore craft. When the report on this expensive failure reached Churchill, he, for all his admiration of offensive intentions, was gravely disturbed, and he told A V Alexander and Pound: 'I was not favourably impressed by Admiral Harwood's account of the Tobruk operation.'[17]

Harwood's view was that Agreement 'was a good try but we had bad losses.'[18] In a letter to Pound, he explained why it had been justifiable to accept 'big risks' in 'a desperate gamble', and it now seemed that the operation 'came nearer to success than we thought at the time'.[19] The operation was praised for being bold and well-conceived, but tragic because whilst the most difficult parts of the plan were successfully accomplished (the arrival of the LRDG and of the MTBs without being spotted), 'it broke down at the critical moment when success was ahead'.[20] In forwarding this letter, Pound isolated Harwood and increased his discomfiture by misrepresenting his earlier remark that 'out of the urge to do something emerged the plan for Tobruk', and telling Alexander, 'Harwood evolved the operation because he had got so bored with doing nothing.'[21]

Churchill and Montgomery distanced themselves from the failure, and neither mentioned the attack in their memoirs, though Montgomery is alleged to have said in the immediate aftermath that he did not place a high priority on the raid. Harwood later attributed many of his difficulties with Montgomery to this ill-starred venture. The heavy losses suffered during the raid on Tobruk achieved little, and Churchill, who had lost confidence in Auchinleck over the fall of Tobruk, now lost confidence in Harwood. He told Alexander: 'We suffered very heavy losses for little or no result.' The naval staff drafted a reply, but as Harwood's full report on Agreement had not been received, Pound stalled for time; 'Keep it until asked for,' he wrote. Churchill did not ask, but the worm in his mind grew.[22]

However, when Harwood met Montgomery, Harwood recalled, the latter 'was very forceful in his views of the Tobruk operation of September last. In my opinion this gave him a bias against me personally.'[23]

17
The Blighter Godfroy

France had fallen to the Germans in June 1940, when Marshal Philippe Pétain, hero of the First World War, signed an armistice agreement which gave him a nominally independent French state based in the French city of Vichy and which included the Mediterranean coast and French overseas possessions. The Vichy French were the legitimate government of France, and regarded the Free French as traitors. Pétain and his Defence Minister, Admiral François Darlan, gave assurances that no French warships would fall into German hands, promises which the British did not think they could rely upon, and French ships which had sought shelter in British ports were seized. On 3 July the French fleet at Mers-el-Kébir near Oran, Algeria, was presented with an ultimatum, intended to keep it out of German hands: come over to the British side or steam to a neutral port. The French admiral refused, several ships were sunk, and some 1,300 Frenchmen killed in a bombardment by Admiral Somerville's Force H. Nevertheless, the battlecruiser *Strasbourg* escaped to Toulon. French ships at Dakar were also attacked. French opinion was soured forever.

There was also a powerful French squadron at Alexandria, commanded by Vice-Admiral René-Émile Godfroy, who until the armistice had been co-operating with Admiral Cunningham's Mediterranean Fleet. Force X, as Godfroy's squadron was known, consisted of the battleship *Lorraine*, four cruisers, three destroyers and a submarine. Cunningham and Godfroy had established good relations, and while Cunningham was prepared to open fire, he chose to avoid fighting and relied upon his negotiating skills. Godfroy might have agreed to scuttle his ships, until he heard news of events in Algeria, but after several hours of high tension, with ships on both sides at action stations, Godfroy accepted terms for demilitarisation.

The agreement was essentially a personal one between Cunningham and Godfroy and no copy was available in London,[1] but the broad terms were that the British would not attempt to seize the French ships by force and the French would not scuttle, attempt to break out or commit any hostile act. French personnel onboard would be reduced while the ships would be maintained in their present material condition, fuel and ammunition would be landed, but the French were allowed to keep their anti-aircraft armament and the British agreed to victual and pay the crews. A codicil to the Cunningham–Godfroy agreement was that in the event of French warships elsewhere being taken over by the Italians or Germans 'this agreement to be reconsidered' and if war were 'declared between England and France a new situation not covered by this agreement will arise.'[2]

Harwood's leave after returning from South America had been broken by an invitation to dine with the Prime Minister on 17 October 1940. Among others present was Vice-Admiral Jack Tovey, who a few months before, in July, had done well in command of the cruiser force at the Battle of Calabria against the Regia Marina, and who was about to become the Commander-in-Chief, Home Fleet.[3] Describing the evening, Tovey told his former chief, Admiral Sir Andrew Cunningham that he was charmed by Churchill, but he was aghast that Churchill 'made astounding statements about naval warfare both at home and abroad'. When Churchill alleged that Cunningham had been 'too pussy-footed in your dealings with Godfroy', Tovey told the Prime Minister that he:

> could not be in full possession of the facts and presumably did not know that at any moment in the discussions you only had to make a two-letter signal and the French fleet was sunk. I asked him which he felt was preferable, to have valuable harbour space cluttered up with wrecks of French ships and to accept the appalling effect throughout the Near East of a battle in Alexandria or to leave the French ships afloat but demilitarised and still a potential resource and even a possible ally.[4]

It is not known whether Harwood was as charmed as Tovey, but he must have remembered the exchange when he met Godfroy in Alexandria.

Operation Bellringer

As ACNS(F) Harwood had thought about the position of the French in the war. They were, he wrote in September 1941 in a think-piece for Pound, broken, and the only way to divert them from their loyalty to Pétain was for them to realise that they had a greater loyalty – to France. De Gaulle was 'completely unreliable', but someone must lead the French, and the British 'must back them to the hilt and so arrange it that it is they who re-enter France and recapture it ... it is only thus that France can redeem herself and make herself worthy of taking her place in the post-war world ... if de Gaulle won't agree, I suggest he must be eliminated.'[5]

In October and November 1941, during Operation Bellringer, the hunt in the Indian Ocean for a convoy of Vichy French merchant ships, Harwood had further occasion to reflect on Anglo-French relations. The Vichy government threatened that if the British seized their ships, Vichy forces would not let British shipping pass 'unheeded' through the Western Mediterranean: Harwood proposed that in this case, the whole of the Western Mediterranean would be declared a war zone and French ships would be sunk on sight. He recognised that this might spark a reaction in metropolitan France and its colonies, in Spain and from the Germans, and urged 'if we intend to force this and the Spanish issues, then we should go whole-hoggedly at an offensive against French trade.'[6] This was a few days before Operation Crusader was about to begin, the British attempt to drive Axis forces out of North Africa: there was much optimism that the Italian army and even the government might collapse. Harwood thought that the Germans might move to occupy Spain, in which case Spanish Morocco, the Canaries, Sicily and Sardinia [*sic*] should be occupied and garrisoned.[7]

Godfroy and Harwood

Cunningham's agreement with Godfroy had been achieved despite some vicious prompting for decisive action from Churchill in London, and it rankled with the Prime Minister that Cunningham had used his initiative to prevent unnecessary bloodshed. Harwood had been present at Chequers when Churchill had accused Cunningham of pussyfooting in his dealings with Godfroy, and before leaving for the Mediterranean he had been given instructions to get the ships to resume the fight for the liberation of France. Harwood had met Godfroy in 1939 when he was commanding a French squadron visiting Bermuda, and had got on well with him. Godfroy had written a generous letter of congratulations after the Battle of the River Plate, and once Harwood had arrived in Alexandria, Godfroy was meticulous in writing further letters of congratulations after British victories and condolences after losses.[8] By May 1942 the French squadron had been lying idle in Alexandria harbour for nearly two years, where Godfroy had become obsessed by his honour, his officers were anti-British and the ships' companies, as Cogswell had astutely observed, were divided into factions. The Free French saw Godfroy's squadron as Fascists who were living at leisure, and paid for by the British, while they fought France's war. The Vichyists saw the Free French as traitors to their country, or worse Communists. A steady trickle of men deserted their ships to join the Free French.

On taking up his new command, Harwood was immediately pitched into lengthy negotiations with Godfroy, who wanted to change the agreement to allow him to repatriate some of his crews,[9] and Harwood had to deal with the Frenchman even while Operation Vigorous was being fought out and Rommel was advancing on Egypt. Harwood was about to reaffirm Cunningham's agreement with Godfroy, with a few minor amendments, when Operation Discretion, the withdrawal of naval forces from Alexandria, was put in motion. Amid a flurry of diplomatic, naval and operational messages from London, from Laval in Vichy, from de Gaulle speaking for the Free French, and Washington (where Churchill was), Harwood got Godfroy's agreement that should Alexandria be menaced by the Axis, Force X would move southwards through the Suez Canal. Godfroy rejected an alternative, which was conveyed in a letter from President Roosevelt, that his ships should be put into the protective custody of the USA.[10] When Godfroy made a counter-proposal, Harwood received a brusque, personal message from Churchill delivered via Richard Casey, the British Minister of State in Egypt: 'You should explain to Harwood that it is out of the question to agree to these ships sailing to Bizerta. Let him clear this idea entirely out of his mind.'[11]

The threat of a German breakthrough into the Delta persisted throughout August 1942, but Harwood's firm advice was to rely on

Godfroy's promise that the French ships would scuttle themselves if any attempt were made by the Germans to seize them. The answer from London was adamant: irrespective of any US proposals 'the most drastic steps must be taken to prevent any of the French ships getting back to France.' However, Harwood kept his head and displayed considerable diplomatic skills, even when the naval staff in London contemplated asking the USA for heavy bombers to help destroy Godfroy's ships.[12]

Operation Torch

Force X took a considerable amount of Harwood's thought and his planning, even as in October he began to prepare for Operation Lightfoot, the British advance from El Alamein and Operation Torch, the Allied landings in North Africa. He was forceful in argument, concluding that if Godfroy did not react to Torch, then the British should do nothing, but if Godfroy tried to bolt or initiated offensive action, he would be sunk.[13] Churchill queried whether a battleship should be sent to Alexandria, and on 5 November sent a stirring message to Harwood:

> Our victory in Egypt and the impending reactions to Torch may give an opportunity for bringing Godfroy to see his duty to France in its true light. You must watch him this moment with the greatest vigilance. We shall also be watching it from here. Your personal influence as one sailor to another may go far. Keep close to him these days and let me know his mood.[14]

On the night of 7/8 November Harwood cleared Alexandria of all shipping, the Army mounted about forty guns all trained on Force X, and twenty-five MTBs were deployed in the harbour. Up until then Godfroy's consistent attitude had been to comply with the terms of his agreements with Cunningham and Harwood, and not to deviate from those terms on the principle that anything that he did would reflect on France and upon her honour.[15] Now, when at 03:00 on 8 November, Harwood sent for Godfroy to tell him about Operation Torch, Godfroy became 'depressed and not very helpful.'[16]

Later that morning Harwood and US General F M Andrews met Godfroy again. Godfroy was obsessed with the sufferings of his poor country, its honour and his honour, and the 1940 Armistice terms, but he was intractable when it was suggested that if Germany invaded Vichy France, Vichy would automatically become one of the Allies. Godfroy agreed 'for a moment but then made excuses for such action by Germany.' It seemed that there might be the opposite risk, that Vichy might declare war on the Allies for invading French North Africa, and Godfroy could think no further than 'scuttling or bolting'. Harwood tried to persuade Godfroy to see him again if Vichy declared war, but the Frenchman would not give this guarantee, and Harwood kept his guns manned and the MTBs in readiness.[17]

Even after the Germans broke the 1940 Armistice and invaded Vichy France on 11 November, Harwood, who wanted to use the port of Alexandria and not hold up the supplies for the Western Desert, felt unable to relax his precautions. At yet another meeting with Godfroy, there could be no accusing Harwood of pussyfooting, indeed, he 'was extremely frank about British point of view and did not mince words about France and the duty of all Frenchmen particularly the navy to resume the fight from which they should never have backed out.'[18] London still seemed to want a dramatic, possibly violent, end to the stand-off: 'It is premature to relax your precautions for dealing with the French ships.'[19]

Then, with the Torch landings successful, Darlan arrived in North Africa claiming to be a representative of Pétain, ordered a ceasefire by Vichy forces, and placed himself at the head of a government of liberation. The Germans confined Pétain, and a hard-line Fascist, Pierre Laval, became effectively head of a puppet French government. Pressure increased on Harwood for a firm line to be taken with Godfroy, Pound signalling that Godfroy's attitude could not:[20]

> ... be continued at the cost of British Exchequer. In view of complete accession to United Nations cause of French North Africa, Dakar and other French possessions new situation has arisen. Either he is for liberation of France or for collaboration with Laval and Germany. You should inform him that in light of Germany's abrogation of the Armistice and the accession of Algiers and Dakar

> forces [to the Allies] it is duty by which we shall judge him – to bring his squadron to the aid of the liberation of France, failing which the [Harwood–Godfroy] agreement of June 20th 1942 must after due notice come to an end.

Harwood summed up the situation in signals and a letter to Cunningham in his capacity as Naval Commander, Allied Expeditionary Force (NCXF). Godfroy was evidently without news of what was happening in France or from other French admirals in North Africa, and would not come over yet, but Harwood had not completely given up hope. It would be easier for him to come over if a stable French government in exile were formed in Algeria, but Godfroy was extremely anti-Gaullist and preferred this to be under someone else. His officers and ships' companies were anti-American and anti-British, still resenting the bombardment of Oran, and blaming the Allied landings in North Africa for provoking the Germans into invading Vichy France.[21]

After Cunningham had met Darlan, who claimed to be trying to bring the whole French fleet over to the Allies, Darlan wrote a personal message exhorting Godfroy to join him.[22] In response, Harwood told Cunningham, Godfroy was very tiresome:[23]

> He won't take the slightest risk and wants 100% certainty so that not only his conscience but also those of his officers can feel perfectly clear ... After a very long session and much rather brutal frankness I gingered him up one night to have a meeting of his Captains after which he came off the fence in a five volume novel full of ifs, buts, etc. The next morning he was extremely fussed and asked that his letter should be washed out ... I can best sum him up by saying that he is the worst time waster I have ever met in my life.

Meanwhile, there was another personal signal in the early hours of 25 November, this one from A V Alexander to Harwood stressing the importance of bringing Godfroy over: 'It will be a great feather in your cap if you bring it off ... We are certain you will do your best ... We want the ships'.[24] There can be little doubt that the 'we' included Churchill.

Harwood was doing his best, and after a day's negotiations replied that he was keeping in touch with Godfroy, but Godfroy was without instructions from France: 'I am in no doubt that he personally is on our side but his principles, possible reprisals to France and general lack of information are clogging his decision.'[25] Harwood supplemented his answer: 'I am doing my best and have used all possible arguments. It will take a long time and it would be fatal to rush it.'[26]

The next day the Germans invaded the French arsenal at Toulon and the French honoured Darlan's pledge that the fleet would not fall into German hands by scuttling seventy-seven vessels, including three battleships, seven cruisers, fifteen destroyers, and twelve submarines which had lain unused during most the war. Harwood received more hassle from London, and he vented his frustration in a letter to Pound, telling him that:

> these blighters have wasted many hours of my time and yours and are still doing so ... I seem to spend most of my life over this tiresome French Admiral Godfroy. I have been very frank with him indeed and I have recently sent him a letter summing up all the views I have given him verbally in a final effort to shake him and his officers out of their rut. They just sit back and talk of their poor country, honour and conscience ... It is as near a hopeless task as I have taken on but I still hope.[27]

Godfroy called on Harwood in the middle of this letter: 'The blighter has just left me. As obstinate as any Frenchman could be ... My parting shot was to ask him what sort of reception Force X would get on its return to a France liberated by Frenchmen who had joined the United Nations.' Harwood saw a silver lining in desertions from Force X: 'Two came over today and expect a lot more in the next few days. I am letting this take its natural course.'[28]

Churchill now tried to apply pressure on Godfroy through the British ambassador in Cairo, Sir Miles Lampson and the Minister of State, Richard Casey. Harwood was quick to point out to Lampson that he had understood that the agreement was between him and Godfroy and that his dealings with the government in London were conducted through the Admiralty. His instructions, which he rehearsed for Lampson, had included personal telegrams from the Prime Minister and the political leader of the Admiralty, and that now was Godfroy's last chance to align himself with the growing forces for the liberation of France. There was, he wrote, no question of Godfroy joining the Free French, but Darlan's message had been handed over, inviting Godfroy to join French forces in North Africa. He, Harwood, was in close touch with both groups of Frenchmen:[29]

> The possibility of bringing financial pressure to bear on Admiral Godfroy has on several occasions formed the subject of communications between myself and the Admiralty. I have consistently tried to avoid this method because I am sure that it is the most certain method to stop him bringing his ships over. Further it would have serious repercussions the most important of which are the probability of Force X being scuttled in the harbour and the crews having to be forced into internment in Egypt. If such a situation should arise it is unlikely that bloodshed and possibly an open battle in Alexandria harbour could be avoided. I can only regret, therefore, that you have brought this suggestion again to the fore. I am afraid it is inevitable that the Free French in Egypt should feel some bitterness towards our actions with regard to Force X. If my object is to bring the ships over, which is the Government policy, I am quite unable to do so without in some way treading on Free French toes.

Harwood explained the situation anew to the Middle East Defence Committee, chaired by Casey. Godfroy, ever loyal to Pétain, was still thinking up every excuse not to commit himself. He kept coming back to the same theme: he could not join Britain because of the attack on Oran in 1940, nor America because of their attacks on French forces during the landings in North Africa, nor the Free French because they were responsible for many of the ills which had affected France since the Armistice in June 1940. Godfroy, Harwood wrote, noted that the Americans had recognised the Darlan government, but feared that the British wished to install a Gaullist government: he could not join the Allies until a stable French regime had been installed in North Africa.

Stoppage of pay

Darlan was assassinated by a Free French hothead on Christmas Eve, 1942, and in January Churchill was once more in Cairo. On 24 January 1943 Harwood and Godfroy met yet again, when the Frenchman had new excuses: he would re-enter the fight but would only do so if Pétain gave up or was replaced by a quisling government. He would, however, support a provisional government agreement provided it did not include any Free French or Communists.

Churchill remained obsessed, and CIGS recalled that two days later he was in the map room in Cairo with General Alexander discussing the advance across the Western Desert with Harwood and others, when the Prime Minister 'turned up' and became embroiled in a long discussion with Harwood, not on the urgent need to open the port of Tripoli, but about Force X. Churchill was 'all for a firmer attitude to these forces to induce them to join the French movement to free France.'[30]

The firmer attitude involved stopping the wages which had been paid to Godfroy's crews since the Cunningham–Godfroy and Harwood–Godfroy agreements. Stopping pay would be a breach of the agreements and, Harwood advised, risked Godfroy scuttling his ships in the harbour, or even a battle, either of which would have a serious effect on Eighth Army supplies. Harwood was convinced that if left to his own devices Godfroy would come over, probably when all Axis forces had been driven out of North Africa. The French ships were no longer of any appreciable fighting value and there was no hurry. No impetuous action should be taken.[31] Nevertheless, by February 1943 Harwood once more considered the need to fortify the harbour.[32] Churchill now turned to Casey and 'your promise to me to see this Godfroy business through to the end. If cutting pay does not suffice we shall have to go on to cutting supplies.'[33]

Ironically, it appears that while Churchill was goading Casey, Lampson and, of course, Harwood, he had already written to Roosevelt as early as 19 December saying: 'We have waited (for Godfroy) for two years or more and there cannot be any particular hurry ... We are bound to get him in the end.'[34] Nevertheless, Godfroy resisted all blandishments and it was only on 17 May 1943, after the Allies had indeed cleared North Africa of Axis forces, and it was clear who was going to win the war, that Godfroy, ignoring orders from Vichy to scuttle his ships, wrote to Harwood's successor expressing the desire 'to join the French Navy in North Africa'. Godfroy was relieved of his command in December 1943 and compulsorily retired as a disciplinary measure He would die of old age at Fréjus, southern France in January 1981, aged ninety-six.

Harwood summed the matter up:[35]

> On both his visits to Cairo I have had to bear the full blast of the Prime Minister's venom against this Squadron. I did my duty and put my views on this question to him, and these views stand recorded ... I quite agree they were received very badly and the whole question was then taken out of my hands and turned over to the Minister of State. After a month and more of meetings with Godfroy, and threats, the view now held out here, but possibly not at home, is just what I put to the Prime Minister and is in accordance with the advice I sent to the Admiralty in my signal 2250/26th January 1943 and many other signals over the last six months ... I can only conclude that I did my duty, unpleasant as it was, and that my advice does not justify censure. I have always said that Godfroy would come over as soon as conditions in France again gave him a chance, but not before we captured Tunisia.

Harwood had followed the wise precedent set by Cunningham, and the latter had supported Harwood's common-sense and moderate approach throughout the months of delicate negotiations with Godfroy.[36]

18
The Clearance of Tripoli

That Harwood had suffered three setbacks, the defeat of Operation Vigorous, the temporary evacuation of Alexandria, and the failure of Operation Agreement, were no deterrent: he saw with some clarity that his duty was to support the land forces who were preparing to push Rommel back from El Alamein. However, any proposals by him to carry out bombardments of the enemy's positions or mount further raiding parties were now vetoed by Tedder, who would not give fighter cover. When Harwood went to see Montgomery in his desert caravan, Montgomery was adamant that he needed all the fighters for the coming land battle and could not afford any to cover naval operations. Harwood vented his frustration in another letter to Pound: 'Montgomery ... was well primed to deter any action by the Navy of any sort. His catchwords were to keep the Navy behind as we need all the fighters for the land battle and can't afford any for you even to bombard. We will do it all by the air. I came back thoroughly depressed.'[1]

The British counterattack at El Alamein opened on 23 October 1942 and the final breakout came on the night of 4/5 November. Mersa Matruh was taken on 8 November, the same day that Operation Torch, the US-led Allied landings in North Africa, began. Bardia fell four days later and Tobruk fell on 13 November. Harwood was surprised at the weight of air power which was used: 'RAF were always supposed to be in such a poor position as regards fighters that none could ever be spared or wasted. When the battle came it seemed that they had great air superiority and I can't help feeling I was cheated of a few fighters which would have enabled me to do more,' and he expressed an opinion held by most naval officers to this day: 'Clearly my experience over this indicates that the Navy must have its own fighters both long range two engine ones and single seater ones or it will be, as I was, at the mercy of RAF charity.'[2]

The relief of Malta

After Operations Harpoon in June and Pedestal in August, both of which suffered heavy losses, no further convoys were run from the west in 1942, while Axis forces still held Tunisia and threatened the route. However, the Army's advance and the recapture of airfields now enabled Harwood to run two convoys to Malta. Operation Stoneage was a convoy of four merchant ships whose arrival in Malta on 20 November is considered to have broken the siege of the island, and caused Brooke, the Chief of the Imperial General Staff, to write in his diary 'Malta convoy of 4 ships arrived safely, thank God! This puts the island safe again for a bit.'[3] Next, Operation Portcullis was a convoy of six merchant ships which took a coastal route to avoid passage through 'bomb alley' and arrived in Malta on 5 December. Four more convoys followed in quick succession in December under the title of Operation Quadrangle. Harwood was able to combine these ships with convoys to Tobruk and Benghazi, now they were again in British hands, and by the end of the year the supply line from Egypt was safe and adequate to supply Malta.

Cunningham returns

In the West, Cunningham was Allied Chief of the Naval Expeditionary Force, and a new command boundary was drawn between Cunningham in the Western Mediterranean and Harwood in the East. In practice, ships and convoys in the Western Mediterranean, as with Harpoon, had usually come under the command of Force H or directly from the Admiralty, so there was little change in Harwood's circumstances or responsibilities. Harwood thought that the division of his nominal command into two parts, the (Western) Mediterranean and the Levant, was logical, and he suggested to Pound that the naval and air commanders-in-chief in the Mediterranean should be co-located with General Dwight Eisenhower, the Supreme Commander, Allied Expeditionary Force.[4]

Supplies to the Army

At the end of November Harwood had told Pound:

> We are well away with the Eighth Army supplies and are ahead of time so far in opening the ports and delivery of ships. The problem

> of supply to the Tripoli coast is a very difficult one as there are no harbours and the winter weather is pretty bad. We are getting out plans to use the reefs and land stores by every known method.[5]

As the Eighth Army advanced westwards, Harwood's Inshore Squadron under Captain Colin Wauchope kept up the delivery of supplies, often landing them over open beaches immediately behind the frontline, and on 21 November Montgomery sent the Navy a congratulatory signal: 'We send the navy our thanks for the part they have played in safeguarding the passage of troops and supplies, without which the offensive would not have been possible.' More aggressive naval operations, for example, raiding ahead of Rommel during his retreat were discussed by the Commanders-in-Chief, Middle East, but decided against because such raids would need fighter protection which Tedder would not give, and troops and tanks which Montgomery would not release.[6]

On 22 December Harwood began a tour of the captured ports, which he described in a long letter to Joan. On the first day he found that Tobruk was a shambles, but ships were being unloaded in an orderly way. Derna had not been badly damaged, but at Benghazi there was hardly a house standing:[7]

> I met the Army authorities and we discovered on the spot all the problems that had to be solved ... Ships that had been sunk had been used by the Germans as jetties and ships were berthed alongside them. Ramps were run to the jetties and used for unloading ... Before [the Germans] left they blew up the ramp and the upper deck and it was cut in half. The oiler was in two parts and one part was still burning when we occupied the place ... At that end of the harbour all the lighters, barges etc. are unloaded, a regular hive of industry. Every kind of war supply from camel beef to ammunition, milk and petrol were passing out and away. The Cathedral mole had been bombed and bombed by us all through the war and yet it was still there and workable, though scarred and battered.

Harwood found time for some early morning shooting, and on Christmas Day he attended Mass in the cathedral at Benghazi. He hoped to fly on to Malta, but a storm turned the airfields to mud and Harwood reluctantly decided that he must return to Alexandria.

Clearance of Tripoli

On 4 October, three weeks before the Allied advance from El Alamein, Harwood had ordered his Superintendent of Salvage, Captain G C C Damant, to draw up plans for Operation Trundle, for the clearance of North African ports beyond Benghazi. Four days later arrangements were put in hand to call forward tugs, schooners, salvage vessels, mobile lighters, and small craft of all sorts. The docking and preparation of suitable ships for the Western Desert run were completed, personnel were allocated, and the stores and explosives to be taken forward by each Port Salvage Party were detailed, Operation Trundle was approved by the commanders-in-chief in committee and on 31 December, after returning from his tour of inspection, Harwood reviewed arrangements with Damant. The South African salvage ship *Gamtoos*, then at Port Said,[8] the Danish tug *Valkyrien* at Tobruk, and the salvage tug *Confederate* in the Red Sea were ordered to move westwards.[9] After this meeting Harwood told Bratt to tell Montgomery: 'I am very concerned about the almost certainty of blocking [by the Germans] but that I do not think they will be able to prevent lighters entering. As a last resort sappers will have to breach the mole. Ships can anchor outside the port with a little lee and discharge into LCTs [landing craft].' Harwood added that the best way to keep the harbour open was for the RAF to sink the three big ships which were in the harbour and which the Germans might use as blockships.[10]

On 8 January 1943 Harwood raised with Alexander and Tedder the need to sink potential blockships at Tripoli before they could be moved into position. Eight bombing raids were mounted without success, and on the night of 18/19 January Harwood authorised Operation Welcome. This was an attack by two underwater chariots or human torpedoes, which succeeded in preventing one blockship being moved into position: both chariots were lost and the crews taken prisoner. Over the next few nights surface ships swept along the coast sinking numerous small craft, and on 20/21 January an attack by MTBs on the mole at Tripoli found the Italian submarine *Santarosa*, and she was torpedoed.

When the leading echelons of the Eighth Army entered Tripoli on 23 January, they were closely followed by the Advance Salvage Party. Their main object was reconnaissance and the preparation of a salvage plan to be put into effect as soon as *Gamtoos* and the main party arrived. They were not idle and blew up some of the upperworks of the wreck of a sunken ship, *San Giovanni Battista*, and quickly made a passage for small craft into the harbour.[11] The naval parties, under the commander of the Inshore Squadron, moved in hard on the heels of the Army. Mine clearance, diving operations and blowing up of the blockships started at once. However, Harwood's Chief of Staff, Commodore J G L Dundas, whose aircraft had broken down for twenty-four hours in the desert, had to come by sea and did not arrive until noon on 25 January. He was followed by the Fleet Salvage Officer, Commander W Rippon, who had left Benghazi on 21 January, having been told not to wait for an air passage as the Tripoli airfields were mined, and who arrived in a minesweeper.

Dundas was about to receive a shock. Going immediately to Navy House he found Wauchope, the Senior Naval Officer Inshore Squadron, about to receive a visit from Montgomery. Dundas:[12]

> Waited for this visit and had a short conversation with the General who told me of the great importance of opening up the harbour as quickly as possible. I assured him that I was fully alive to this and that as soon as the first salvage ship arrived the work would start on the maximum scale. I said that the *Gamtoos* was expected to arrive that evening. I also told him that as I had not seen any Salvage Officer or visited the wrecks I could not possibly give any idea of the time likely to be required. I told him that I did not think it could be less than several weeks particularly in view of the probability of bad weather, but of course at this time I did not know that the concrete ship would be the easiest to tackle. At the same time I said that in fair weather merchant ships could unload in the outer roads as soon as clear berths had been established. This, he quite rightly pointed out, was not nearly good enough. He now had the task of capturing Tunisia and he must build up his reserve supplies at the full capacity rate of the port.

This was not quite true, as de Guingand, Montgomery's chief of staff revealed, 'the Army needed a rest and time to check up on things.'[13] Indeed, the matter was of such little import that Montgomery did not mention it in his memoirs, and the author of a three-volume hagiography of Montgomery did not know which was the port where clearance had been an alleged issue.[14]

Nevertheless, Montgomery said he would send his chief engineer to see Dundas and that evening Dundas, Rippon and Wauchope held a conference with Brigadier F H Kisch, Montgomery's Commander, Royal Engineers.[15] The meeting was cordial and Kisch promised every help with men and materials in the spirit of previous port clearances. Later Dundas told Harwood:[16]

> Nothing that occurred at the meeting suggested to me that I should be on the alert for future accusations against the Navy ... My signal to you, made that night, gave the list of stores required and in particular those required by air passage to replace some that had been sent by road. Again, had I known of subsequent recriminations, I should have included explosives in the requirements so that we could have been entirely independent of the Army. Nor would the Fleet Salvage Officer, had he had similar knowledge, have accepted what he thought was a good offer. It was all unnecessary and must also be remembered that he had not had time to visit the *Gamtoos* which had only anchored late that evening.

At the end of the conference Rippon gave his opinion, which he would have to confirm by daylight, that a passage could be made for tank landing craft in a few days, and for cargo vessels in about a fortnight. Next morning Dundas was sent for by Montgomery: Dundas's reception was 'very cold and critical ... including sceptical remarks to the Navy's intended hours of work.' Dundas was curtly informed that arrangements for uncorking the harbour at Tripoli were totally inadequate both as regards personnel and equipment. The whole resources of the Eighth Army were at the Navy's disposal, and all concerned must get on with the job. Montgomery told Dundas that he wanted no recriminations, and Dundas assured Montgomery that there were sufficient stores and equipment, that more were readily available, that work would continue day and night, and, unless the weather intervened, ships should be able to enter the harbour in fourteen days. Montgomery brusquely repeated his criticism without further comment, adding that he wanted his message conveyed to Harwood.

That afternoon when Dundas met Kisch on board *Gamtoos*, where work was already well in hand, he told Kisch that his report to Montgomery must have been very exaggerated, that the Navy could have 'got on just as fast without assistance', and that thanks to his report, Dundas had 'a most unpleasant message' to deliver to Harwood.

It was clear to Dundas that Kisch had little idea of the complexity of salvage operations, and he expected to see work in full swing on all blockships simultaneously. The need for a survey and a plan was not understood, nor that working several separate teams of divers was impracticable. Rippon pointed out it was better to employ the divers on one job at a time, any divided control when using explosives under water was dangerous, and that the use of too many divers simultaneously was risky, as one bomb falling within a quarter of a mile would kill them all.

The first supply convoy, composed of landing craft, had left Benghazi two days before Tripoli fell, and the first merchant ship convoy sailed simultaneously from Alexandria. By the 25th a small passage had been cleared to enable landing craft to enter; next day the first proper convoy arrived, but had to anchor outside. On the 26th a beginning was made by getting 370 tons of cargo discharged, and thereafter matters improved rapidly. Then a violent storm caused damage among the landing craft, and delayed clearance and salvage work. The same storm struck Benghazi and damaged the moles so badly that it was reduced to a fair-weather port. Nonetheless by the 29th the gap in the blockships in Tripoli was wide enough for LCTs to enter, and 1,000 tons of cargo were discharged next day. Soon an average of 1,500 tons per day were being delivered, and on 4 February the Army admitted that for the previous two days, delivery from ships had exceeded what they could unload and clear.[17]

Churchill was again in North Africa and on 4 February, when he, the CIGS and General Alexander visited Tripoli, they witnessed two

9,000-ton merchant ships enter the harbour through a newly created gap, 100ft wide and 24ft deep between the blockships.[18] In London Pound was reassuring A V Alexander: 'I consider the Navy under Harwood's direction has done very well in opening up Tobruk, Benghazi etc. and in getting them going so quickly after they had been captured, particularly as the enemy had done everything possible to make them unusable.'[19]

The General jokes

Meanwhile, the atmosphere in Montgomery's headquarters mess, which had become very uneasy for the sailors, became worse after Montgomery made a rare joke, that 'what was wanted was people who could uncork harbours rather than bottles'. Word travelled like wildfire, creating a most unfortunate impression among the men of the Inshore Squadron, the salvage ships and the naval beach parties, all of whom had toiled for months, often under the most trying and dangerous circumstances, to 'uncork' the harbours needed to supply the Army – and had all too often to cork them up again when they were abandoned during the Army's retreats. These feelings were exacerbated when Montgomery's congratulatory message on the capture of Tripoli was read out: it contained well-deserved tributes to all services and branches, except the Navy, about which not one word was said. Bratt discussed the strained and uncomfortable situation in which he found himself and the congratulatory message with Brigadier Sir Brian Robertson, Montgomery's head of administration. Robertson had no illusions at all regarding the debt owed by the Army to the sea services during the long advance, but he also felt that the preparations for the clearance of Tripoli could have been better organised. No one desired good relations between the Army and Navy on all levels more than Robertson, but he warned Bratt that Montgomery's whole attitude was coloured by his poor opinion of Harwood.

When Harwood's Deputy Chief of Staff, Commodore H G Norman, also visited Tripoli, and while he was lunching in Montgomery's mess, he too mentioned the congratulatory message, and suggested that some mention of the Navy's part might have been included. Norman at once received a sharp kick under the table from Brigadier 'Freddie' de Guingand, who was sitting opposite him and who gestured to him to keep quiet. After the meal was over de Guingand took Norman aside and explained that his suggestion did not stand a chance of acceptance by Montgomery as long as Harwood was naval commander-in-chief, but that he, de Guingand, would see that the Navy's efforts received proper acknowledgment. Thanks either to Robertson's or de Guingand's sympathetic understanding, Montgomery did later visit the ships engaged on clearance work and made an appreciative speech to their companies. But, pointedly, it was not until the end of the campaign in April, when Harwood had been relieved, that Montgomery signalled that 'without the safe conduct of tanks, petrol and other munitions of war to Tobruk, Benghazi and Tripoli, the Eighth Army would have been unable to launch the offensive'.

Post-war, both Churchill and Montgomery eventually paid tribute to the speed with which the port of Tripoli had opened up, but perhaps the best accolade came from the Germans who expected that their demolition of the harbour would prevent the British from using the facilities for four weeks, but instead 'The enemy [ie the British] is already using Tripoli port in spite of the enormous destruction which we had carried there.'[20] There was little delay in clearing the harbour and the Army's progress did not suffer.

Montgomery's stab

Montgomery had little understanding of or sympathy for the Navy, feelings which were to become reciprocal. Cunningham's view of Montgomery was that 'he is a bit of a nuisance; he seems to think that all he has to do is say what has to be done and everyone will dance to the tune of his piping ... [General] Alexander appears quite unable to keep him in order.'[21] Cunningham would later have bitter experience of Montgomery, when in 23 August 1943 Montgomery told Eisenhower at a meeting of commanders-in-chief that the Army was ready to execute Operation Baytown, the crossing of the Messina Straits, but they were held up by the Navy and, furthermore, they were unwilling to operate at night. Cunningham told Alexander, 'I find that, not only were the statements incorrect, but that General Montgomery had at no time been in direct touch with the Senior Naval Office of the Expedition and that his statements were, in fact, completely unfounded.'[22]

For now, in Tripoli in January 1943, Montgomery had told Dundas that he wanted no recriminations, but this also was untrue. Though the reasons are obscure, for they had only met a few times, Montgomery, the aesthete, had developed a personal dislike of Harwood. Harwood smoked, drank in moderation, was corpulent, and lived in comfort in Alexandria, while Montgomery lived in a caravan in the desert. Perhaps he resented that, while Harwood was one tier above him in the Middle East hierarchy, he was one rank below in substantive rank. Perhaps Montgomery, the son of a Northern Irish Protestant minister, was antipathetic towards a Roman Catholic admiral.

Whatever the cause of Montgomery's dislike, before Dundas returned to Cairo on 27 January he lunched with Montgomery, where he formed the impression that the general's criticisms had been resolved. This sorry disturbance of the happy relations between the Army and the Navy, which had been sustained through the many months of wear and tear of the Mediterranean campaigns might perhaps have subsided,[23] but Montgomery wrote over the head of his own immediate superior, Alexander, the Commander-in-Chief, Middle East Forces, to General Sir Alan Brooke, the Chief of the General Staff, who was in Cairo in Churchill's entourage. Montgomery complained to Brooke that the clearance of Tripoli was not proceeding quickly enough. The letter arrived with Brooke just before dinner on 27 January when he told Churchill, 'We ought to do something,' and Churchill sent for Harwood at 23:00 that evening. Churchill told Harwood of the Army's dissatisfaction and their great surprise that fourteen days would be required to clear the port. He made the very wounding charge that the Navy had let the Eighth Army down.[24] Although next morning Churchill sent for Damant, the Superintendent of Salvage, and after close questioning became 'most reasonable and his only intention appeared to be to spur us on to greater efforts', the damage had been done.[25]

Harwood wrote to General Alexander, explaining that his main anxiety had been that the time estimated to open Tripoli was over-optimistic, 'in view of the extremely difficult task to be undertaken', and highlighting that his advice to Montgomery as to the date when cargoes could be landed was seven to ten days after entry, whereas

1,150 tons had been discharged on the sixth day. Harwood thought that if Montgomery had not allowed for the naval advice, 'then it is not quite fair to lay the blame on the Navy'.[26]

Harwood also warned Pound by signal that, when back in London, Churchill might repeat what he had been told by Montgomery:[27]

> On the return of the Prime Minister to London I fear you may be troubled by suggestions that the Navy has not done all that it could to expedite clearing a deep draught passage into Tripoli harbour. Complaint to this effect was made to him by the Army without my knowledge. Since the end of December I have been impressing on the Army the likely effects of successful blocking and though impatience is perhaps inevitable, there could be no justification for surprise or for planning on an unduly optimistic basis ... There has been much uninformed criticism with regard to shortage of personnel and gear on the assumption that greater resources would enable more work to be carried out simultaneously ... The original inter-service official estimate of the earliest arrival of the first convoy through swept and defended waters was 7 days after the Army's arrival ie. 30th January. Actually due to successful minesweeping the convoy arrived on 26th January and LCTs started unloading on that day. By 30th Jan. 2,500 tons had been unloaded after 2 days of bad weather. The last two days have averaged 1,500 tons per day and weather permitting I hope this will be maintained. This fulfils Army's highest expectations at this early stage.

In a separate signal a pained Harwood told Pound: 'I am very cross with Eighth Army Commander for this backhander but am keeping discreet.'[28] After an exchange of signals, Pound satisfied himself about what had transpired in Tripoli and before writing to Churchill. His letter was factual, but did suggest that there should have been more liaison with the Army beforehand about provision of explosives and allocation of manpower. Pound stressed that the rate of unloading exceeded the Army's highest expectations and it was illogical to suggest that military plans could have been affected by supposed shortcomings of the salvage service:

> The Army does not appreciate that underwater salvage work is inevitably slow and methodical. It is true that the additional gear and spares required at a later stage were dispatched by a slow form of transport but this was rectified in ample time. Comment was no doubt justified but certainly not outside the Mediterranean Command ... in my opinion there has been no delay and no lack of material on the spot. Nothing but the weather will cause delay.[29]

However, a few days later, after Brooke had returned to London, Pound wrote in the opposite sense to Harwood:

> I must be quite frank, however, and say that the story as a whole leaves me with the definite impression that insufficient supervision had been taken on the highest level to ensure that an operation [the clearance of Tripoli harbour] which was so vital to the Army, and on which everyone's attention was focused, had behind it all the drive and forethought which it demanded.[30]

Apparently, Brooke had returned with a message from Churchill that the Army no longer had confidence that the Navy would in all circumstances give the Army the necessary support.[31] Reflecting on the matter later, it was clear to Harwood that Montgomery's views of the Navy's work to unblock Tripoli were open to suspicion, and he had judged the situation on the flimsiest information without in any way learning or wishing to know the facts,[32] nevertheless, facts were not to be allowed to influence opinion. Any objective and close investigation of the clearance of Tripoli does not reveal any serious neglect or delay on the Navy's part. Nor was there any delay to the Army's advance for, as de Guingand, the Chief of Staff, noted, the Army needed a rest, and did rest for several weeks. The sad conclusion is that Montgomery, from whatever motive, used an unfounded accusation as a pretext for undermining an officer of another service. Regrettably, there was deeper mischief afoot.

19
Harwood's Relief

In early 1943 Harwood was still only a substantive rear-admiral but on 6 February he was promoted to vice-admiral, while retaining his rank as acting-admiral and his appointment as Commander-in-Chief, Mediterranean. Two weeks later, British naval command in the Mediterranean was changed to bring it into kilter with the Allied command organisation. Cunningham, who as Naval Commander, Allied Expeditionary Force (NCXF), had commanded the sea areas of the Allied landings on the Atlantic and Western Mediterranean coasts of North Africa, now resumed the title of Commander-in-Chief, Mediterranean. Harwood, who had already suggested something similar to Pound a few months before,[1] became Commander-in-Chief, Levant. Harwood, who had been starved of resources for operations in the Levant and had already lent MGBs and MTBs to Cunningham in the West, now lost his successful 10th Submarine Flotilla to Cunningham as well. A revised command boundary was drawn, joining southern Italy in a dogleg to the Libya/Tunisia border, placing Sicily and Malta under Cunningham.

On 14 February, before these boundary changes came into effect, Harwood heard from A V Alexander, offering him the appointment of Second in Command, Eastern Fleet. The offer took Harwood by surprise, but he had once before been nominated to relieve Admiral Sir James Somerville, who now commanded the Eastern Fleet, and he saw no reason why after a period as second in command he should not succeed to the principal command. He told Joan:

> I have just had a signal saying that this job has not enabled me to get to sea and now that I am a Vice Admiral I should change and get to sea. I have therefore been offered the job of 2nd in Command Eastern Fleet to be relieved here in May. I have of course accepted

> and asked if I can come to UK between the appointments ... I never dreamt of it even ... [but] ... This is a shore job and I had to go to sea again and the sooner the better. If it leads to No. 1 the sooner the better. If it leads to No 1 it will be a very good job.

Alexander's message had been 'a nice signal', he told Joan, which 'called attention to the Battle of the River Plate, my forceful tactics and how the Admiralty had hoped that further opportunities would have occurred and so on'.[2] Harwood was already making plans for his leave, writing to Joan on 20 February: 'I shall hope for some leave in June. I wonder how long I shall get. I ought to be able to spin it out to a month but of course part of the time will have to be in London. Where shall we stay?'[3]

Pound's unnecessary letter

Harwood had little time to savour the prospect of his new command, for the First Lord's message was closely followed by a letter from Pound, dated 20 February, which began 'I most heartily subscribe to what the 1st Lord said in para 1 of his telegram and I shall be glad to see your flag flying afloat again', and ended 'You have clearly made a great name for yourself as a sea commander and I am sure, given the opportunity which your new appointment should do, you will do so again.' That is all that Pound needed to say, but between these two sentences he packed a punch. Harwood himself had wondered to Joan about the sudden announcement: 'It is hard to judge at this distance what it all means'. Pound answered Harwood's apprehensiveness: 'You will be wondering why the change has been decided on so suddenly and I think it is only fair you should know'. Pound took responsibility for advising Alexander that Harwood should be relieved, and he listed several complaints. Casey, the Minister of State, considered that naval representation on the commanders-in-chief committee was not as strong as that of the other services; Brooke, on return to London, had been 'quite definite that the army had lost confidence that the navy would in all circumstances give them the necessary support'; and, specifically, that the arrangements for the clearance of Tripoli had been largely responsible for this attitude. Harwood was astonished. He had already dealt at length with Montgomery's unfounded accusation, and wrote at once to Casey to ask what he had said, and to Commodore Geoffrey Norman in Cairo for background information.

The complaint about naval representation in Cairo was a canard: a matter which had been raised by Casey's predecessor, Lyttleton, with Cunningham in his first tenure as Commander-in-Chief, Mediterranean, and which Cunningham had dealt with robustly in June 1942 while he was in London and between appointments:[4]

> The question of the inter-service co-ordination of command in the Middle East has been the subject of some controversy during the last two years. Various solutions have been tried, one of these was the establishment of an additional Chief of Staff to C-in-C, Mediterranean. This does not however appear to have satisfied the other two services though in my view it worked efficiently and perhaps had the arrangement been more heartily accepted it would have been still more efficient. The latest solution is the maintenance of an establishment in Cairo by the C-in-C, Mediterranean. The effect and intention of this arrangement is that the C-in-C, Mediterranean, should spend a large proportion of his time in Cairo. I view this arrangement with concern. We are at present going through a most critical time in the Mediterranean and I regard it as of cardinal importance that the Admiral should be in the closest touch with his Fleet, with his small craft and with the Merchant Navy. It is illusory to suppose that this can be effectively done if the Admiral is 100 miles from the sea for half the week. When hard fighting and difficult conditions have to be met the leader should not be 100 miles away from his forces ...

On 7 March 1943 Norman, the additional chief of staff, gave Harwood his views. He knew that the Minister of State separately, and that Alexander and Tedder together, had sent cables to London recommending that Harwood should spend more time in Cairo than Cunningham had. Despite best intentions, this had not been possible. However, Harwood had not refused to come up to any meeting when he had been required, nor had Norman ever been reproached by Casey or either of the other commanders-in-chief for failing to get an answer or decision on any naval matter. Alexander himself rarely spent long periods in Cairo and 'frequently attended meetings without having read his papers beforehand'. Norman might have added that the commanders-in-chief had different geographical areas of responsibility, and that the other services had operational headquarters, for example at Eighth Army and the RAF groups, for which there was no equivalent in the Navy. [5]

A snake in the grass

Harwood's first note to Casey does not seem to have survived, but Casey's reply was bland. He admitted that he had told Churchill that naval representation on the commanders-in-chiefs committee was not as strong as the other services, but 'I went into no greater detail ... My remarks were general and comparative. I don't know what more I can say about it ... I think you know that I have a great respect and liking for you ... and I am personally sorry if any remarks of mine might be thought to have had any effect on your professional career.'[6] This was clearly unacceptable and Harwood drafted a reply:[7]

> As I see it you have two ways of doing your duty – either to criticise the Head of a Service or to defend him against political intrigue and venom. Clearly you felt it necessary to adopt the former course and of that I cannot complain, though I profoundly disagree, but my point is that surely I should be told the reason why you found it necessary to criticise my handling of my duties. In view of the interest which my removal, very largely at your dictates, will arise now and in the post war books, letters and at the War Colleges, I do feel that the question ought to be thrashed out.

Harwood believed that the root cause of his humiliation was:

> Venom ... in political circles at home about Force X – I certainly failed to get them over and no doubt incurred much displeasure but ... If you had cause for complaint over my handling of this difficult problem I suggest that you could have told me; indeed have given me political directions. As you did neither I would suggest that I was entitled to expect your support on this question if and when I was attacked. It was clear to me when you returned from England

> that you had been directed to force the pace on Force X and override my recommendation. I feel that today you would not be prepared to criticise my views in this respect and if so this seems to be a point on which even now I could receive your assistance.[8]

Harwood was very hurt and very angry:

> The ostensible reason of your complaint given to me was that my representation on the C-in-C's Committee was not as strong as the other services. This quite frankly I deny and I can't see how, never having attended one of these meetings, you could possibly be justified in making such a statement. As regards the Defence Committee on which you preside, I have been through the records of our meetings and I can find no items that we discussed that were likely to lead you to feel that I had not adequately reported my views ... The situation is now that I am being removed from my Command largely because of a statement you made and partly because of some remarks by the Army. As regards the latter I have forwarded a full explanation to the 1st Sea Lord and I can only suggest on the political plane that you should equally place on record with the 1st Lord of the Admiralty the reasons that led you to express criticism of the way in which I carried out the not strictly naval portion of my duties. I would appreciate, but cannot do more than ask, for a copy of this letter.[9]

There is no knowing where this correspondence would have gone, but sensibly Harwood did not send his riposte.

The Army's lost confidence

It was the charge that the Army no longer had confidence that it could rely on the Navy in all circumstances to give it support which hurt most. It was a grave reflection on the Navy and on Harwood. Norman, who had been in Cairo for nearly two years was best-placed to refute this, and was adamant: 'I ... can state without fear of contradiction that there is no foundation whatsoever for the allegation. In fact the reverse is the case and I am almost embarrassed at times at the eulogies I have to listen to on the Navy's and Merchant Navy's work in support of the

Army.' Norman was clear that Brooke had been given this information by Montgomery, but, he wrote:

> You heard yourself what LGA [Lieutenant General Administration – Robertson] had to say at the morning meeting you attended on Saturday [6 March?] ... he has consistently paid tribute to the work of the Western Desert shipping both Naval and Mercantile throughout the Eighth Army's campaign and I know that he adopts this attitude at all meetings whether or not there are Naval representatives present.[10]

Norman reminded Harwood of two other factors, first that Churchill's cables showed his close interest in supplies to the Western Desert and the rate of discharge at Tripoli, but these signals were addressed to Robertson and not copied to Harwood. Norman also noted the Eighth Army's cover plan while it sat and recuperated before a further advance 'from Tripoli on to the Mareth Line has been throughout the difficulty of opening up and maintaining supplies through Tripoli'. (The Eighth Army sat in Tripoli from the end of January until it began its attack on the next westward objective, the Mareth line, on 16/17 March.[11]) The regrettable inference of the cover plan was indeed that the Navy had failed the Army, but whatever the reason for this long delay at Tripoli, it was not a shortage of supplies arriving through the port: 'the figures for the discharge should, I suggest, be an adequate answer to this.'[12]

Cunningham's sympathy

In the middle of this crisis for Harwood, on 15 March, he met Cunningham to agree details of their division of responsibility for the Mediterranean and the Levant. They 'had a very good meeting ... and ... quickly reached agreement on all points'.[13] Harwood did not use the opportunity to tell Cunningham about Pound's letter, and when Cunningham did hear about it, presumably through Norman, with whom he maintained a private communication, he told Pound that Harwood was very upset by the reasons for being relieved. Montgomery's claim that there had been 'dilatoriness in opening up Tripoli', he told Pound, 'is quite untrue. In my opinion Tripoli was most expeditiously cleared and opened up and any statement to the contrary is quite untrue ... I feel that Harwood has been very hardly dealt with. Nor will this tend to improve relations between the Navy and the Army which are usually excellent. Montgomery, I gather, is not given to appreciate what the Navy does for him and wants pulling up'.[14]

This drew a rare reprimand from Pound: Harwood had been relieved 'on my recommendation ... I am very sorry for Harwood but with a blood pressure of 255, which no one knew about until after Tripoli, it is not surprising that he was not up to the mark. I am surprised at your expressing such a definite opinion about his relief when you only know one side.'[15] This comment on Harwood's health came from a man who had himself been ill for many months, frequently lapsed into sleep at meetings, and was soon to die of a brain tumour. However, to Harwood, Cunningham wrote:[16]

> Ramsay [*sic*] has told me about the reason you are leaving the Mediterranean and I think you are being extremely badly treated. I have written to Dudley Pound and told him so but of course it will make no difference. Of course you will know that at first I opposed your appointment as CinC Med. Nothing personal but it meant that all the vice-admirals were cut off from an appointment which I thought a very bad thing. Having been in the job however I do think you should have been properly supported.

Cunningham thought it was 'a sad story': Pound, he told Roskill, who was writing his book of *Churchill and the Admirals*, was inclined to condemn officers without hearing what they had to say. Perhaps on this occasion Pound felt remorse, because when Cunningham became First Sea Lord after Pound's death on Trafalgar Day 1943, he found that many important letters, like those about Harwood, were missing. He speculated that they had been destroyed by Pound.[17]

Harwood's health

Harwood wrote an eight-page exoneration, rehearsing many of the arguments which have already been set out here. It would do no good, except perhaps to annoy Pound. Harwood was inclined to corpulence and, though he played golf and tennis, shot and fished when he could, he had been criticised for his lack of physical fitness since W W Fisher's warning in 1933. In 1934–36 he had been accompanied by Joan, but since then he had been confined to a ship, or the Stygian living conditions of the Citadel, or his headquarters in Alexandria, and beyond reach of her care. On 20 March 1943 he suffered a heart attack. His doctors found that his blood pressure was 240/140 and, on their advice, at the end of March 1943 he returned to England by air and spent two weeks in the Royal Masonic Hospital followed by a year of sickness and unemployment. His appointment as Vice-Admiral Commanding the 3rd Battle Squadron and 2nd in Command of the Eastern Fleet, which had been publicly announced on 6 March, and was to have taken effect on 17 April, was cancelled.

Undoubtedly, the stress brought on by Pound's letter had contributed to his heart attack.

20
Finis

Harwood was on foreign service and sick leave for a year until appointed in his substantive rank of vice-admiral, to be Admiral Commanding, Orkneys and Shetlands. There he remained until March 1945 when he was invalided from the service in August and promoted admiral on the retired list. The war in Europe was coming rapidly to a close and there was little excitement in the islands which had once been a base for the Home Fleet and a barrier to the German navy. Montgomery, now a victorious field-marshal, visited the islands and was hosted by the Harwoods, and the occasion passed off without rancour.

Harwood had one last service to give. He chaired a committee on the training of officers which looked at the future of the Royal Naval College, Greenwich. The committee made ambitious, far-reaching and well-argued proposals for turning Greenwich into the university of the Royal Navy, but in post-war, economy-minded Britain these ideas fell on deaf ears.[1] In retirement there were dinners, ceremonies and speeches, but Harwood's work was done.

Retrospect

Harwood's early life and naval career were a metaphor of his age. He was well reported on throughout his naval career, as a staff officer, as a leader of men, a diplomat and someone possessed (*pace* Hastings) of intelligence, imagination, ambition and fighting spirit. Perhaps the only unusual feature was that he was a Catholic and he bore quiet witness to his faith without provoking anyone, except perhaps the Ulsterman, Bernard Montgomery. His private letters to Joan reveal his love for her and, a feature of their correspondence, an almost permanent concern for their finances.

His time as Commodore, South America made the man. Before sailing from Plymouth in 1936 Harwood wrote to Joan, 'I have the best job in the Navy; my own squadron, and am virtually my own boss in a part of the world I know and love'. In the following years he understood that showing the flag, support to the local British communities and the furtherance of British interests were an important part of his duties. Gone by the 1930s were the happy-go-lucky days in *Southampton* when, as soon as the formalities were completed, the officers were whirled off into the interior to enjoy their shooting and fishing. Harwood was quick to appreciate how circumstances were changing and to adapt visits to foreign ports both to be more meaningful for the local authorities and British communities, and to counter the growing influence of the totalitarian regimes of Germany and Italy. In his speeches to British audiences in North and South America he was forthright about the need to re-arm and about Britain's ability to protect trade, while with the South Americans he concentrated on their links to Britain which had been forged in their fight for independence and their subsequent economic development. His open and friendly character quickly won him the friendship and trust of the South American people, which on the outbreak of war was to reap rewards.

His junior officers learned that parties were primarily duty engagements where dowagers had to be charmed before their daughters. Harwood made clear that officers could not fulfil their duties without learning at least a smattering of Spanish, and ships' companies too understood their part in showing the flag. The anonymous authors of the *Cruise of HMS Exeter* showed their pride in ceremonial activities, an enjoyment in giving concert parties, and a pleasure in hosting visitors. The behaviour of the ship's company ashore and the low incidence of leave-breaking showed that *Exeter* was a happy ship and, as he had in *London* in the Mediterranean, Harwood succeeded in making *Exeter* the winner of more sporting trophies than any other ship in the squadron and, despite lack of facilities, in bringing her to the highest degree of fighting efficiency.

Harwood threw himself wholeheartedly into the social and representational side of his job and monitored every detail to ensure he provided generous and impressive personal hospitality on board. The cost of Harwood's duty entertaining far exceeded the allowance provided by a parsimonious Admiralty, and though he had no appreciable private income, his menu cards were embossed with his broad pennant, his brandy glasses displayed *Exeter*'s ship's badge, and his cigarettes were specially rolled with his broad pennant motif which made them highly attractive souvenirs.

Harwood displayed an easy, outgoing manner and was intuitively trusted. He was equally at home at diplomatic receptions as he was with the British communities, and his ability to make speeches, and even crack jokes, in Spanish endeared him to all. He was a demanding but very human and understanding captain. Noel Kemble of *Exeter*, and previously of *London*, wrote of Harwood, 'With an obstinate officer like myself he had quite a problem on his hands. Nevertheless his sometimes deliberately fierce demeanour never really hid his real understanding of the problem or of the person with whom he was dealing'. One officer told Joan: 'The commodore is terrible when he looks at you through his eyebrows', but beneath those beetle brows there was a soft heart. When one of his officers got engaged to a girl ashore, Harwood, who knew the officer's parents, had them both to lunch and wrote to assure the parents that she came from a respected local English family and would make a daughter-in-law they would be proud of (the marriage proved a long and happy one).[2]

He made a point of befriending South American naval officers, and in Montevideo he conducted simple exercises with the Uruguayan navy, most notably with the old cruiser *Uruguay* commanded by Commander José Rodriguez Varela. Varela would later be the head of the Uruguayan inspection team sent to assess *Graf Spee*'s readiness for sea. Montevideo became the proxy home port for *Exeter* in South America, and although it did not have the bright lights of Buenos Aires, Rio de Janeiro or Valparaíso, the population was friendly and pro-British. Harwood made special friends with the ambassador, Eugen Millington-Drake, who eased his relations with the local community. Probably through Lloyd Hirst, whose intelligence work had continued, Harwood also met Rex Miller (elsewhere known under the pseudonym of Ray Martin), the head of MI6 in South America. All were to play important parts in the *Graf Spee* story.

McCall, the naval attaché, wrote: 'Much of the goodwill ... was due to Harwood's work. He was a popular man who got what he wanted by friendliness'. Another admirer wrote: 'It was obvious that he had made a very intensive study of all the many problems which he might be faced in that area should war eventuate ... he could talk Spanish fluently and there was little doubt that he had made a great impression with the S American countries'.

Though out of sight and often out of mind of the Admiralty, Harwood succeeded well in his years in command of the South American Division, and in his last peacetime report on Harwood, his commander-in-chief wrote that he could confidently recommend Harwood for promotion to admiral in important sea commands. When war started, Harwood deployed his slender forces with skill, and though his sources of intelligence were slim, it was not just luck when on the morning after he had announced his intention to 'attack at once by day or night', he met the German *Graf Spee*. The Battle of the River Plate, between his three cruisers and a much heavier pocket battleship, earned Harwood a permanent place in history. His daring won him worldwide respect and admiration, and the gratitude of the First Lord of the Admiralty, Winston Churchill.

It is hard to determine what direct input that Harwood, during his time as Assistant Chief of Naval Staff (Foreign), had in operations such as Menace, but he gave policy advice at the highest level on a range of subjects important to the war. He enjoyed the confidence of Churchill, who recognised Harwood's fighting spirit and urged that he should be promoted to high command.

Cunningham disapproved of Harwood's appointment as Commander-in-Chief, Mediterranean, because other more senior officers were 'passed over' and because he thought that Harwood's talent would be better employed in a seagoing command. Harwood took up his duties when the Mediterranean Fleet had been depleted by losses and its two battleships disabled, but the Army was in Tobruk, far to the West, and preparing to advance. Operation Vigorous, a convoy to relieve Malta, was entirely feasible while the coast of Cyrenaica and its airfields were in British hands, but the operational environment was entirely changed by Rommel's pre-emptive attack which swept British forces back hundreds of miles to El Alamein. The convoy would still have stood a good chance of success had it been reinforced by the Eastern Fleet, a reinforcement which Churchill vetoed. Harwood skilfully manoeuvred the Vigorous convoy out of range of the Italian fleet, but he was denied success by Tedder's failure to provide adequate offensive and defensive air support, and by Vian's illness, which robbed the latter of his customary decisiveness.

Harwood's time as Commander-in-Chief, Mediterranean and then of the Levant was marred by a succession of other reverses. While Rommel readied himself for an advance into the Delta, British civil and military forces burned their papers and began to evacuate non-essential personnel. As the most westerly and most exposed of British infrastructure in Egypt, Harwood felt obliged to evacuate the naval base at Alexandria: compared to the loss of airfields in the Western Desert, it was a brief, precautionary abandonment, but nevertheless it irked Churchill.

Operation Agreement, a major raid on enemy-held Tobruk, was an event in the spirit of the Zeebrugge raid in 1918 and the raids on St-Nazaire and Dieppe in 1942, and which appealed very much to Churchill. It started well and might have succeeded, but the withdrawal was turned into a disaster by, once again, Tedder's failure to provide air cover.

Harwood brought to Alexandria the diplomatic skills which he had honed in South America, and he applied these to the problem of Godfroy and the French Force X. Harwood pursued the same policy towards Godfroy as his predecessor, Cunningham, and it is to their joint credit that no fighting took place in Alexandria and that the harbour was not littered with scuttled French ships. The matter vexed Churchill, and caused further loss of confidence in Harwood, though it was Harwood's policy towards Godfroy which in the end proved right.

Montgomery's complaint about the clearance of the harbour of Tripoli, over the head of his superior to Brooke and Churchill, was malicious, and however comprehensive Harwood's explanation, it was wilfully misunderstood. Any statement by Montgomery that the Army had lost confidence that the Navy would in all circumstances give the necessary support was simply not true. All other reports were in the opposite sense. The Navy in the Eastern Mediterranean had helped the Army to an extent probably unexampled in history, and one of the main factors in the Army's advance was Harwood's Fleet Air Arm aircraft, attached to 201 (Naval Co-operation) Group, and his submarines. It would have been more pertinent to complain that Tedder only paid lip-service to the concept of naval co-operation.

Likewise, Casey's complaint about Harwood's attendance at meetings in Cairo was a canard, a criticism which had been decisively put to bed by Cunningham. Cunningham had said that, having given Harwood the command in the Mediterranean, he should have been fully supported, but Churchill proved fickle and transferred his faith to Montgomery, and Pound followed suit. Pound's letter to Harwood explaining why he was relieved was unnecessary. Pound and Harwood had often enjoyed a master-servant relationship, and the latter had been ineffably polite and long-suffering, even when Pound had been at his most insufferable, but one can only wonder whether Harwood's appointment to second in command of the Far East Fleet would have withstood Harwood's angry response to Pound's letter telling him why he was being re-appointed.

Illness intervened, the year in Orkney and Shetland was fallow, and Harwood only enjoyed a few short years of retirement. Since his death, on 9 June 1950 at the premature age of sixty-two, post-war analyses, starting with Roskill's investigation in the 1950s and continuing in Correlli Barnett's *Engage the Enemy More Closely* in 1991, have tended to deal harshly with Harwood's reputation. However, Henry Harwood will be forever known as the victor on 13 December 1939 of the Battle of the River Plate, the first major naval battle of the Second World War and a battle won in the greatest traditions of the Royal Navy. The nature of the victory by lesser, lighter forces against a more powerful enemy, an attack pressed home regardless of loss and won against the odds harked back to the frigate actions of the Nelson era. Winston Churchill said of this in 1939 that 'The warrior heroes of the past may look down, as Nelson's monument looks down upon us now, without any feeling that the island race has lost its daring or that the examples which they set in bygone centuries have faded as the generations have succeeded to one another.'[3] Churchill was delighted with Harwood for having driven an enemy pocket battleship into a neutral harbour, 'in spite of her far heavier metal and commanding range'.[4] This was the sort of battle that fired Churchill's imagination, and confirmed that the Royal Navy could still be counted upon to outstrip its rivals in the qualities that mattered most: aggressive spirit, tactical skill, courage, and determination. In the sombre, first, dark winter of the war, the Battle of the River Plate was in Churchillian prose 'a flash of light and colour ... a great action which will long be told in song and story'.[5] Nothing can take this triumph from Harwood.

Notes

Sources

The sources for this biography of Henry Harwood are noted in the endnotes. The principal, personal papers are in eight, uncatalogued boxes at the Imperial War Museum. Some papers have been transcribed by Henry Harwood's sons and privately published as *Letters, Papers and Speeches*, and an unpublished draft entitled Mediterranean. Other papers have been retained by the family and have yet to be deposited in an archive. archive. Unless otherwise stated references are to HFP, many of which can also be found in IWM. references are:

CAC	Churchill Archives, Cambridge
HFP	Harwood Family Papers
IWM	Imperial War Museum, London
LPS	Letters, Papers and Speeches
NHB	Naval Historical Branch, Portsmouth
TNA	The National Archives, Kew

Chapter 1

1 Harwood, C H H, ***History of the Harwood Family*** (Gosport: Ashgate Colour Press, 2009). See also IWM 60/95/1. Henry Harwood's grandfather, born Henry Penny, traced his descent from King Edward III, but he assumed his mother's maiden name of Harwood in 1853. His father, Surtees Harwood, a London barrister, died in 1892 when his only son was just four. His mother Mary Ullathorne came from a staunchly Catholic Yorkshire family who traced their descent from St Thomas More.

2 Charnock, John, ***Biographia Navalis; Or, Impartial Memoirs of the Lives and Characters of Officers of the Navy of Great Britain, from the Year 1660 to the Present Time*** (London: Printed for R Faulder, Bond-Street, 1794), vol I, p166. Thomas Harwood learned his business under 'brave Sir Thomas Ayscough' who was 'a match for Van Tromp or De Ruyter whom, in the first Dutch war, he engaged and conquered'. Little more is known of Thomas Harwood except that his fortunes survived the Glorious Revolution of 1688 and in 1694/95 he was Sheriff of Berkshire.

3 TNA ED 35/944 Fareham: Stubbington House, Question of Recognition for Purposes of Teachers' Registration Regulations 1903–21. See also https://en.wikipedia.org/

wiki/Stubbington_House_School. The school moved to Ascot in 1962 and closed in 1997.

4 https://en.wikipedia.org/wiki/List_of_Victoria_Crosses_by_school#Victoria_Crosses_by_school_and_campaign

5 Captain Evelyn Twysden Wickham (1888–1973), see ADM 196/144/257, etc.

6 Admiral Sir Tom Phillips (1888–1941), given his short stature, was nicknamed 'Tom Thumb', Deputy Chief of the Naval Staff (later Vice Chief of the Naval Staff) 1 June 1939 to 21 October 1941, commanded Force Z during the Japanese invasion of Malaya, when the battleship *Prince of Wales* and battlecruiser *Repulse* were sunk by Japanese aircraft.

7 Henry and Stephen Harwood, *Letters, Papers and Speeches from the Collection Of Admiral Sir Henry Harwood KCB OBE (1888–1950)* (Gosport: The Better Book Company, 2012), henceforth LPS. The originals are uncatalogued in the Imperial War Museum, but there is a bound copy of LPS in IWM 60/95/8. LPS 1/3 and 1/4 Harwood to his mother, June 1904.

8 LPS 1/6 from *London* at Beirut, 5 Aug 1904.

9 LPS 1/7 from *London* at sea, 20 Aug 1904.

10 HMS *Bramble*, built by W H Potter and Son in Liverpool in 1898, complement eighty-five officers and men, armed with two 4in and four 12pdr guns, sold in Bombay in 1920.

11 Commander the Hon R O B Bridgeman, second son of the Earl of Bradford, awarded the DSO in 1915 during the East Africa campaign when he 'displayed great courage and coolness ... though subjected to a heavy and accurate fire ... worthy of the best traditions of the Royal Navy', died at sea after his seaplane's engine failed during a reconnaissance flight over the Rufiji River delta in 1917.

12 Admiral Sir Henry Ruthven Moore (1886–1978), ACNS(Trade) 27 Jul 1940, then VNCS 21 Oct 1941 to 7 June 1943.

13 The German ship's correct name was *Admiral Graf Spee*, but to the British she was known as *Graf von Spee* or simply *Graf Spee*: the simpler form is used throughout this work, except where it is verbatim.

14 Admiral John Henry Godfrey (1888–1970), Director of Naval Intelligence 1939–42 and supposedly Ian Fleming's model for the fictional James Bond's boss, 'M'.

15 LPS 1/30 Speech at dinner given by Merchant Venturers, Bristol during visit of HM Ships *Warwick* and *Velox*.

Chapter 2

1 Captain William Henry Wake Ridley (1887–), see ADM 196/51/23.

2 Captain Arnold Maitland-Dougall (1887–), see ADM 196/92/29.

3 Vice-Admiral Sir John Gregory Crace (1887–1968), known as Jack or 'Crack' was an Australian-born officer of the Royal Navy who commanded Task Force 44, at the Battle of the Coral Sea in 1942. See ADM 196/51/55 and ADM 196/92/43.

4 Rear-Admiral Henry Montagu Doughty (1870–1921), second captain of *Royal Sovereign* Jul 1917 to 16 Jun 1919.

5 Pre-war, the German Heinrich Beck had built and patented a new searchlight: the war caught him in the USA. See http://www.skylighters.org/beck/index.html.

6 Admiral Sir Thomas Hunt (1866–1943), first captain of *Royal Sovereign* 3 Mar 1916 to Jul 1917, and Commander-in-Chief, South America Station 9 Mar 1919 to 1921.

7 LPS 1/13 onboard *Royal Sovereign*, 27 Nov 1918.

Chapter 3

1 Vice-Admiral Sir Theodore John Hallett (1878–1956) retired in 1933 but was recalled and served as a beachmaster for the Dunkirk evacuation in 1940, as a member of the expeditionary force to Narvik in Norway in 1942 and then as director of training for the commandos.

2 When Hunt visited Asunción in Paraguay in HMS *Petersfield* in Aug 1920, it was the first visit of a British warship so far inland, possibly since

the Battle of Obligado in 1845.
3 LPS R/12 Speech at the Torpedo & Anti-Submarine Officers' Dinner, 28 Oct 1949.
4 Lloyd Hirst, *Coronel and After* (London: Peter Davies, 1934), p141.
5 Millington-Drake, Eugen, *The Drama of Graf Spee and the Battle of the River Plate* (Peter Davies: London, 1964), pp19–21.
6 Admiral Sir John Hereward Edelsten (1891–1966) was ACNS(U-boat Warfare and Trade) in 1942: as 'Banderas' he wrote *Sporting Reminiscences of South America, 1919–1921, HMS Southampton* (London: Riddle, Smith and Duffus, 1922).

Chapter 4
1 IWM 60/95/5. Contains Harwood's papers of the Committee on the Royal Naval College, Greenwich 1945–46 and background papers including a history of the lieutenants' course.
2 Professor Sir Geoffrey Callender (1875–1946) taught history at the Royal Naval College, Osborne 1905–13, when he wrote *Sea Kings of Britain* (3 vols, 1907–11), was the first professor of history at the Royal Naval College, Greenwich, headed the Society for Nautical Research's campaigns to save HMS *Victory* for the nation and to found a naval and maritime museum for the United Kingdom, and was director of the National Maritime Museum 1937–46.
3 Admiral the Hon Sir Reginald Aylmer Ranfurly Plunkett-Ernle-Erle-Drax (1880–1967), often referred to as Reginald Plunkett or (after 1916) as Reginald Drax, and one of the founders of *The Naval Review*.
4 Command 1343 of 1921.
5 Stewart, Ninian, *The Organisation of the Naval Staff within the Admiralty and the Ministry of Defence* 1927–1999 (Unpublished).
6 Admiral of the Fleet David Richard Beatty (1871–1936).
7 Admiral Sir George Hamilton D'Oyly Lyon, KCB (1883–1947).
8 Phillips, a school friend from Stubbington days, and Godfrey, a term-mate from *Britannia* days and a fellow China hand. See Brodhurst, Robin, *Churchill's Anchor: The Biography of Admiral of the Fleet Sir Dudley Pound* (Barnsley: Pen & Sword, 2000), p50: they 'were an impressive collection'.
9 Admiral Sir Hugh Dudley Richards Watson (1872–1954) was Naval Secretary 1921–23.
10 Admiral Sir Barry Edward Domvile (1878–1972) who was interned during the Second World War as a Nazi sympathiser.
11 LPS 2/6 Harwood to Joan, 4 Aug 1925.
12 Admiral Sir George Knightley Chetwode (1877–1957) commanded *Queen Elizabeth*, then *Warspite* 1926/27, and Naval Secretary 1929–32.
13 Admiral of the Fleet Sir George Creasy (1895–1972) in war Director of Anti-Submarine Warfare, flag captain to the Commander-in-Chief, Home Fleet, Chief Staff Officer to the Naval Commander-in-Chief of the Allied Expeditionary Force. An advocate of naval air power.
14 Admiral of the Fleet Bruce Austin Fraser, 1st Baron Fraser of North Cape (1888–1981) Controller of the Navy 1939–42, Second-in-Command and then Commander-in-Chief, Home Fleet 1942–44, Commander-in-Chief, Eastern Fleet 1944, later First Sea Lord 1948–51.
15 William Stephen Richard King-Hall, Baron King-Hall (1893–1966), naval officer, writer, politician and playwright. He resigned from the Navy in 1929 but continued to write about it.
16 Robin Brodhurst, *Churchill's Anchor: The Biography of Admiral of the Fleet Sir Dudley Pound* (Barnsley: Pen & Sword, 2000), pp53–9.
17 Rear-Admiral Royer Mylius Dick (1897–1991) was flag-lieutenant to Vice-Admiral W H D Boyle, Flag Officer 1st Cruiser Squadron, when he witnessed Pound at work and play in 1926/27.
18 LPS 2/8 Harwood to Joan, a letter begun on 5 Aug 1925 and apparently finished on 7 Aug.

19 Halpern, Paul G (ed), *The Mediterranean Fleet, 1919–1929* (Farnham: Ashgate for the Navy Records Society, 2011), pp457–60.
20 TNA ADM 1/8711/146 Exercise MU Passage of the Fleet to the East, through the Malacca Straits under wartime conditions. Alternative routes, fuelling arrangements.
21 Roskill, Stephen, *Naval Policy between the Wars: The Period of Anglo-American Antagonism 1919–1929* (London: Collins, 1968), pp534–6. But see also Friedman, Norman, '*Review of the Royal Navy in Eastern Waters 1935–1942*', *Mariner's Mirror*, 103:3 (2017), 370, where Friedman refutes Roskill.
22 Brodhurst, pp54–5.
23 Stephen Roskill, *Naval Policy Between The Wars: The Period of Reluctant Rearmament 1930–1939* (London: Collins, 1976), p465n. As Roskill remarks, lower-deck names given to senior officers are often both witty and shrewd.
24 LPS 2/7 Harwood to Joan, *Queen Elizabeth* at Malta, 4 Aug 1925.
25 LPS 2/11 Harwood to Joan, *Queen Elizabeth* at Corfu, 10 Aug 1925.
26 LPS 2/12 Harwood to Joan, *Queen Elizabeth* at Corfu, 11 Aug 1925.
27 LPS 2/13 Harwood to Joan. *Queen Elizabeth*, Krystos Bay, Greece, 21 Aug 1925.
28 LPS 2/10 Harwood to Joan, *Queen Elizabeth* at Thasos, Greece, 1 Sep 1925.
29 LPS 2/17 Harwood to Joan, *Queen Elizabeth* at Thasos and Lemnos, 1 Sep 1925.
30 LPS 2/17 Harwood to Joan, *Queen Elizabeth* at Thasos and Lemnos, 1 September 1925.
31 LPS 2/20. Harwood to Joan, *Queen Elizabeth* at Thasos, 16 September 1925.
32 Brodhurst, p59.

Chapter 5

1 Vice-Admiral Arthur Lionel Snagge (1878–1955), see TNA ADM 196/44/444, etc.
2 Admiral of the Fleet Sir Reginald Yorke Tyrwhitt (1870–1951), see TNA ADM 196/43, etc.
3 Temple Patterson, A, *Tyrwhitt of the Harwich Force* (London: The Military Book Society, 1973), pp236–73.
4 LPS 11/85 Tywhritt to Harwood, undated.
5 LPS 1/30 After dinner speech given during visit Bristol, Summer 1930.
6 LSP 2/30. Bristol. Lord Mayor's Banquet on same occasion.
7 Vice-Admiral Ronald H C Hallifax (1885–1943).
8 A search at the RCDS does not reveal who the staff were nor who Harwood's fellow students were.
9 Sir Henry Robert Moore Brooke-Popham (1878–1953), Oxfordshire Light Infantry, transferred to the Air Battalion, Royal Engineers, in 1912 and the newly founded Royal Air Force in 1919. He was the first Commandant of the Royal Air Force Staff College (1921–26), the first RAF officer to be Commandant of the Imperial Defence College (1931–33) and Governor and Commander-in-Chief of Kenya (1937–39). Recalled to service he was Commander-in-Chief, Far East (the first RAF officer to hold such a post) but was retired in May 1942.
10 IWM 60/95/5 A memoir by an old friend who first met Harwood when shipmates on the South American station in HMS *Southampton*. 'It was obvious that he had made a very intensive study of all the many problems which he might be faced in that area should war eventuate ... he could talk Spanish fluently and there was little doubt that he had made a great impression with the S American countries'.
11 Halpern, Paul G, *The Mediterranean Fleet, 1930–1939* (Oxford: The Navy Records Society with Routledge, 2016), pp3–11.
12 Admiral of the Fleet Alfred Ernle Montacute Chatfield, 1st Baron Chatfield (27 Sep 1873 - 15 Nov 1967), Beatty's flag captain at the Battles of Heligoland Bight 1914, Dogger Bank 1915 and Jutland 1916. In the interwar years Commander-in-Chief, Atlantic Fleet and then Commander-in-Chief, Mediterranean Fleet before serving as First Sea Lord in the 1930s when

he won back the Fleet Air Arm from the RAF. Some argue he should have been recalled as First Sea Lord instead of Pound, but served as Minister for Co-ordination of Defence in the early years of the Second World War. (See footnote on W W Fisher below.)

13 Admiral Sir William Wordsworth Fisher (1875–1937) Commander-in-Chief, Fleet 1932–36, probably the outstanding British admiral of the interwar period who would have become First Sea Lord instead of Pound, but died in office as Commander-in-Chief, Portsmouth.

14 Gerald Strickland, 6th Count della Catena, 1st Baron Strickland (1861–1940), a Maltese and British politician, was in succession governor of the Leeward Islands, Tasmania, Western Australia and New South Wales. Formed the Anglo-Maltese Party in 1921 which amalgamated with the Maltese Constitutional Party to become the Constitutional Party under his leadership, was leader of the opposition 1921–27. In 1924 he won Lancaster for the Conservatives in the United Kingdom elections, was made a peer in 1928, and from 1927–30 was fourth prime minister of Malta.

15 Count Sir Michael Gonzi (1885–1984), elected as a Labour senator in the Malta legislative assembly in 1921, resigned halfway into his term to be ordained as the Bishop of Gozo in 1924, and became Archbishop of Malta in 1943.

16 Halpern, Paul G (ed), ***The Mediterranean Fleet, 1930–1939*** (Oxford: The Navy Records Society with Routledge, 2016), pp26–8

17 LPS 11/77 Vice-Admiral Sir Bertram Ramsay to Harwood, 21 October 1940.

18 Cock of the fleet: a sporting trophy competed strongly for between ships of the fleet.

19 IWM 60/95/2. George K Chetwode, ***Some Notes on Boat Pulling and Regattas*** (HMS ***Warspite***, 1926) which Chetwode, as an admiral, supplemented with further notes in 1932.

20 LPS 2/21 Harwood to Joan, London, 14 Jul 1933.

21 Captain L F Potter, commanding the cruiser HMS ***Devonshire***; Surgeon-Commander E C Holton, principal medical officer in HMS ***London***; Paymaster-Commander W G Enright; Roman Catholic chaplain Thomas Basil Bruce-Cooke; and (?) Paymaster-Midshipman R W Bell.

22 TNA ADM 196/92/53 Confidential report by W W Fisher.

23 Vice-Admiral John Knowles im Thurn (1881–1956), commanded HMS ***Hood*** 1923–25 on her world tour, ACNS 1931–33 when he was appointed admiral commanding 1st Cruiser Squadron in the Mediterranean Fleet.

24 TNA ADM 196/92/53.

25 Presumably using CB 3011 War Game Rules (1929): see TNA ADM 186/78.

26 Admiral Sir Ragnar Musgrave Colvin (1882–1954) commanded the Royal Australian Navy at the outbreak of the Second World War; Rear-Admiral Arthur George Talbot (1892–1960); and Vice-Admiral Sir John Mansfield (1893–1949).

27 IWM 60/95/2. Attack on and Defence of Trade, a syllabus of six lessons, Summer session 1936.

28 HFP (see also IWM 60/95/2) Captain J A Heenan RCNR to J I Hornby (who was then considering a biography of Harwood), dated 8 Nov 1962

29 LPS R/12 After dinner speech to Torpedo & Anti-Submarine officers at HMS ***Vernon***, 28 Oct 1949.

30 LPS 4/14. Harwood to Joan, probably from ***Achilles***, Jan 1940.

31 LPS R/12 After dinner speech to Torpedo & Anti-Submarine officers at HMS ***Vernon***, 28 Oct 1949.

32 LPS 11/4 Harwood to Pound, end Jan 1940.

Chapter 6

1 Admiral the Hon Sir Matthew Robert Best (1878–1940), commander on the staff of the British commander-in-chief at the Battle of Jutland, Commander-in-Chief, America and West Indies Station 1934–37. Relieved on 28 May 1939 by Vice-Admiral Sir Sydney Meyrick.

2 Tute, Warren, The *Cruiser* (London: Cassell & Co Ltd, 1955), an epic novel of the Navy in peace and war.
3 Rear-Admiral Philip John Mack (1892–1943) the eldest of three brothers in the RN, he was a destroyer captain in the Mediterranean in the Second World War, but was killed in an air crash off Gibraltar.
4 TNA ADM 1/8728/173 Proposals for Appointment of an Assistant Naval Attache in South America, 1928.
5 Vice-Admiral Stephen Harry Tolson Arliss (1895–1954), also a successful destroyer captain in the Mediterranean.
6 Admiral Sir Henry William Urquhart McCall (1895–1980).
7 TNA ADM 1/10220 Naval Reporting and Control Network in South America.
8 Hirst's daughter, Barbara, was a frequent and popular visitor whenever *Exeter* was in Montevideo. Harwood made her an honorary member of the ship's company and issued her with service documents recording her badges and promotion to leading girl.
9 Rear-Admiral Sir (Charles) Philip Clarke (1898–1966).
10 Weekes: it was the custom for a paymaster officer to follow his 'star' and to take rank from his chief's, thus Weekes became an Acting Paymaster Captain as secretary to a Acting-Admiral Harwood.
11 Wickham, in charge of *Exeter*'s after 'Y'-turret, the last to keep firing during the Battle of the River Plate, was subsequently killed in 1944 in the coastal forces on the East Coast.
12 Cogswell, Reginald, *Exeter: A Cruiser of the Medium Size* (Liskeard: Navy Books, 2017), p34.
13 Hirst, p272.
14 Admiral Sir Sydney Meyrick (1873–1979) became Commander-in-Chief, American and West Indies Station on 15 April 1937.
15 LPS 4/37 Notes in Spanish for a lunch/dinner on board *Exeter* at Iquique, Chile, Sep 1937.
16 LPS 6/37 Extract from newspaper *Mercurio*, 24 Sep 1937.
17 LPS 11/37 Notes in Spanish for a lunchtime speech on board *Exeter*, Buenos Aires, Dec 1937.
18 LPS 12/37 British Society lunch, Buenos Aires, 14 Dec 1937.
19 Cogswell, p31.
20 Admiral Sir Charles Woodhouse (1893–1978), *Ajax* 1938–40, *Howe* 1942–44, Commander-in-Chief, East Indies 1948–50.
21 https://en.wikipedia.org/wiki/Freeman_Freeman-Thomas,_1st_Marquess_of_Willingdon.
22 *Padua* was one of the famous flying P-liners owned by the Laeisz shipping company in Hamburg. In 1938, under her master Richard Wendt, she sailed from Germany via Chile to Australia and back in eight months and twenty-three days, a world record that has never been broken. *Padua* survives as the Russian-flagged *Kruzenshtern*. The author is grateful to Dr Jann M Witt for help in identifying this ship.
23 Anon, *The Cruise of HMS Exeter* (London: W H Smith & Son, 1940), pp105–6.
24 Cogswell, pp150–1.
25 *The Cruise of HMS Exeter*, pp108–9.
26 Cogswell, p151.
27 Cogswell, p156.
28 Cogswell, p157.
29 Hirst, pp10, 22.
30 *The Cruise of HMS Exeter*, p216.
31 Cogswell, p182.

Chapter 7

1 Cogswell, pp187–9.
2 Raeder, Erich, *Der Krieg Zur See 1914–1918: Der Kieuzerkreg in den Ausländischen Gewässern* (Berlin: Mittler & Sohn, 1922), vol I. Vol II was printed in 1923. A third volume was published in 1937 by Eberhard v Manten about raider warfare by auxiliary cruisers, ie disguised merchant ships.
3 TNA ADM 116/5307 Fuehrer Conferences on Naval Affairs, 1939, p14.
4 Ibid, p8.
5 TNA ADM 223/68 Account of cruise and destruction of *Graf Spee* in River Plate action: The German Story. TNS ADM 223/69 Despatches from Naval Attaché, Buenos Aires concerning River Plate action: 'Dau was a

reserve officer of the old school, who had been a prisoner of the last war in England, and bore us a grudge. He was a stern disciplinarian, feared, respected and disliked. The crew were merchant service, a hard-bitten discontented lot ... on board the *Altmark* the *Admiral Graf Spee* maintained a naval guard, between whom and the ship's crew there was constant friction amounting sometimes to free fights'.

6 TNA ADM 223.69 Langsdorff was 'a very courteous, charming gentleman, a man of high though socialistic ideals ... though the Captain was pro-Nazi, he was not rabidly so, and was disgusted with the rapprochement between Germany and Russia ... he was obviously a man of very high character and he was proud of the fact that he had not been the cause of a single death as the result of any of his various captures.'

7 TNA ADM 223/68.

8 TNA ADM 116/5307 Fuehrer Conferences on Naval Affairs 1939, p11.

9 TNA FO 370/592 Diaries of men from *Graf Spee*.

10 TNA ADM 53/108160 Log of *Cumberland*.

11 TNA ADM 1/10678 HMS *Cumberland* Reports of Proceedings in South Atlantic 1–31 October 1939. TNA ADM 1/10512 South America Division, Report of Proceedings, HMS *Cumberland* 28 August to 30 September.

12 LPS 4/1 Harwood to Joan, 25 Aug 1939.

13 LPS 4/2 Harwood to Joan, 14 Sept 1939.

14 Ibid.

15 Ibid.

16 LPS 4/7 Exeter, 20 Oct 1939. The original of this letter has been destroyed.

17 LPS 4/8 Exeter notepaper, probably from *Ajax*, 'Buenos Aires tomorrow'.

18 TNA ADM 196/92 Meyrick to Secretary to Admiralty, 14 Jan 1939.

19 Other prefixes were AAA – under attack by aircraft, SSS – under attack by submarine, and, added later in the war, QQQ – under attack by disguised enemy raider.

20 TNA FO 370/592.

21 TNA ADM 1/10723 Actions with the Enemy (3): Voyage of German Battleship *Graf Spee*: narrative compiled from conversations with captured British Merchant men.

22 Naval Staff and Grove, E (nd), *German capital ships and raiders in World War II: Volume I From Graf Spee to Bismarck, 1939–1941* (London: Frank Cass), p8.

23 NHB War Diary (Naval) 1–31 Oct 1939 (2)

24 TNA ADM 53/108161. Log of *Cumberland*.

25 Harwood received this report in the mail on 7 December and forwarded it, without comment, on 12 December to the Admiralty in London with a copy to Lyon.

26 TNA ADM 1/10723.

27 LPS 4/9 Harwood to Joan, 3 Nov 1939.

28 TNA ADM 116/5307 Fuehrer Conferences on Naval Affairs, 1939, p37.

29 TNA ADM 223/464 History of Naval Intelligence and the Naval Intelligence Department 1939–1945 including raids of the *Scharnhorst, Gneisenau* and *Graf Spee*.

30 LPS R16 Royal Navy Club of 1765 and 1785, dinners to Commemorate the Battle of the River Plate. 28 Mar 1950 and 11 Dec 1980.

31 TNA ADM 223/464 History of Naval Intelligence and the Naval Intelligence Department 1939–1945 including raids on the *Scharnhorst, Gneisenau* and *Graf Spee*.

32 Dudley Pope, *The Battle of the River Plate* (London: William Kimber & Co, 1956), p100.

33 310 hectometres = 33,790yds (or 16.7 nautical miles): German gunnery ranges were given in hectometres or units of 100 metres. British measurements were in yards, with 1 cable = 200yds and at 10 cables or 2,000yds = 1 nautical mile.

34 LPS 4/17 F E Rasenack, 26 September 2001.

35 TNA ADM 223/68 Account of cruise and destruction of *Graf Spee* in River Plate action: The German Story.

36 Other, politer versions of Bell's words exist, but these are the words which

Harwood family lore holds.

Chapter 8

1 S D Waters, ***Official History of New Zealand in the Second World War 1939–45: The Royal New Zealand Navy*** (Wellington: Department of Internal Affairs, 1956), p45.

2 Some commentators doubt whether *Graf Spee* was able to split her fire in this way, but see Vice-Admiral Friedrich Ruge, 'Ruckblicke: Panzerschiff *Graf Spee*', ***Marinezeitschrift***, 12.5 (1954) 'In the beginning *Graf Spee* fired with one turret at each of the two groups but soon concentrated her heavy fire on the more dangerous ***Exeter***'. See also Paul Schmalenbach, ***Die Geschichte Der Deutschen Schiffsartillerie*** (Berlin: Koehlers Verlagsges, 1993), p159 and Alan D Zimm, 'The Battle of the River Plate: A Tactical Analysis', in ***Warship 2018*** (Oxford: Osprey Publishing, 2018), pp28–45. The author is grateful to Drs Eric J Grove and Jann Witt for their advice.

3 Holman, Gordon, ***The King's Cruisers*** (London: Hodder & Stoughton, 1947), p28.

4 Captain R E Washbourn (1910–), born in Nelson, entered RN 1928, served Achilles, 1939–42, Commodore Superintendent, Devonport dockyard 1948–50.

5 ***Naval Review***, 1940 vol 3, 'The Battle of the River Plate compiled from despatches'.

6 Holman, Gordon, ***The King's Cruisers*** (London: Hodder & Stoughton, 1947), p32.

7 Ibid, p34.

8 Holman, p42.

9 TNA ADM 1/10727 Analysis of W/T signals during River Plate Action shows necessity for W/T H/F receiving watch at Falkland Islands.

10 Ibid.

11 Eugen Millington-Drake, ***The Drama of Graf Spee and the Battle of the River Plate*** (Peter Davies: London, 1964), p298.

12 TNA ADM 1/110727.

13 TNA ADM 116/4320. Harwood had broadcast a warning to all shipping shortly before 1125 GMT.

14 Holman, p36.

15 Holman, p42.

Chapter 9

1 ADM 223/69 *Graf Spee*: copy of despatches from Naval Attaché, Buenos Aires concerning events subsequent to River Plate action.

2 Waters.

3 Millington-Drake, p337.

4 '1912–2012. 100 AÑOS DE LA ESTACIÓN COSTERA CERRITO RADIO', La Galena Del Sur, 2018 <https://lagalenadelsur.wordpress.com/2012/01/31/1912-2012-100-anos-de-la-estacion-costera-cerrito-radio/> [5 January 2018].

5 https://en.wikipedia.org/wiki/Pursuit_of_Goeben_and_Breslau#First_contact. The pursuit of the German battlecruiser ***Goeben*** and the light cruiser ***Breslau*** occurred in the Mediterranean Sea at the outbreak of the First World War when the British Mediterranean Fleet failed to engage the German ships whose arrival in Constantinople brought the Ottoman Empire into the war on the side of the Central Powers. Winston Churchill, who was First Lord of the Admiralty, wrote in his ***World Crisis*** that ***Goeben*** had brought 'more slaughter, more misery, and more ruin than has ever before been borne within the compass of a ship.'

6 TNA CAB/65 War Cabinet 114 (39). Conclusions of a Meeting of the War Cabinet held at 10 Downing Street, S.W. 1, on Thursday, December 14, 1939, at 10 A.M.

7 Holman, p8.

8 B&J, chap 5.

9 Millington-Drake, pp316ff. This episode was dramatised in the 1956 film and in subsequent popular stories into fictional calls between the offices of the British ambassadors in Buenos Aires and Montevideo using insecure telephone lines.

10 TNA CAB/65 War Cabinet 116 (39). Conclusions of a Meeting of the War Cabinet held at 10 Downing Street, S.W. 1, on Friday, December 15, 1939, at 11-30 A.M.

11 Holman, p39.

12 LPS 4/10 Harwood to Joan, 17 Dec 1939.

13 Lord Strabolgi, *The Battle Of The River Plate* (London: Hutchinson & Co, 1940), pp188–90.
14 TNA ADM 116/5307 Fuehrer Conferences on Naval Affairs, 1939, pp60–1.
15 Waters, p65.
16 Waters, p66.
17 Holman, p40.

Chapter 10

1 LPS 4/11* AJAX. 21 Dec 1939. Discusses Tactical Problems. Describes Scuttling.
2 LPS 11/33 Professor Sir Geoffrey Callender to Harwood, 14 Dec 1939.
3 HFP Notes concerning HHH made by Lady Harwood noted by CHHH, 4 Mar 2000.
4 LPS 11/43a From Admiral Sir Frederick Dreyer, 18 Jan 1940.
5 LPS 11/78 From 'Riddles'.
6 LPS 11/41 From Admiral Sir Andrew Cunningham.
7 LPS 11/54 From Admiral Sir William Goodenough.
8 LPS 11/37 Admiral Sir Walter Cowan to Harwood, undated.
9 LPS 4/20 Harwood to Joan, 1 Mar 1940.
10 LPS 11/55 From Captain T J Hallett.
11 Private communication to author by Lord Digby dated 11 Sep 2017. The messenger pronounced Montevid(ay)o): 'Montevideo' said Churchill in his English accent.
12 LPS 11/92 From Captain 'Wickie' Wickham.
13 LPS 11/65 Captain Arnold Maitland-Dougall to Joan.
14 LPS 11/38 From Rear Admiral 'Crack' Crace.
15 LPS 11/57 From Captain E J Hardman-Jones.
16 IWM 60/95/4. The supply departments apparently performed well and did not merit separate reports, only in *Exeter* was it noted that there were insufficient leather boots and gloves for fire and repair parties, but the arrangements for action messing worked well.
17 LPS 11/3 From Pound, 11 Jan 1940.
18 LPS 11/4 From Harwood to Pound (typed copy of draft).
19 TNA ADM 116/5307 Führer Conferences on Naval Affairs, 1939, p62.
20 TNA ADM 116/5307, pp65–7.
21 LPS 4/11 * AJAX. 21 Dec 1939. Discusses Tactical Problems. Describes Scuttling.

Chapter 11

1 RNZN, p71.
2 For a full account of the extraordinary work undertaken to make *Exeter* in all respects ready for sea, see Cogswell, pp269–83.
3 LPS 4/15. Harwood to Joan, 19 Jan 1940.
4 LPS R1 Friends of Uruguay Lunch, Dec 1945.
5 Waters, p71.
6 LPS 11/71 From Vice-Admiral Sir Tom Phillips.
7 LPS 4/19 Wood to Joan, 27 Feb 1940.
8 Ibid.
9 Ibid.
10 Baptiste, Fitzroy André, *War, Co-operation, and Conflict: The European Possessions in the Caribbean* (New York: Greenwood, 1988). Nevertheless, in March 1940 the President of Panama, on behalf of the Neutrality Committee, sent a formal complaint to the British government protesting against *Dorsetshire*'s alleged violation of the Pan-American Security Zone.
11 LPS 4/17 Harwood to Joan, 1 Feb 1940.
12 LPS 4/18 Harwood to Joan, 25 Feb 1940.
13 LPS 4/25 Harwood to Joan, 31 May 1940. In 1950 Copello, cardinal archbishop of Buenos Aires for over a quarter of a century, celebrated a requiem mass for Harwood.
14 Naval Staff and Eric Grove, *German Capital Ships and Raiders in World War II: Volume I From Graf Spee to Bismarck, 1939–1941* (London: Frank Cass).
15 TNA ADM 116/4109.
16 LPS 4/25 Harwood to Joan, 31 May 1940.
17 Foley, Thomas, *I Was an Altmark Prisoner* (Not known: Francis Aldor, 1940).
18 Dove, Patrick, *I Was Graf Spee's Prisoner* (Not known: Cherry Tree, 1940).

19 LPS 4/27 Harwood to Joan, 25 Jun 1940.
20 *The Battle of the River Plate* (1957) [film], UK: J Arthur Rank Film Distributors. When work began on 13 December 1955, the anniversary of the battle, the HMS *Ajax* and River Plate Association sent a message to the producers: 'Hope your shooting will be as successful as ours'. Harwood was played by Anthony Quayle.
21 TNA ADM 234/435 The Battle of the River Plate, BR 1877 formerly CB 3052.
22 LPS 4/27 Harwood to Joan, 25 Jun 1940.
23 See chapter 7. NHB War Diary (Naval) 1–31 Oct 1939 (2).
24 TNA ADM 53/108161 Log of HMS Cumberland.
25 TNA ADM 205/4 First Sea Lord's Records 1939–1945 ff 5, Lyon to Tennant 1 February 1940.
26 Albert Victor Alexander, later 1st Earl Alexander of Hillsborough (1885–1965) was a Labour MP and First Lord of the Admiralty, ie its political head, 1929–31 and 1940–46 and Minster of Defence 1946–50. Not to be confused with General Alexander.
27 LPS 11/24 From The Secretary The Right Honourable The Viscount Halifax KG GCSI, etc, etc, etc.

Chapter 12

1 CAC AVAR 5/4/58
2 CAC AVAR 5/4/56
3 CAC DUPO 2/2 to Blake to Donald McLachlan.
4 Simpson, Michael, *The Cunningham Papers: Vol I The Mediterranean Fleet 1939–1942* (Aldershot: Ashgate for the Navy Records Society, 1999), p208.
5 CAC AVAR 5/4/68 (a) Alexander/Churchill 18/19 Nov 40 and (b) Alexander to Pound 18 Nov.
6 Joan in her copy of Roskill's *Churchill and the Admirals.*
7 CAC AVAR 5/4/72 Alexander/Pound, undated.
8 Tute, Warren, *The Cruiser* (London: Cassell & Co Ltd, 1955), an epic novel of the Navy in peace and war.
9 LPS 11/166. From Cardinal Hinsley, undated.
10 LPS 4/27. Harwood to Joan, 25 June 1940.
11 IWM 60/95/3 Harwood 'Requirements for the Defence of Bases', 20 Sep 1941.
12 Halpern, Paul, *The Keyes Papers: Vol III 1939–1945* (London: Allen & Unwin for the Navy Records Society, 1981), pp102–6.
13 IWM 60/95/3.
14 Simpson, Michael, *The Cunningham Papers: Vol I The Mediterranean Fleet 1939–1942* (Aldershot: Ashgate for the Navy Records Society, 1999), p208.
15 IWM 60/95/3. Harwood to 1SL, 22 Jul 1941.
16 Ibid, Harwood to VCNS, 13 Aug 1941.
17 Ibid. Harwood to VCNS, 15 Oct 1914.
18 Ibid. Harwood to VCNS, 19 Oct 1941.
19 Ibid. Harwood entitled 'Eastern Fleet', 7 Jan 1942.
20 Ibid. Harwood entitled 'Eastern Fleet', undated.
21 Ibid. Harwood, 16 February 1942.
22 Ibid. Harwood to 1SL 13 March 1942.
23 Ibid, Harwood, entitled 'The American Pacific Problem', undated.
24 Ibid. Harwood entitled 'Appreciation of the Capture of Certain Atlantic Islands', dated 26 July 1941 and undated and unentitled memorandum on Operation Puma.
25 Simpson, Michael, *The Cunningham Papers: Vol I The Mediterranean Fleet 1939–1942* (Aldershot: Ashgate for the Navy Records Society, 1999), p583.
26 CAC EDSN 1/2 Cunningham to Edelsten, 23 Apr 1942.
27 HFP.

Chapter 13

1 CAC ROSK 8/4 an unpublished note by S W Roskill entitled 'Montgomery and the Admirals'.
2 Cunningham of Hyndhope, Admiral of the Fleet Viscount, *A Sailor's Odyssey* (London: Hutchinson & Co, 1951), p458. See also Playfair, I S O, F C Flynn, C J C Molony, and T P Gleave, *The Mediterranean and Middle East: Vol III British Fortunes Reach Their Lowest Ebb* (September

1941 to September 1942) (London: HMSO, 1960), pp177–80.
3 Hinsley, F H, *British Intelligence in the Second World War: Vol II Its Influence on Strategy and Operations* (London: HMSO, 1981), p22 et seq.
4 Ibid, p636.
5 TNA ADM 205/8. Remarks on General Ismay's note to CAS, 20 August 1941.
6 Simpson, vol I, Cunningham to Pound, 14 Oct 1941, p514.
7 General Sir Claude Auchinleck, later Field Marshal (1884–1981) was Commander-in-Chief of the Indian Army in 1941, when he was Commander-in-Chief, Middle East (land) Forces, but when the war in North Africa turned against the British, he was relieved by Alexander in mid-1942 during the El Alamein campaign.
8 Simpson, vol I, Cunningham to Willis, 20 Nov 1941, p533.
9 Simpson, vol I, Cunningham to Pound, 15 Mar 1942, pp582–3.
10 HFP Troopers to MIDEAST signal, 4 Apr 1942.
11 IWM 60/95/3 Harwood to the Prime Minister, 2 Jul 1941.
12 Simpson, vol I, Cunningham, p415.
13 TNA ADM 205/8 File no 1 part D September to October 1941. Conclusion of a conference held between CAS and CNS at Chequers on 4 Oct 1941.
14 TNA AIR 23/1376 CinC Mediterranean to AOCinC Middle East, 21 Dec 1941.
15 CAC ROSK 5/99 Harwood to Pound, 28 Nov 1942.
16 AIR 23/1376 Tedder to Portal, 16 May 1942.
17 Poland communication.
18 Ibid. CinC Mediterranean to Admiralty signal, 25 May 1942.
19 CAC ROSK 5/99 Harwood to Pound, 28 Nov 1942.
20 David Balme and Peter Hore, *Enigma: The Untold Story* (Dunbeath: Whittles Publishing, 2016), pp100–1.
21 Kenneth Poolman, *Night Strike From Malta: 830 Squadron RN and Rommel's Convoys* (London: Jane's, 1980), pp149–50.
22 TNA AIR 23/1376 No. 201 Naval Co-operation Group 1941–42. Simpson to Harwood, 9 Oct 1941 and Harwood to Tedder, 29 Oct 1941.

Chapter 14

1 TNA ADM 223/558. Governor and CinC Malta signal, 20 Apr 1320.
2 Ibid. Chiefs of Staff signal, 23 Apr 2230.
3 Ibid. Governor Malta signal, 26 Apr 2200Z.
4 Ibid. Mideast signal, 6 May 1430.
5 John Wingate, *The Fighting Tenth: The Tenth Submarine Flotilla and the Siege of Malta* (London: Leo Cooper, 1991), see pp191–2.
6 NHB 14. Prime Minister's letter M.168/2 of 8 May 1942.
7 Ibid. CinC Mediterranean signals, 15 May 1801C and 17 May 1351C.
8 Ibid. Admiralty signal, 9 May 1931B and CinC Mediterranean signal 16 May 1720C.
9 Ibid. CinC Mediterranean to Admiralty signal 1932C/18 May.
10 Ibid. CinC Mediterranean signal 1720C/16 May.
11 Ibid. Cunningham to Admrialty 1248B/28 Mar 1942.
12 Ibid. CinC Mediterranean to Admiralty for 1SL signal, 22 May 1842C.
13 Ibid. Admiralty signals, 2 May 2310 and 22 May 2315.
14 Ibid. 1SL to CsinC Mediterranean and Eastern Fleets signal, 23 May 2228B.
15 Admiral of the Fleet Sir Philip Vian (1894–1968). See his *Action This Day* (London: Frederick Muller Limited, 1960).
16 NHB 14. CinC Mediterranean to CinC Eastern Fleet signal 24 May 1324C. Admiral Sir William Tennant (1890–1963), Rear-Admiral, 4th Cruiser Squadron 1942–44 and later Acting Vice-Admiral and Flag Officer, Levant & Eastern Mediterranean.
17 Ibid. Personal from 1SL 3 June 0213B.
18 Ibid. Admiralty to Vice-Admiral Malta and CinC Mediterranean signal, 5 Jun 0018.
19 Ibid. Chief of Staff to Britman, Washington signal 5 Jun 1044Z containing a request for more heavy bombers.

20 Ibid. Mideast 'Most Secret and Personal for Chiefs of Staff from CsinC', 4 Jun 1520Z.
21 Ibid. From Chiefs of Staff, 7 June 0900Z.
22 Operation Vigorous has been written about several times, most recently by Vincent O'Hara, ***In Passage Perilous: Malta and the Convoy Battles of June 1942*** (Indianapolis: Indiana University Press, 2017) whose account has the merit that it used both British and Italian sources. This account is based on (a) Harwood's report of proceedings and Vian's narrative account of the operation in TNA ADM 1/12377 Convoys and Escorts: Operation Vigorous (relief of Malta from Egypt, (b) the naval staff history by Pitcairn-Jones, L J and J Owen, with a new preface by Malcolm Llewellyn-Jones, ***The Royal Navy and the Mediterranean Convoys*** (London: Routledge, 2007) (c) the official history by Roskill, Stephen W, ***The War at Sea: The Period of Balance Vol II*** (London: HMSO, 1956) and has been illuminated by an account of the air operations over Vigorous in TNA AIR 25/799. The various accounts clearly demonstrate the time difference between the transmission and receipt of radio messages in 1942: there are also unaccountable differences of several minutes and sometimes hours in various accounts. Where these are irreconcilable the author has used Harwood's times.
23 NHB 14 CinC Mediterranean to Admiralty, 3 Jun 1303C
24 Ibid. CinC Mediterranean, 8 June 1203C.
25 Ibid. CinC Mediterranean, 12 Jun 1702C 'use Duke of York's callsign'. HMS ***Duke of York*** was at Scapa Flow.
26 John Wingate, ***The Fighting Tenth: The Tenth Submarine Flotilla and the Siege of Malta*** (London: Leo Cooper, 1991).
27 Lorna Almonds Windmill, ***A British Achilles: The Story Of George 2nd Earl Jellicoe*** (Barnsley: Pen & Sword Military, 2005), pp30–42.
28 NHB 14 CsinC Middle East to Chiefs of Staff signal 10 Jun 1400. 'Convoy Vigorous will sail on 12th June being preceded by a diversionary convoy of four ships which will sail for Port Said on 11th'.
29 Ibid. CinC Mediterranean to Admiralty signal, 12 Jun 2246C.
30 Richard Casey, ***Personal Experience 1939–1946 by Lord Casey*** (New York: David McKay Co, 1962), p106.
31 NHB 13 Vian to Harwood. 2315C/14 Jun 1942, f 390.
32 Ibid. Harwood to Vian. 0021C/15 Jun 1942, f 387, and 0131C/15 June 1942, f386.
33 Ibid. Harwood to Vian. 0325C/15 Jun 1942, f382.
34 Ibid. CinC Mediterranean, 15 Jun 0705C.
35 Ibid. CinC Mediterranean, 15 Jun 1153C
36 TNA AIR 25/799 No. 201 (General Reconnaissance) [*sic*] Group.
37 Almonds, p38. See also TNA WO 373/40.
38 TNA ADM 205/56. Complaint by CAS that 1SL criticised the skill of the RAF in a memorandum to PM 15 May 1942.
39 TNA ADM 205/20. Air Force Co-operation with the Navy and Army COS (42) 155 and 264.
40 TNA ADM 205/56. Pound's correspondence with CAS about maintenance of torpedoes in the RAF. Tedder to Portal signal 16 June 2016 marked 'Personal'.
41 AIR 25/799 No. 201 (General Reconnaissance) Group.
42 O'Hara, pp213–14.
43 Correlli Barnett, ***Engage the Enemy More Closely: The Royal Navy in the Second World War*** (London: Faber and Faber, 1991), p509.
44 See Richard Woodman, ***Malta Convoys, 1940–1943*** (London: John Murray, 2000).
45 Max Hastings, ***Finest Years: Churchill as Warlord 1940–45*** (London: Harper Press, 2010).
46 O'Hara, pp172, 214.
47 Barnett, p506. See also ADM 234/353 Battle Summary No 32 Malta convoys 1942.
48 ***Daily Telegraph***, 'Surgeon Lt-Cdr Paul Houghton', 2009 <http://www.telegraph.co.uk/news/obituaries/medicine-obituaries/6409316/Surgeon-Lt-Cdr-Paul-Houghton.html> [19 February 2018].

49 CAC ROSK 5/95 Vian to Roskill, 28 Nov 1954.
50 Ibid.
51 CAC ROSK 5/95 Cunningham to Roskill, 6 Nov 1956?
52 CAC Rosk 5/95 Cunningham to Roskill, 16 November 1956?
53 TNA ADM 196/92.
54 *Daily Telegraph*, 'Surgeon Lt-Cdr Paul Houghton'. For Vian's malaria see TNA ADM 196/56.
55 Philip, Admiral of the Fleet Sir Vian, *Action This Day* (London: Frederick Muller Limited, 1960), pp97–8.
56 Harwood to Pound, 28 Nov 1942.

Chapter 15

1 Churchill, *Second World War*, vol IV.
2 Churchill, p349. Letter. Churchill to Auchinleck. 24 June 1942.
3 LPS.
4 Francis de Guingand, *Operation Victory* (London: Hodder & Stoughton, 1947), p126.
5 Ibid.
6 Roskill, Stephen W, *The War at Sea: The Period of Balance* (London: HMSO, 1956).
7 TNA ADM 205/8. Ismay to Pound, 9 Jun 1941.
8 LPS.
9 Unwin, Vicky, *Love and War in the WRNS* (Stroud: The History Press, 2015), pp117–25.
10 Med War Diaries.
11 LPS.
12 De Guingand, p126.
13 Casey, p112–13.
14 Ibid.
15 Hinsley, F H, *British Intelligence in the Second World War: Its Influence on Strategy and Operations* (London: HMSO, 1981).
16 CAC ROSK 8/4.

Chapter 16

1 Stephen Roskill, *Churchill and the Admirals* (London: Collins, 1977), p323. See also TNA ADM 205/14 Churchill 21 Jul 1942, etc.
2 ROSK 5/98 Undated note by SWR and ACNS(F) to 1SL, 23 Jul 1942.
3 ROSK 5/99 Harwood to Pound, 28 Nov 42. At 04:15 on 29 August 1942 Edridge shelled Axis positions off El Daba, Egypt, but was hit by a torpedo fired by an Italian motor torpedo boat, disabled and had to be towed into Alexandria.
4 Ibid, 323. See also TNA ADM 204/52 Harwood 12 Jul and Moore 18 Jul 1942.
5 Casey, p125.
6 Appendix 5A2. Report by Chief of Staff, Cdre Norman to C-in-C. 7 Mar 1943. Extract (CM15).
7 Minutes-C.C. (42) 29th Meeting.
8 Most Immediate signal No CST/134 of Eighth August.
9 General Sir Harold Alexander, later Field Marshal and 1st Earl Alexander of Tunis (1891–1969), Commander-in-Chief Middle East (land) Forces in succession to Auchinleck from 15 August 1942 to February 1943. See Casey, p126.
10 Appendix 5A3. By Field Marshal Alexander of Tunis. Supplement to the *London Gazette*, 5 February 1948.
11 CAC ROSK 8/23 Cdre Norman to Roskill, 7 Mar 1962.
12 De Guingand, p158.
13 Chief Engine Room Artificer Lewis in his book *Lost Voices of the Royal Navy* recounts that when HMS *Sikh* fuelled there the crew of the oil lighter greeted them with 'You go Tobruk, no?'
14 HFP Prime Minister to CinC, Signal 1639A/13 Sep.
15 CinC to 1st Sea Lord, 0200 14 September 1942.
16 Appendix 5A4. C-in-C Med to First Sea Lord, 17 September 1942, Signal timed 1731A. Report on Operation "Agreement" (CM6) Personal and Private for First Sea Lord.
17 Roskill, *Churchill and the Admirals* (Bk 12).
18 Appendix 5A9. CinC to 1st Sea Lord, 28 November 1942. Extract.
19 In a letter to the First Sea Lord (App 5A8).
20 NHB ACNS(F) Telegrams Operation Agreement Raid on Tobruk, September 1942 f 1.
21 Pound to the 1st Lord dated 4 January 1943.
22 Ibid, 324 TNA ADM 205/14 Churchill, 28 [September] 1942.
23 Harwood to Pound, 16 Mar 1943.

Chapter 17

1 NHB 11. French Squadron at

Alexandria, April 1941–July 1943 ff 50–247. War Cabinet WP (41)137, 30 Mar 1942 Vichy Squadron at Alexandria, Cunningham-Godfroy Agreement, 7 July 1940.
2 Ibid, ff 269 Cunningham to Admiralty 2355/13 Apr 1941.
3 Roskill, *Churchill and the Admirals* (London: Collins, 1977), p122.
4 Simpson, vol I, p169.
5 IWM 60/95/3 Harwood entitled 'The French Situation', 23 September 1941.
6 Ibid. Harwood to Pound 'Vichy French Ships', 2 November 1941.
7 Ibid. Harwood to Pound untitled, 12 October 1941.
8 LPS 11/137 from Contre-Admiral Godfroy, 18 Dec 1939.
9 NHB 11 ff 27–269 War Cabinet to Harwood 1620B/20 May 1942.
10 Ibid, ff 189–285.
11 Ibid, ff 201. Churchill to Casey 2215Z/7 July.
12 Ibid, ff 189. Pound to Harwood 1901C/23 Aug 1943; f 216 Pound (approved by Churchill and Alexander) to Harwood 0152B/3 Jul; and f 229 Alexander to Harwood 0205/30 Jun 1942.
13 Ibid, ff 181 Harwood to Admiralty 2015C/13 Oct 1942.
14 Ibid, ff 167 Churchill to Harwood 130A/5 Nov 1942.
15 Harwood to Middle East Defence Committee, 23 January 1943.
16 LPS 6/4 Harwood to Joan, airgraph, 13 Nov 1942.
17 CinC to Admiralty 1626B/8 Nov 1942.
18 NHB 11 Harwood to Admiralty 2026B/14 Nov 42.
19 Ibid. Pound to Harwood 1356A/15 Nov 42.
20 Admiralty to C-in-C, 25 Nov 1942.
21 Simpson, vol II Harwood to Admiral Cunningham, 14 November 1942, pp46–7.
22 NHB 11, Cunningham (NCXF) to Harwood 1142A/27 Nov 42.
23 Ibid, p 52, Harwood to Cunningham, 3 Dec 1942.
24 Admiralty Personal from First Lord to CinC. 0240/25 Nov 1942, and Admiralty Fm 1st Sea Lord (Approved by 1st Lord) to CinC Copied to NXCF. (Cunningham) Signal 0329/28 Nov 422.
25 CinC to Admiralty and NCXF (Cunningham) 2051/25 Nov.
26 CinC to Admiralty, 26 Nov 1942.
27 CAC ROSK 5/99 Harwood to Pound, 28 Nov 42.
28 CAC ROSK 5/99 Harwood to Pound, 28 Nov 42.
29 CinC to Ambassador in Cairo (Lampson), 31 December 1942.
30 Alanbrooke, p370, 26 January 1943 (Cairo).
31 CinC to Minister of State (Casey), 15 February 1943.
32 NHB 11, ff 59 Harwood to Admiralty 2350B//12 Feb 1943.
33 Ibid, ff 50 Churchill to Casey 2325Z/21 Feb 1942.
34 Ibid, ff 70 Former Naval Person to the President, T1730/2 of 19 Dec 42.
35 Harwood to Pound, 12 March 1943.
36 LPS 6/13 Cdr VG Weekes to Lady Joan Harwood, 27 Aug 79.

Chapter 18

1 Harwood to Pound, 28 Nov 1942.
2 Ibid.
3 Alan Francis Brooke Alanbrooke, Alex Danchev and Daniel Todman, *War Diaries, 1939–1945: Field Marshal Lord Alanbrooke* (London: Phoenix, 2003), p342.
4 CAC ROSK 5/99 Harwood to Pound, 28 Nov 42.
5 CAC ROSK 5/99 Harwood to Pound, 28 Nov 42.
6 Pound to A V Alexander, 4 Jan 1943.
7 LPS 6/8 Harwood to Joan, from Alexandria, Jan 1943 in 2 parts.
8 Vic Weinerlein, 'HMSAS GAMTOOS, 1942–1945 A South African Salvage Vessel In The Second World War', Military History Journal Of The South African Military History Society, 13.5 (2006) <http://samilitaryhistory.org/vol135vw.html> [Accessed 23 February 2018].
9 Harwood to Pound, 2 Feb 1943. On the return of the Prime Minister.
10 Harwood to General Alexander, 1 Feb 1943.
11 Harwood to Pound, 12 Mar 1943.
12 Commodore Dundas, Chief of Staff to Harwood, 3 Feb 1943.
13 De Guingand, pp231–4.
14 Hamilton, Nigel, *Monty: Master of the Battlefield 1942–1944* (London:

Hamish Hamilton, 1983) 'the dilatory performance by the Royal Navy in getting Benghazi [*sic*] harbour fully operational (for which Admiral Harwood was sacked) threatened to upset the whole "Fire-eater" plan', p108.

15 Frederick Hermann Kisch (1888–1943), a Zionist leader and as a brigadier one of the highest ranking Jews to serve in the British Army.

16 Dundas, 3 Feb 1943.

17 Harwood to Pound signal 1144B, 4 Feb 1943. 'Eighth Army (Q) side admits that unloading from ships was beating what army ashore could unload and clear for the last two days. Unloading from the ships in future depends largely on the weather.'

18 Brooke, diary 4 Feb 1943, pp378.

19 Pound to A V Alexander, 4 Jan 1943.

20 CAC ROSK 5/98 Cunningham to Pound, 28 April 1943.

21 CAC ROSK 5/98.

22 Simpson, vol II, p126. Cunningham to General Alexander, 26 Aug 1943. See also Cunningham, pp212–13. Cunningham diary, 15 July 1944, 'Montgomery thought Cherbourg was not going fast enough. I was very firm with him [CIGS] and told him that Montgomery must learn to believe that the men entrusted with opening up the harbour, who are great experts, are doing their best – and that I wasn't going to have another Tripoli nonsense.'

23 Ian Stanley Ord Playfair, C J C Molony and W G F Jackson, ***The Mediterranean and Middle East: The Destruction of Axis Forces in Africa*** (London: Naval & Military Press, 2004), p256.

24 Alan Francis Brooke Alanbrooke, Alex Danchev and Daniel Todman, ***War Diaries, 1939–1945: Field Marshal Lord Alanbrooke*** (London: Phoenix, 2003), p371. See also CAC 8/4 Cdr Barry Duckworth to Roskill.

25 HFP Harwood to Pound signal 2020 on 4 Feb 1943.

26 Appendix 8A10. CM10. CinC letter to General Alexander. 01/02/43.CM10).

27 Harwood to Pound on 2 Feb 1943. Harwood had already written a similar note to General Alexander on 1 February.

28 Harwood to Pound signal timed 1005, 3 Feb 1943.

29 Pound to Prime Minister, 6 Feb 1943.

30 Pound to Harwood, 15 Feb 1943.

31 Playfair IV, p256.

32 Harwood to Pound 16 March 1943.

Chapter 19

1 CAC ROSK 5/99 Harwood to Pound, 28 Nov 42.

2 LPS 6/11 Harwood to Joan, 20 Feb 1943.

3 LPS 6/10 Harwood to Joan, 16 Feb 1943.

4 Simpson, vol I, p327. Cunningham 's Memorandum on Command in the Middle East, 10 June 1942.

5 LPS HFP Mediterranean App 8A5. Commodore Norman to CinC Levant, 7 March 1943. (CM15) RN, GHQ, Middle East.

6 LPS HFP Mediterranean App 9A4. From Minister of State, Cairo. (Casey) to CinC (CM17), 13 March.

7 Appendix 9A5. CinC to Minister of State, 15 March 1943. (CM17a).

8 Ibid.

9 Ibid.

10 Norman.

11 Playfair, vol IV, p334.

12 Norman.

13 Simpson, Cunningham papers, vol 11, p72.

14 Simpson, Cunningham papers, vol 11, p71.

15 Simpson, vol II, p95. From Pound, 23 April 1943, p72.

16 HFP Cunningham to Harwood, 15 Mar 1943.

17 Cunningham to Roskill, 12 November 1956 (?).

Chapter 20

1 TNA ADM 116/5786 Harwood Committee on Royal Naval College Greenwich.

2 LPS 3/1. Harwood to Lady Pelly, wife of Admiral Sir Hugh Pelly, 24 January 1938. Their son Lieutenant Douglas Pelly had just become engaged to Miss Catherine 'Kitty' Lorraine Conran of Buenos Aires.

3 WSC, GUILDHALL, 23 February 1940.

4 WSC, BBC broadcast, 18 December 1939.

5 WSC, onboard HMS ***Exeter***, 15 February 1940.

Bibliography

1912-2012. 100 AÑOS DE LA ESTACIÓN COSTERA CERRITO RADIO', *La Galena Del Sur*, 2018 <https://lagalenadelsur.wordpress.com/2012/01/31/1912-2012-100-anos-de-la-estacion-costera-cerrito-radio/> [Accessed 5 January 2018]

Alanbrooke, Alan Francis Brooke, Alex Danchev, and Daniel Todman, *War Diaries, 1939–1945: Field Marshal Lord Alanbrooke* (London: Phoenix, 2003)

Anon, *The Mediterranean Fleet: Greece to Tripoli* (London: The Admiralty, 1943)

Auphan, Admiral Gabriel, and Jacques Mordal, *La Marine Française Dans La Seconde Guerre Mondiale* (Paris: Editions France-Empire, 1967)

Balme, David, and Peter Horc, *Enigma: The Untold Story* (Dunbeath: Whittles Publishing, 2016)

Baptiste, Fitzroy André, *War, Co operation, and Conflict: The European Possessions In The Caribbean* (New York: Greenwood, 1988)

Barnett, Correlli, *Engage the Enemy More Closely: The Royal Navy in the Second World War* (London: Faber and Faber, 1991)

Bennett, G H, and R Bennett, *Hitler's Admirals* (Annapolis, Md: Naval Institute Press, 2004)

Bennett, Geoffrey, *Battle of the River Plate: Sea Battles in Close-Up* (London: Ian Allan, 1972)

Black, Nicholas, *The British Naval Staff in the First World War* (Woodbridge: Boydell Press, 2009)

Bragadin, Marc'Antonio, *The Italian Navy in World War II* (Annapolis: United States Naval Institute, 1957)

Brodhurst, Robin, *Churchill's Anchor: The Biography of Admiral of the Fleet Sir Dudley Pound* (Barnsley: Pen & Sword, 2000)

Casey, Richard, *Personal Experience 1939–1946 By Lord Casey* (New

York: David McKay Co, 1962)

Chetwode, George K, *Some Notes on Boat Pulling and Regattas* (HMS *Warspite*, 1926)

Cogswell, Reginald, *Exeter: A Cruiser of the Medium Size* (Liskeard: Navy Books, 2017)

Cunningham of Hyndhope, Admiral of the Fleet Viscount, *A Sailor's Odyssey* (London: Hutchinson & Co, 1951)

de Guingand, Francis, *Operation Victory* (London: Hodder & Stoughton, 1947)

Dove, Patrick, *I Was Graf Spee's Prisoner* (Not known: Cherry Tree, 1940)

Edelsten, John S, *Sporting Reminiscences of South America, 1919–1921, HM. Southampton*, 1st edn (London: Riddle, Smith and Duffus, 1922)

Edwards, Kenneth, *Men of Action* (London: Collins, 1943)

——, *Seven Sailors* (London: Collins, 1945)

Foley, Thomas, *I Was an Altmark Prisoner. The First Authentic Account of the 'Graf Spee's Activities, Life Abroad the Raider, and Life Aboard the Hell Ship 'Altmark' by One of Her Prisoners* (Not known: Francis Aldor, 1940)

Friedman, Norman, 'Review of the Royal Navy in Eastern Waters 1935–1942', *Mariner's Mirror*, 103:3 (2017), 370

Greene, Jack, and Alessandro Massignani, *The Naval War in the Mediterranean, 1940–1943* (London: Chatham Publishing, 1998)

Gregory-Smith, Frank, *Red Tobruk: Memories of a World War II Destroyer Commander* (Barnsley: Pen & Sword, 2008)

Grove, Eric J, *The Price of Disobedience: The Battle of the River Plate Reconsidered* (Stroud: Sutton Publishing, 2000)

Halpern, Paul G (ed), *The Keyes Papers: 1939–1945* (London: Allen & Unwin for the Navy Records Society, 1981)

——, *The Mediterranean Fleet, 1919–1929* (Farnham: Ashgate for the Navy Records Society, 2011)

——, *The Mediterranean Fleet, 1930–1939* (Oxford: The Navy Records Society with Routledge, 2016)

Hamilton, Nigel, *Monty: Master of the Battlefield 1942–1944* (London: Hamish Hamilton, 1983)

Hammond, Richard, 'British Aero-Naval Co-Operation in the Mediterranean 1940–45', in *A Military Transformed?* (Solihull:

Helio & Co, 2016), pp229–245

Harwood, C H H, ***History of the Harwood Family*** (Gosport: Ashgate Colour Press, 2009), IWM 60/95/1

Harwood, Henry and Stephen, ***Letters, Papers and Speeches from the Collection of Admiral Sir Henry Harwood KCB OBE (1888–1950)*** (Gosport: The Better Book Company, 2012)

Harwood, Henry Harwood, 'The River Plate Battle', ***Supplement to the London Gazette*** (1947), 2759

Hastings, Max, ***Finest Years: Churchill as Warlord 1940–45*** (London: Harper Press, 2010)

Hinsley, F H, E E Thomas, C F G Ranson, and R C Knight, ***British Intelligence in the Second World War: Its Influence on Strategy and Operations vol II*** (London: HMSO, 1981)

Hirst, Lloyd, ***Coronel and After*** (London: Peter Davies, 1934)

——, ***Britons at Maldonado*** (Novus Orbis: Montevideo, 1975)

Holman, Gordon, ***The King's Cruisers*** (London: Hodder & Stoughton, 1947)

Kennedy, John, ***The Business of War: The War Narrative of Major-General Sir John Kennedy*** (London: Hutchinson, 1957)

Jurens, William J, 'Under the Guns: Battle Damage to ***Graf Spee*** 13 December 1939', in ***Warship 2018*** (Oxford: Osprey Publishing, 2018), pp46–66

Lavery, Brian, ***Churchill Goes to War: Churchill's Wartime Journeys*** (London: Conway Maritime, 2007)

'List Of Victoria Crosses By School', <https://en.wikipedia.org/wiki/List_of_Victoria_Crosses_by_school#Victoria_Crosses_by_school_and_campaign> [Accessed 5 December 2017]

Marder, Arthur Jacob, and introduction by Barry M Gough, ***Operation Menace: The Dakar Expedition and the Dudley North Affair*** (Barnsley: Seaforth Publishing, 2016)

Miller, Geoffrey, ***Superior Force: The Conspiracy Behind the Escape of Goeben and Breslau*** (Hull: University of Hull Press, 1996)

Millington-Drake, Eugen, ***The Drama of Graf Spee and the Battle of the River Plate*** (Peter Davies: London, 1964)

Naval Staff, and Eric Grove, ***German Capital Ships and Raiders in World War II: Volume I From Graf Spee to Bismarck, 1939–1941*** (London: Frank Cass)

O'Hara, Vincent P, *Struggle for the Middle Sea: The Great Navies at War in the Mediterranean, 1940–1945* (Annapolis: Naval Institute Press, 2009)

——, *In Passage Perilous: Malta and the Convoy Battles of June 1942* (Indianapolis: Indiana Universtiy Press, 2017)

Pitcairn-Jones, L J, J Owen, and new preface by Malcolm Llewellyn-Jones, *The Royal Navy and the Mediterranean Convoys* (London: Routledge, 2007)

Playfair, I S O, F C Flynn, C J C Molony, and T P Gleave, *The Mediterranean and Middle East: Vol III British Fortunes Reach their Lowest Ebb (September 1941 to September 1942)* (London: HMSO, 1960)

Playfair, Ian Stanley Ord, C J C Molony, and W G F Jackson, *The Mediterranean and Middle East: the Destruction of Axis Forces in Africa*, 4th edn (London: Naval & Military Press, 2004)

Poolman, Kenneth, *Night Strike From Malta: 830 Squadron RN and Rommel's Convoys* (London: Jane's, 1980)

Pope, Dudley, *The Battle of the River Plate* (London: William Kimber & Co, 1956)

Raeder, Erich, *Der Krieg Zur See 1914–1918: Der Kieuzerkreg In Den Ausländischen Gewässern* (Berlin: Mittler & Sohn, 1922)

Roskill, Stephen W, *The War at Sea: The Defensive Vol I* (London: HMSO, 1954)

——, *The War at Sea: The Period of Balance Vol II* (London: HMSO, 1956)

——, *The War at Sea: The Offensive Vol III Pt I* (London: HMSO, 1960)

——, *Naval Policy between the Wars: The Period of Anglo-American Antagonism 1919-1929* (London: Collins, 1968)

——, *Naval Policy between the Wars: The Period of Reluctant Rearmament 1930-1939* (London: Collins, 1976)

——, *Churchill and the Admirals* (London: Collins, 1977)

Ruge, Friedrich, 'Ruckblicke: Panzerschiff Graf Spee', *Leinen Los! – Die Monatszeitung Des Deutschen Marinebundes E.V*, 12 (1954)

Schmalenbach, Paul, *Die Geschichte Der Deutschen Schiffsartillerie* (Berlin: Koehlers Verlagsges, 1993)

Simpson, Michael, *The Cunningham Papers: Vol I The Mediterranean Fleet 1939–1942* (Aldershot: Ashgate for the Navy Records Society, 1999)

——, *The Cunningham Papers: Vol II The Triumph of Allied Sea Power*

1942–46 (Aldershot: Ashgate for the Navy Records Society, 2006)
Smith, Peter Charles, *Massacre at Tobruk* (London: William Kimber, 1987)
Stephen, Martin, *The Fighting Admirals: British Admirals of the Second World War* (London: Leo Cooper, 1991)
Stewart, Ninian, *The Organisation of the Naval Staff within the Admiralty and the Ministry of Defence 1927–1999* (Unpublished)
Strabolgi, Lord, *The Battle of the River Plate* (London: Hutchinson & Co, 1940)
Tedder, Arthur William Tedder, *With Prejudice* (London: Little, Cassell, 1966)
Temple Patterson, A, *Tyrwhitt of the Harwich Force* (London: The Military Book Society, 1973)
The Battle of the River Plate (UK: J Arthur Rank Film Distributors, 1957)
The Cruise of HMS Exeter (London: W H Smith & Son, 1940)
The Daily Telegraph, 'Surgeon Lt-Cdr Paul Houghton', 2009 <http://www.telegraph.co.uk/news/obituaries/medicine-obituaries/6409316/Surgeon-Lt-Cdr-Paul-Houghton.html> [Accessed 19 February 2018]
Tute, Warren, *The Cruiser* (London: Cassell & Co Ltd, 1955)
Unwin, Vicky, *Love and War in the WRNS* (Stroud: The History Press, 2015)
Vian, Philip, Admiral of the Fleet Sir, *Action This Day* (London: Frederick Muller Limited, 1960)
Waters, S D, *Official History of New Zealand in the Second World War 1939–45: The Royal New Zealand Navy* (Wellington: Department of Internal Affairs, 1956)
Weinerlein, Vic, 'HMSAS GAMTOOS, 1942–1945 A South African Salvage Vessel In The Second World War', *Military History Journal Of The South African Military History Society*, 13 (2006) <http://samilitaryhistory.org/vol135vw.html> [Accessed 23 February 2018]
Williams, Hamilton, *Britain's Naval Power: A Short History of the Growth of the British Navy from Trafalgar to the Present Time* (London: Macmillan & Co, 1904)
——, *Britain's Naval Power: A Short History of the Growth of the British Navy from the Earliest Times to Trafalgar* (London: Macmillan & Co, 1902)

Windmill, Lorna Almonds, *A British Achilles: The Story of George 2nd Earl Jellicoe* (Barnsley: Pen & Sword Military, 2005)

Wingate, John, *The Fighting Tenth: The Tenth Submarine Flotilla and the Siege of Malta* (London: Leo Cooper, 1991)

Winton, John, *Ultra at Sea* (London: Leo Cooper, 1988)

Woodman, Richard, *Malta Convoys, 1940–1943* (London: John Murray, 2000)

Woodman, Richard, *The Battle of the River Plate: A Grand Delusion* (Barnsley: Pen & Sword, 2008)

Zimm, Alan D, 'The Battle of the River Plate: A Tactical Analysis', in *Warship 2018* (Oxford: Osprey Publishing, 2018), pp28–45

Index